ADVANCE PRAISE FOR

If You Can Stand the Heat

"A **valuable and amusing** collection of tales and tips from back- and front-of-house industry leaders. The books will both entertain and inform food lovers, professionals, and anyone thinking of going into this exciting business."

—Bradley Ogden, author of *Breakfast, Lunch, and Dinner*

"An **inspiring, practical, and insightful** chronicle of the men and women responsible for today's American culinary scene. A true kitchen drama."
—Vincent Schiavelli, author of *Papa Andrea's Table*
and *Bruculinu, America*

"**Great** profile of what happens behind the scenes of our industry, told with wit, meaningful quotes, and plenty of reference material. If you are thinking of going into the restaurant business, this is a must-have book." —Lidia Matticchio Bastianich of Becco, Felida, and Frico Bar,
author of *Lidia's Italian Table*

"This book has captured the essence of what we refer to as 'the calling': that all-consuming passion that chooses you as its mate to do the most satisfying of work, cooking in a professional kitchen. Striving to be the best every day as chefs, we have our own language, lifestyle, code of ethics, and hierarchy. **Dawn Davis has cracked that code**."
—Gale Gand and Rick Tramonto, authors of *American Brasserie*

"Americans are starving for accurate knowledge about the work of the professional chef—not the phony romanticized version in food magazines, but the real stuff. **Dawn Davis serves up the real stuff**—story, information, and elegant portraits of great American chefs—in *If You Can Stand the Heat*. The book is an important addition to the small but growing body of journalism exploring this fascinating work and the unusual souls who devote their lives to it."
—Michael Ruhlman, author of *The Making of a Chef*

PENGUIN BOOKS

If You Can Stand the Heat

A graduate of Stanford University and a Techniques of Fine Cooking class at Peter Kump's School of Culinary Arts, Dawn Davis lives in New York City with her library of more than 150 cookbooks and culinary magazines dating back over ten years.

Krista Olson is a graphic designer and photographer living in New York City. Since the age of sixteen she has worked in restaurants and professional kitchens, both in the kitchen and in the dining room. She has also worked at the James Beard Foundation, where she photographed numerous chefs in San Francisco and New York City.

 PENGUIN BOOKS

If You Can
Stand the Heat

TALES FROM CHEFS
& RESTAURATEURS

BY *Dawn Davis*

Photographs by Krista Olson

PENGUIN BOOKS
Published by the Penguin Group
Penguin Putnam Inc., 375 Hudson Street,
New York, New York 10014, U.S.A.
Penguin Books Ltd, 27 Wrights Lane,
London W8 5TZ, England
Penguin Books Australia Ltd, Ringwood,
Victoria, Australia
Penguin Books Canada Ltd, 10 Alcorn Avenue,
Toronto, Ontario, Canada M4V 3B2
Penguin Books (N.Z.) Ltd, 182–190 Wairau Road,
Auckland 10, New Zealand

Penguin Books Ltd, Registered Offices:
Harmondsworth, Middlesex, England

First published in Penguin Books 1999

10 9 8 7 6 5 4 3 2 1

LIBRARY OF CONGRESS CATALOGING-IN-PUBLICATION DATA
Davis, Dawn.
    If you can stand the heat : tales from chefs & restaurateurs / by
Dawn Davis : photographs by Krista Olson.
       p.   cm.
    ISBN 0 14 02.8158 4
    1. Cooks—United States Biography.   2. Restaurateurs—United
States Biography.   I. Title.
TX649.A1D38   1999
641.5'092'273—dc21
[B]   99-26563

Printed in the United States of America
Set in Fairfield
Designed by Mia Risberg

For my mother, Leona Davis,
who by her deeds provides me with the
kind of nourishment that makes
all else possible

You watch the Food Network the way others watch the news, as if David Rosengarten or Mario Batali is going to report some vital piece of information you'll need to navigate through the day. You subscribe to more cooking magazines than you truly have time to peruse in one month, let alone cook from, and your bookshelves are sagging under the weight of all your cookbooks. Just this past weekend, though you are fatally allergic to nuts, you went out and bought *The Walnut Cookbook: Walnuts in Every Guise Imaginable.* You're so obsessed with the idea of cooking that when you should be preparing a legal brief, an ad campaign, or a homework assignment, you find yourself fantasizing about food or enrolling in cooking schools instead.

Until now, you've been content to just daydream about food. But suddenly, reading about it in *Food & Wine* and *Bon Appétit* or watching someone else prepare it on television no longer satisfies you. You want to actually *be* a chef, but you realize that you don't have any idea how to break into the industry. Fortunately, the twenty or so chefs profiled in *If You Can Stand the Heat* do, and here they share their wisdom and experience. Having worked in a broad range of restaurant and hotel kitchens across the country, they can speak to everything from what it's like to be a woman in the industry to how to make the transition from being a chef to a chef-owner, from the differences between catering and working in a restaurant to what to consider when planning a profitable menu. They also reflect on the culinary revolution that has occurred in the United States in the last twenty-five years, a journey that, expressed most simply, has taken us from iceberg to mesclun.

Is their advice worth taking seriously? They've won their share of James Beard Awards and International Association of Culinary Professionals honors. Their restaurants are usually crowded; they get great reviews and they have the respect of their peers. A few are affiliated with restaurants that top those surveys in which locals rate a city or region's best restaurants. And if the critics and the diners agree, then they must be on to something.

Where did I find them? Restaurant and food critics at newspapers across the country referred some of the chefs to me. Others were referred by fellow chefs; still others I approached directly, after I ate one of their meals or read about them in a magazine. As I combed through various lists, I wasn't necessarily looking for the "best" chef in town or those whose stories are widely available, though there are certainly chefs of that caliber here, but rather a mix of people whose experiences would be informative and inspiring to the aspiring professional and the armchair "foodie" alike. I was also looking for people whose stories had a little twist. With a former ballerina, a cowboy, and a chef–cum–acclaimed novelist, I found what I was looking for.

Of course, this grouping of chefs is subjective, and anyone who would attempt a similar exercise would come up with an entirely different group. Sometimes I'd no sooner left a city than I'd hear about a chef that I just "had to meet" there. As I looked into their backgrounds, I would often start to fret. Should I have included this one? Would that one have talked about a different segment of the business? But inevitably, with a little more research, I found that no matter how unusual their stories were, there was also something in their background that resonated with themes other chefs in the book had already raised. This isn't to say that all the chefs in the book agree on everything. Some advise going to cooking school, for example, and others don't. Some apprenticed abroad, others didn't. Some dream of having their own restaurant, others would rather lose their money "at the track." But because many of the same themes kept surfacing—the importance of mentors, the hierarchical yet democratic ways of kitchens, and the long hours and incredibly exhausting hard work, to name a few—I was ultimately convinced that this group was representative.

The book is divided into four parts, with boxes on an array of subjects. There's a box on positions in the kitchen, for example, and a couple on prominent food organizations. For those who decide after reading this book that they *can't* stand the professional heat, there's even a list of culinary vacations. In addition to those sidebars, there are also several appendixes that provide information on everything from how to contact the organizations referenced (in boldface) in the book to culinary scholarships.

Part 1, "Breaking In & Moving Up," provides all sorts of advice on how to break into the industry and on what to expect once you get started. Andrew Pforzheimer of Barcelona and Luna in Connecticut, a twenty-year veteran of the food industry, suggests that you "beg and plead your way into your first job, and work for nothing if you have to." To that, Anthony Bourdain, who has worked in a number of prestigious kitchens in New York, including the Rainbow Room, would add that when you're just starting out, "you have to get rid of any preconceptions about how you should be treated as a human being because you will be asked to do unreasonable and demeaning things" until you work your way up and gain the trust of the cooks above you. Other chefs have advice on how to make the best of your education, whether it's formal or not. Patricia Williams of Drew Nieporent's City Wine & Cigar warns cooks to "carefully plan your job moves . . . [and] constantly think about what kind of cuisine you eventually want to pursue"; and Marc Jolis, who has spent the last several years specializing in vegetarian cuisine, shows, by example, that it's possible to move into the industry even in midlife.

When they weren't giving advice on what to expect the first several years, it seemed that most of the chefs wanted to talk about food. And, interestingly, in a true sign of the times, they wanted to talk not so much about French or Italian food as about regional American cuisines, which is the ground covered in Part 2, "A Taste of America's Regional Cuisines." This is not to say that Italian and French food, in particular, weren't important to this group of almost exclusively American chefs and restaurateurs. On the contrary, the importance of French training emerged as a theme of special significance to chefs throughout the book. In two sections, a French education was of particular importance: to Michael McCarty of Michael's in Los Angeles and New York and Alan Wong of the eponymous restaurant in Hawaii. However, many of these chefs came of age when, to paraphrase Michael McCarty, they were discovering food right in their backyard. And when it came to reflecting on their own food philosophy, more than a few of them wanted to talk about America's regional foods. Edna Lewis and Scott Peacock take great pride in southern traditions. Tom Perini would not even be a cook if it weren't for ingredients and traditions that he finds right on his ranch in Texas. Not every region is included. Indeed, a hotbed of much activity recently, the Pacific Northwest, is missing. But there is a sampling—from the South to the Pacific, from the Southwest to the West.

Other chefs were less interested in what was happening regionally and more focused on foods and flavors from abroad. As the chefs in Part 3, "Border Crossing," indicate, we're living, eating, and cooking in a truly postmodern world. It's no longer a matter of an immigrant family's coming to America and opening a restaurant featuring the home cooking of their native country. Now American-born chefs are looking outward, embracing the cuisines and foodways of cultures to which they are not native. In "Border Crossing" you'll find examples of both. There's the De Monteiro family, who came here from Cambodia. They cook flavorful Cambodian cuisine at their restaurants in the Boston area; and there's Chicago's Rick Bayless, a self-described "gringo," who is widely considered one of the country's leading experts on the food of Mexico. Linda Rodriguez is a Filipino-American from the South who is an enthusiast about the food of Japan. Also in Part 3, you'll find Sonia Urban, the only pastry chef profiled in the book. She's a double border-crosser—in terms of both her geographical influences and her work experience. She's heavily influenced by her Caribbean background, using jalapeños, pepper, and tropical fruits, for example, to compose a fruit soup. But she has also crossed the "line" between the kitchen *and* the pastry kitchen. While one pastry chef's story could never adequately describe that segment of the business, it is hoped that her tale does shed light on what the similarities and differences between the two worlds are.

Inevitably all the chefs profiled in *If You Can Stand the Heat* are businessmen and -women, even if they don't own or co-own their restaurants. To highlight just a bit of what falls under their domain, they're responsible for keeping good food costs, managing the cooks who report to them, and inventory control. Because so much of their job is about managing resources and people, I've ended with their thoughts on the "Business of the Business," Part 4. Seth Price of Bubby's in New York provides some thoughts on the economics of brunch and breakfast, whereas Bobby Flay of Mesa Grill reminds cooks to be as concerned with flavor as they are with entrepreneurialism. Frank Brigtsen of Brigtsen's and Anne Kearney of Peristyle, both in New Orleans, address the importance of filling tables consistently and budgeting as accurately as possible. The chefs' advice in this section is supplemented by counsel from a number of experts in the industry, some talking on the value of good service, some on restaurant and menu design, some on forecasting an accurate start-up budget. Though they all had different things to say about the business of running a restaurant, one theme was expressed a number of times: At the end of the day, no matter how glamorous a notion, a restaurant is still a business— sinks have to be unclogged, bills have to be paid, the payroll has to be met. One restaurateur, Steve Poses of Frog-Commissary, the father of the Philadelphia renaissance, started in the industry with some romantic notion that he'd have a social impact on the city, that people would meet in restaurants the way in the "olden days" people met in candy stores. But some years later, he realizes that he's had a more significant *economic* impact on the city than a social one, which is just fine by him. "I've created jobs and careers for people, and I've come to think that's one of the most important things a person can do."

Still, to the outside world anyway, there *is* a certain romance linked with being a chef or a restaurateur. I was certainly caught up in it, which is why I set about interviewing all these chefs and restaurateurs. I too find myself fantasizing about opening night at my hypothetical restaurant. I too dine out with almost reverential interest in the work of cooks and chefs, and have far more of their cookbooks, I confess, than I could ever hope to learn from. Why so much interest on my part and those of my fellow "foodies"? Maybe we're drawn to the platonic idea of being a chef or restaurateur because as Jonathan Waxman, a chef-restaurateur with national influence, once explained to me, a chef's work is both physical and intellectual; it's a combination of blue-collar and white-collar work. Or maybe we are drawn to it simply because there is joy in the *idea* of making people happy, of "restoring" them—to go back to the Latin roots of the word *restaurant*. That's certainly the appeal for Frank Brigtsen, anyway. Seeing the smiling faces at the end of each night is what motivates him to work the line, "because if you can do that, you've got something." A similar impulse inspires Thomas Keller of The French Laundry in Napa Valley. When asked why of all the professions in the world he chose one that demands so much of his time and energy, he responded that giving his diners more, "in turn, gives me more"; the payoff for him, then, is in part spiritual, a notion the French have long respected. According to Dominique Simon, a French maître d' who has worked in restaurants the world over and whose story is revealed here, people are drawn to this industry because "dining is about people coming together, breaking bread and drinking wine, which is one of the oldest symbols of sharing we have."

But to bask in the romance is to disregard what life in the industry is really like. And when I asked these chefs to reflect on their food philosophies, career paths, and lifestyles, I told them to be painfully honest. Most dispelled the romance. Alan Wong was most succinct: "It's hard work, it's greasy, it's hot. Your legs get sore, your feet get sore, your back gets sore. It's not glamorous. When everyone is out partying, you're *providing* the party." In other words, if you're thinking about being a chef, think twice.

But as Bobby Flay theorizes, "someone will read this and insist on opening up a restaurant anyway." And for those people here's a thought, emphasized by many of the chefs whose stories follow: While they have achieved some degree of fame, the majority of chefs labor in obscurity. Anne Kearney, who is the youngest of the crew, but no less wise than the others, put it best: "Fame can't be your motivating factor, because you can work hard your whole life and fall through the cracks with no one ever taking notice."

ACKNOWLEDGMENTS

Were it not for the incredible access that the chefs included in this book provided me, there would be no tales to tell. Whether you met me in the middle of your work night, picked me up from a train station, fed me, or invited me, a total stranger, into your home so that we could continue our interview well into the evening, I am grateful for your hospitality as well as your honest, thoughtful reflections. Some of you even talked to me when this book was but an idea without a home, and for that I'm especially grateful. I also thank your family and staff for helping with the logistics: Jennifer Fite of Frontera Grill, Marna Brigtsen and Rob Weiss of Brigtsen's, Stephanie Banyas of Mesa Grill, Tom Sand of Peristyle, Delilah Staton of Michael's, the Frog-Commissary catering crew, Dawn Alvin at BondSt, and Mona Taga at Alan Wong's. Thanks also to the entire dinner crew at Sullivan's, who more than compensated for my mistakes when Anthony Bourdain insisted I not just write about the work of chefs but actually get behind the line. To the many consultants and experts who helped me paint a broader portrait of the industry—Nicole Aloni, Larry Bogdanow and Iva Kravitz, Gary Goldberg, Karen Karp, Brendan Keenan, Charles Legalos, Linda Lipsky, Dominique Simone, and Candy Wallace—I can only say the obvious: I could never have completed this project without your assistance.

For carefully reading different sections of the book or supplying me with resources, thanks also to the people at various food organizations and publications: Towley Aide at Greenbrier, Dan Strehl of the Los Angeles Public Library, who led me to Karen Berk of Zagat in Los Angeles, Mitchell Davis and Phyllis Isaacson at the James Beard Foundation, John Halligan of the RIHGA Royale's Halcyon Hotel, Francie King of CC2000, Abigail Kirsch of Les Dames d'Escoffier International, and Terri Pittaro of the ACF.

Thanks also to the chefs whose knowledge, which I learned from interviews, and experiences implicitly inform this book: Chef Ashbel (whose biscuits are to die for), Jennifer Beastie, Carla Gahr (a chef and photographer whose graceful photograph of Edna Lewis and Scott Peacock perfectly captures their friendship), Roger Hoyt, Neela Paniz, Jonathan Waxman, and Michael Wild. On the pastry side, David Brown, Marty Peikoff, and Patrick Terrail. And for the insights into how management fits in, John O'Neill at Rosa Pistola in San Francisco.

Krista Olson's photographs are priceless, though having worked with her, I can better understand how the cliché "a picture is worth a thousand words" arose. Thanks for having such a great eye and being a trustworthy sounding board. It's foodies like you, Ashley Collins, Gideon Hollis, Lionel Leventhal, Jennifer Marshall, Joe McGuire, Jodi Peikoff, Lisa Queen, Paul Rankin (who provided the title), Michele Rubin, Maurice Russell, and Gay Young, who remind me that it's okay to be one of those who live to eat.

My agent, Jane Dystel, never doubted this project, and without her early commitment it would have remained a figment of my imagination. I was lucky to have the guidance of two editors: Carole DeSanti, whose wise advice works like a dash of ginger or a sprig of rosemary—just a bit goes a long way—and Alex Babanskyj, who is so indefatigable, she proved time and again that she definitely *can* stand the heat. Thanks, Alex, for the scrupulous edit, when and where the manuscript needed it most, and the Balducci cookies and other pick-me-ups when I did. Thanks also to the design and production team at Penguin. For reading and rereading drafts and encouraging me nonetheless, thank you, Leona Davis, Dr. Noah Guynn, Mac LaFollette, Courtney Manino, Greg Miller, Erica Motley, and Theresa Baldwin Robert. For helping me to test the recipes in that damn kitchen in New Milford, my thanks again to Noah, an intuitive cook. For help with the French, thank you, Sara, mother of Thea. For running an extra twenty miles every week so that you could try "just one more dish," my loving gratitude to Mac.

Finally, thanks to all the friends and family who went neglected while I set off to see where my compulsion would lead, particularly David Troutt, Dorothy Regan, the Hawaii crew, D'Kota's nana, my aunt Stella and my mother, both of whom cooked big bowls of gumbo and batches of tacos when I most needed a dose of home cooking.

Preface vii / Acknowledgments xiii /
List of Recipes xviii

Part 3 · Border Crossing

Part 4 · Chef-Owners on the Business of the Business

LIST OF RECIPES

Soups
California Gazpacho
Sweet Potato Soup with Smoked Chiles and Blue and Gold Corn Tortillas
Butternut Shrimp Bisque
Chilled Soup of Spring Peas Infused with Garden Mint

Fish and Shellfish
Sautéed Shrimp with Garlic and Sherry Sauce

Portuguese Seafood Stew

Royal Catfish Enrobed with Coconut Milk and Lemongrass

Sea Scallop Ceviche with Grilled Red Onion
    and Mango-Tortilla Salad

Gratin of Louisiana Oysters with B&B, Spinach,
    Italian Sausage, and Romano Cheese

Bluefish Provençale

Game and Poultry
Foie Gras with Fiery Leeks and Tamarind Sauce
Roasted Salt-Brined Turkey (see also holiday menu)
Bacon-Wrapped Dove Breast or Quail Breast

Beef
Perini Ranch Steakhouse Rub

Lamb
Grilled Lamb Chops with Macadamia-Coconut Crust,
Cabernet Sauvignon Jus, and Coconut-Ginger Cream

Pork
Grilled Tenderloin of Pork with Apples and Calvados
Tomatillo-Braised Pork Country Ribs with Mexican Greens

Vegetarian Dishes and Vegetables

Lucky Seven Vegetable Tunisian Stew

Sweet Potato Casserole (see also holiday menu)

Roasted Beets in Gingered Syrup (see also holiday menu)

Corn Pudding

Vegetarian Matsutake Hari Hari Nabe

Pasta

Hand-Rolled Ravioli with Roasted Tomatoes,
Mushrooms, and Goat Cheese with Artichoke Brown Butter

Desserts

Lane Cake

Exotic Fruits in Consommé

Fresh Berries in Champagne Vanilla Sabayon with Pecan Pound Cake

Crème de Farine with Poached Golden Delicious Apples,
    Candied Apple Ice Cream, and Cinnamon Stick Syrup

Breakfast/Brunch

Banana or Plantain Walnut Pancakes

Holiday

Roasted Salt-Brined Turkey

Sweet Potato Casserole

Roasted Beets in Gingered Syrup

Corn Pudding

Lane Cake

kitchen

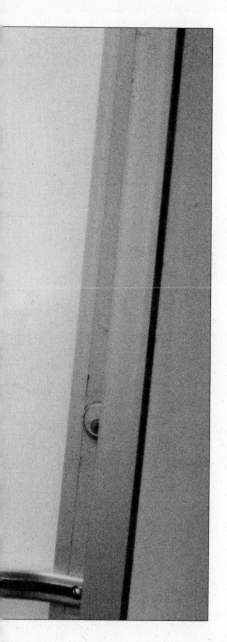

* PART 1

---

*Breaking In
& Moving Up*

Patricia Williams

THE IMPORTANCE OF
BEING A WELL-ROUNDED COOK

With high cheekbones and long legs, Patricia Williams looks more like a former model than a former ballerina, and nothing like a typical chef. After dancing nationally for more than a decade, she traded in her toe shoes for a whisk and her tutu for a chef's toque and began working in some of the most popular kitchens in Manhattan: Arizona 206, 150 Wooster, and the Supper Club among them. In 1996 she landed an opening spot as executive chef at Drew Nieporent's City Wine & Cigar Co., where she began with a menu that blends European, southern, and Latin flavors in such dishes as risotto with hominy and ham or in guava-glazed tuna with cucumber and toasted pumpkin-seed vinaigrette. One of the growing number of women to enter the mostly male clique of nationally recognized gourmet chefs, Williams proffers advice on what, if any, special considerations women face in the profession. She also addresses why it is critical for all new chefs—male and female alike—to diversify their skills before homing in on one type of cuisine.

I applied for my first job wearing high heels and skintight pants. That's not the way you're supposed to dress for an interview," particularly one at the Quilted Giraffe in Manhattan, which was then a four-star restaurant, but for Williams, a former ballerina, dressing theatrically was *de rigueur*.

Williams was born and raised in Texas but left the Lone Star State to pursue a dance career that would take her around the world. She danced with New York City's Harkness Ballet, the Chicago Ballet, and eventually the esteemed New York City Opera Ballet. She loved the physicality and creativity of it all. But dance careers have a short shelf life, and Williams chose to get out before hers expired. She'd been dancing professionally since she was fifteen. By the time she was twenty-eight, she was ready to retire. "I could have danced until I was thirty-five or thirty-six, but I wanted to quit when I was at my best." The whole time she danced, she was in classes, on the road, or on stage, and almost always on a diet. Once she retired, she had more free time than she knew what to do with, and absolutely no idea what to do with her life.

Since she had always enjoyed performing in Paris, she bought a plane ticket to France. "I took all the money I had, said goodbye to my mother, and went there to live." As one friend after another took her on tours of the countryside, she was struck by the local farmers' markets and vineyards. One of her favorite experiences was shopping for truffles, which she likens to watching a drug deal. "The best truffle man would sell only to the people he liked. He'd go to the back of his car, open up his bag, and take out this little gram scale. It was so exciting." She also remembers watching with something akin to awe while a friend, a chef, wended his way through the hills of Provence, ascending and descending for twenty-five miles before he found the perfect baby lettuces. Williams was so utterly intoxicated by the food that she gained twenty pounds. "If you know anything about dancers, you know there is a lot of major food deprivation going on. France was an eating extravaganza."

After living in France for three months, Williams returned to the United States. While she wasn't sure a career in the food industry was the way to go, cooking professionally had enough in common with dance to make it appealing:

> *After working as a ballerina, I knew I had to do something physical. And with cooking you're constantly moving. It's also creative. There's always something to*

learn, always something new to do. It's not a career that is stagnant. And you can do it for a long time, which was really important to me.

Dancing and cooking are also both art forms that revolve around giving pleasure to strangers—the dancer gives pleasure to the audience, and the restaurant chef to the patron. Sufficiently intrigued, Williams decided to apply for the beginning cooking course at the **New York Restaurant School.** She was instantly hooked. "I didn't even finish the course before I went and asked for a job at the Quilted Giraffe, one of the top-rated restaurants at the time.* "I said to them, 'I don't really know how to do much. But will you hire me anyway?' They said yes on the spot."

How could they resist high heels and skintight pants?

If the people at the Quilted Giraffe thought Williams was going to burn out, as most newcomers do, they were wrong. Forbidden to do almost anything, Williams started out as a very lowly dessert plater; her sole responsibility was to slice and plate desserts. As in ballet, where trainees repeat one position hundreds of times, new kitchen assistants were required to repeat a task until they got it right. From there, Williams worked her way up the kitchen hierarchy, moving from cold to hot appetizers and finally to the line. She remembers her time there as rigorous and demanding:

> *The Quilted Giraffe's kitchen was the most consistent I have ever worked in. You didn't cook anything in the beginning. You'd watch someone do it ten times; then someone would do it with you ten times. If you did it wrong, the person doing it with you got yelled at those ten times—you didn't. After the tenth time, however, if you did it wrong, you got yelled at. Everybody in the kitchen would come over to you and say, I'm sorry, I will not accept that plate going out.*

After a year, she left the Quilted Giraffe to go to Arizona 206, where she worked the day shift. At the time, it was one of the more exceptional restaurants in town and its innovative chef, Brendan Walsh, was one of the first chefs to use organic food from California. "At 206 we saw things that were so beautiful. You don't see anything like it to this day,

*Its other alumni include Tom Colicchio of Gramercy Park and Wayne Nish of March, both in New York.

mostly because of price. The menus and food of the 1980s were *so* expensive. Men with expense accounts, people plunking down two, three hundred dollars a night for a meal. It was nothing for them."

After working at Arizona 206 for several months, Williams figured she'd learn more if she moved on to something new. As she explains it, diversifying their skills is one of the most important things chefs can do:

> *You have to carefully plan your job moves, to constantly think about what kind of cuisine you eventually want to pursue. When I started, I made a list of the people with whom I wanted to work. I knew their reputation because I had their cookbooks and had eaten out at their restaurants, making mental notes about each chef along the way. Often the better the restaurant, the less the pay, but it's more money for you later on because you're getting an education.*

This time she wanted to learn volume, which she did by working with Ali Barker, who had just left Danny Meyers's Union Square Cafe, where he had earned three stars as opening chef, to open up 150 Wooster. Not surprisingly—in light of his success at Union Square, which to this day is consistently rated as one of the top restaurants in the nation—the Mediterranean-style food at 150 Wooster was extraordinarily popular. And big crowds meant Williams got to practice her hand at maintaining quality while learning how to handle volume. Williams's next goal was to nail breakfast. When a job at a popular brunch place, Sarabeth's Kitchen, opened up, she jumped at the opportunity. Other jobs followed, including one at a hotel, which offered yet a different kind of experience. "I wanted to be well rounded: consistency, among other things, at Quilted Giraffe; organic cuisine at Arizona 206; breakfast and lunch at Sarabeth's; and volume at 150 Wooster."

Once Williams had diversified her skills, she felt that she could concentrate on one type of food. Southwestern was one of her personal favorites—it was closest to what she had grown up eating as a half-Cherokee, half-Mexican kid in Texas. So when Drew Nieporent (of New York City's Montrachet, Nobu, Tribeca Grill, Layla's, et al.) approached her about opening City Wine & Cigar, a wine and cigar club as well as a restaurant, she knew it was a perfect fit. Her mission was to design a menu of southwestern-influenced foods that, with their strong flavors, could stand up to tobacco and spirits. "I wanted the menu at City Wine to be ethnic in a daring way, so I developed a menu that draws a lot on Indian (indigenous South American) and Latin flavors, which share many of the same ingredients—chile, cinnamon, coriander." Items on the menu reflect not only her background but also ideas from Latin cookbooks, which she reads voraciously, and lingering memories of her food extravaganza in France. A typical dish is Foie Gras with Fiery Leeks and Tamarind Sauce, a Latinized interpretation of a classic French dish.

As executive chef at City Wine & Cigar, Williams designs menus, controls inventory, orders food, and manages people. She mines her own past not only for food and menu ideas but also for the best management techniques. For example, she instills the same consistency she learned at Quilted Giraffe in her kitchen at City Wine & Cigar. "Nothing goes out until it's right. No exceptions, because if you let it slide once, you will the second, the third, and the fourth time as well. It's important to me because my name is out there, and I won't accept anyone putting out a bad plate." And, like the best restaurant chefs with whom she's worked, she's learned to listen to the people she employs. She has two sous chefs—one who is very experienced and one who has had less time on the line. But she listens to both of them equally, because an inexperienced cook may put something together that she hasn't considered, precisely because of his or her inexperience. "As a manager, you don't hire the people with whom you work the most closely and not listen to them."

She has other considerations when it comes to hiring and working with people. For starters, she tries to maintain the right mix of people with whom to work in the kitchen. Because she's a woman in a male-dominated field, one might assume that she likes working with other women. But in fact she prefers to have a balance:

> Too many women in the kitchen and everyone starts worrying about how you feel. I say, "Who cares how you feel? There's work to be done." Too many men in the kitchen and there's too much testosterone. I call it the "cowboy kitchen"—"I'm better than you; I'm faster than you." A balance makes it much easier for everyone. Guys feel more comfortable and women feel more secure.

Until recently, when the effects of an increasing number of women in key positions could be felt, striking a balance was difficult because there were so few women in professional kitchens. "When I started, approximately fifteen years ago, some places wouldn't interview women. In one interview, someone actually asked me whether if I got raped and mugged on the way home, I would still come to work the next day. Then they asked why my husband allowed me to work." She declined the job.

Much has changed since that dreadful interview, and women restaurateurs such as Alice Waters of Chez Panisse, Nora Pouillon of Restaurant Nora and Asia Nora, and Ella Brennan of Commander's Palace have paved the way for a new generation of women restaurateurs (such as Mary Sue Milliken and Susan Feniger of Border Grill in Los Angeles, Nancy Oakes and Traci des Jardins in San Francisco, and Lydia Shire of Biba in Boston); but cooking professionally is still not necessarily a female-friendly industry. (For a list of resources for women in the restaurant industry, see page 169.) It's an environment, where men feel free to constantly come on to women and make crude anatomical references and jokes. The rough behavior of men aside, kitchens also lack glamour. There's no time to make oneself up—and no point to it—because after hours of dicing, deboning, and moving animal flesh around a hot grill, makeup and hairdos become smudges and hair don'ts. "It's not a job where your appearance is very appealing. I rarely wear makeup, and I never wear nail polish because I don't want chips in the food. You have to project a really clean image."

There's also the "costume" to worry about. Though kitchens are opening up and allowing their staffs to be a bit more creative in what they wear, the iconographic chef's whites still prevail. "Those whites look great on the male chefs, but dumb on women," according to Williams. At best, women "look as if they have their father's clothes on." At worst, "those great big pants make us look like a bear or a mushroom walking down the street."

Dating is also much more difficult for women than it is for men. In reflecting on her own experiences and those of her male peers, Williams found that women will wait for a man, but men won't wait for women: "I don't finish working until between twelve midnight and two A.M., every night. My schedule caused problems with my first marriage. My husband worked during the day, and I was very devoted to my work and worked all night long. We had other problems, but that was part of the breakup." As a result of the pressure on her social life, until she recently remarried, Williams tended to socialize with friends in the business but only date men outside the industry—no other chefs, no waiters, no bartenders or managers. "Before I remarried, I dated people who had a whole life themselves, so that it wasn't necessary for me to be there with them all the time. They could come in for dinner and I'd try to sit down with them later at night. But they had to be very secure within themselves, and I didn't meet very many of those people."

As with her male counterparts, however, attention to her personal life comes only after her work as an executive chef is done. And at this stage in her career, Williams's main responsibility is to live up to and improve upon the initial reviews for City Wine & Cigar—"Light, aggressive, very tasty. . . . The menu breaks new ground. . . . Williams has thrown out all the conventional notions of cooking for smokers. This is not a red meat and potatoes menu, but a carefully constructed group of dishes that stand up to cigar smoke and big wine through the sheer power of flavor."[1] She is under considerable pressure. In an era when the average start-up cost of opening a restaurant has risen dramatically, the owners of City Wine have much more at stake financially than restaurateurs did twenty years ago. The responsibility, of course, falls disproportionately on the chef's shoulders, even though restaurant design and service (see pages 100 and 238, respectively) are an integral part of a restaurant's success. And it's not just the restaurant's future that's hanging in the balance but Williams's own future as well. "I'm forty-three, and a fifty-year-old line cook is an ugly thing. You have to think about the reviews in terms of your marketability and what it will bring you in the future."

Just as she did as a dancer, Williams plans to continue only for as long as she is at the top of her game. And for now, that's more than enough. "When I danced, I gave it my utmost, and it was fulfilling. It's the same with cooking. It's introduced me to people and opened up opportunities for me that I would never have experienced otherwise."

Note: In early 1999, Williams left Drew Nieporent's Myriad Restaurant Group to pursue other opportunities. Wherever she lands, she'll bring her experiences at City Wine & Cigar to bear. Meanwhile, in a move that may be interpreted as the beginning of the end of cigar trendiness, the Myriad Group is transforming the space that was formerly City Wine & Cigar into a seafood restaurant.

Patricia Williams's

✕

Foie Gras with Fiery Leeks
and Tamarind Sauce

Chef's note: *As a kid growing up in Texas, I used to love to drink a soda made of tamarind. When I opened City Wine & Cigar Co. and was working on a foie gras dish, I thought back to that sweet, tangy drink, and I also came up with the idea of adding fiery leeks to complete the dish. The most important part of this dish is the quality of the foie gras. The next is the heat of the pan. And finally, you'll want to sauté the foie gras until it has a crisp, golden skin.*

(Serves 4)
Fiery Leeks

5 ounces leeks (white parts only), julienned
4 tablespoons butter
1 cup water
1 tablespoon garlic confit*
½ tablespoon chipotle pureed until smooth†
2 tablespoons Champagne vinegar

*For garlic confit, blend ½ head of garlic with ¼ cup of olive oil and cook over the lowest flame possible until the garlic is softened and golden brown. The garlic is strained out of the oil and processed or mashed with a fork until smooth. The extra garlic confit will last in the refrigerator for two weeks.
†Cans of chipotle peppers in adobo sauce can be found in most gourmet and Hispanic markets. Puree the peppers until smooth.

1. In a heavy-gauge saucepan, sweat the leeks in *2* tablespoons of butter in a covered pan over medium heat for 2 minutes.

2. Add the water and remaining ingredients, including the remaining 2 tablespoons of butter. Slowly cook the leeks until they are completely softened, not at all stringy, approximately 15 to 20 minutes. If the leeks become dry, add water to complete the cooking process.

Tamarind Glaze

4 ounces garlic, chopped
2 teaspoons olive oil
15 Szechwan peppercorns
1 cup pomegranate juice*
1 tablespoon tamarind concentrate†
1 cup veal demiglaze

1. Coat the garlic with the oil. Put the garlic and peppercorns in a heavy-bottomed saucepan. Slowly heat the garlic and peppercorns and sauté the garlic until golden. (Be careful not to heat the garlic too quickly, or the peppercorns will burn and become bitter.)

2. Add the pomegranate juice and reduce to a glaze-like consistency. Add the tamarind concentrate and demiglaze, reduce for 5 minutes, and strain.

To Sauté the Foie Gras

steel pan
kosher salt
fresh black pepper
Four 3-ounce slices of foie gras

*Pomegranate juice can be found in Middle Eastern food markets.
†Tamarind concentrate can be found in Middle Eastern or Asian food markets.

1. Heat the steel pan until it is very hot.
2. Sprinkle the salt and the pepper on the foie gras.
3. Place the foie gras slices in the hot pan and gently press them into the heat to ensure a crust.
4. Turn the foie gras when the crust is achieved and cook on the remaining side until the foie gras is soft to the touch.

To Assemble the Dish

1. Gently warm the leek mixture and place in the center of the plate.
2. Place the foie gras atop the leeks.
3. Spoon the warm tamarind glaze on the foie gras and around the plate.

Andrew Pforzheimer

BREAKING IN AND MOVING UP

"You've come a long way, baby" is an apt expression that applies not only to just how far chefs have come in terms of respect and prestige—a transition from blue-collar workers to celebrities of sorts—but also to how far Andrew Pforzheimer has come since the days of his college campus fast-food job at Paco's Tacos. Over the course of a twenty-year career, Pforzheimer has worked the line at one of San Francisco's most prized restaurants, composed burgers for Los Angeles's celebrities, and drawn raves for his work at New York's '21' Club. He's now the owner of three restaurants in Connecticut. Having worked his way up from fast-food prep cook to chef and from chef to entrepreneur, Pforzheimer has done it all. Below, he offers his suggestions on how someone with no connections in the industry can break into the business and—if not deterred by the long hours and hard work—move up.

If you want to break into this industry, I think the best way to get started is to beg and plead your way into your first job, and work for nothing if you have to." In the business, this is known as a *stage,* or *trailing,* working for free or next to nothing as a chef's apprentice, while you observe and gradually help a cook or cooks at their stations. Not only do you learn a great deal, but at the end of your training period you also have something to put on your résumé.

Pforzheimer is not advising anything he hasn't tried himself. As a major in philosophy and Russian literature at Harvard College, Pforzheimer worked at Paco's Tacos in Harvard Square, refrying precooked food. It wasn't exactly haute cuisine, but it provoked his interest in food—so much so that by his sophomore year, he was spending more time shopping and preparing for the *Harvard Lampoon*'s weekly dinners than on either Plato or Turgenev. By the end of his junior year, while others were plotting how to get into business school, Pforzheimer had decided to take an eating tour of New Orleans. With a friend, he went to twenty restaurants in eight days, consuming everything in sight and taking scrupulous notes along the way. Full of things Creole and Cajun, he decided to take a leave of absence from Harvard in order to pursue this budding passion more seriously.

A family friend gave him the name of André Parra, the chef-owner of L'Ermitage in Burgundy. Since epicures more experienced than himself told him that France was the way to go, Pforzheimer wrote to Parra requesting an apprenticeship. But rather than stick around nervously checking the mail, he decided to go to France anyway. Pforzheimer started with a bike tour of the French countryside, planning to end in Burgundy, right in L'Ermitage's courtyard. Halfway through his tour, he called home to see if there had been word from France. As Pforzheimer feared, Parra had written back to say he couldn't offer an apprenticeship, owing to the French immigration laws. Unfazed, prepared to beg and plead if necessary, Pforzheimer bicycled to L'Ermitage anyway. A shocked Parra tried, to no avail, to turn him away. Exhausted by the effort, Parra finally promised Pforzheimer one thing—a bed in a cinder-block shed out back, where he could figure out how to get back to the States. Since that was where the apprentices were sleeping, it was about as close to the kitchen as Pforzheimer could expect to get. Undeterred, Pforzheimer initially tried to charm Parra. When that didn't work, he resorted to wiliness. He volunteered to teach Parra's daughter English, figuring that if she took to it, Parra would ask him to stay. It worked. Parra agreed to let him work through the end of the summer.

Dull though his prep assignments were—chopping parsley, shelling peas, and eviscerating duck—Pforzheimer was ecstatic. Not only did he do the tasks competently and without complaint; his enthusiasm also set him apart from his French colleagues, who were less focused, in part because they were much younger. "The second it was three o'clock, the French apprentices would be out like a shot. Because I didn't have any friends and I didn't speak any French, I'd work straight through. They loved my work ethic."

He started out as a basic apprentice before being promoted to apprentice *poissonier,* a job that no one else wanted. Sure it was fun to learn how to prepare beautiful fish entrées. But that wasn't all the apprentice *poissonier* did. As Pforzheimer would soon learn, he also had to make biweekly runs to the train station to pick up boxes of whole fish, which he then had to clean and scale. By the end of the day, he couldn't even count the number of punctures on his hands from the fish spines. Several months after Pforzheimer's arrival, the *poissonier* just up and disappeared. When the three people who, in the hierarchy of the kitchen, were ahead of Pforzheimer tried and failed to do the job, he was, finally, promoted. It was the opportunity he had been waiting for.

When he returned to Harvard to finish school a year later, fluent in both the French language and the ways of French kitchens, he knew without a doubt that he wanted to be a chef. Indeed, he had come up with a master blueprint for his entire career. He'd start with a two-year learning period, followed by five years as a line cook and two years as a sous chef. By the time he was thirty, he wanted to have his own place. Pforzheimer unwittingly did what many an experienced chef explicitly advises. For example, in the wonderfully informative *Becoming a Chef* by Andrew Dornenburg and Karen Page, Chef-owner Michael Foley of Printer's Row and Le Perroquet in Chicago advises:

> *The only way a person can be happy with the routine of "chop, slice and dice" is if you set up a program of goals. . . . The goals have to be related to the industry, such as learning as much as you can about fish or meat. . . . Then you should learn as much as you can about operations, how to work a station properly. Always put your goals into a time frame.*[2]

Pforzheimer started immediately. He got to work, even as he was finishing college. During his last two years at Harvard, he took a part-time job working the garde manger station at Upstairs at the Pudding, a fancy northern Italian restaurant in Cambridge.

After he graduated from Harvard, Pforzheimer initiated phase two of his plan. He started looking for a place where he could work the line, a position he considers the most crucial training period in any cook's career. Before the annual restaurant issues of *Esquire* and *Gourmet,* there were few places Pforzheimer could go for information. So he consulted a magazine people frequently read for the articles: *Playboy.* "Once a year, they listed the top twenty-five restaurants in the country. Nobody else really did this fifteen years ago, because back then nobody gave a damn about chefs or cooking in general." He applied to two of the featured restaurants, New York's Lutèce and Le Bec-Fin in Philadelphia, both of which turned him down. Then he tried another route. He flew out to San Francisco to "meet *the* chef, a man named Jeremiah Tower."

Born in the United States and educated in England and Australia, Tower, like Pforzheimer, went to Harvard College and then the Harvard Graduate School of Design, where he got a master's degree in architecture. Though Tower is now known as one of the authority figures of California food, his start in cooking was purely accidental. While he was looking for work as an architect in 1972, he took a job in a restaurant. Bitten by the restaurant bug, he was working with Alice Waters at Chez Panisse in Berkeley shortly thereafter. Waters, a graduate of the University of California at Berkeley, where she majored in French Cultural Studies, opened what has long been considered one of America's best restaurants, Chez Panisse, in 1971. Since her first days as a chef and restaurateur, she has opened two more restaurants; written several books, including *The Chez Panisse Menu Cookbook* and *Chez Panisse Vegetables;* and blazed many trails that now seem familiar: the use of local, seasonal ingredients versus an overreliance on canned or imported foods; and the use of a broader variety of ingredients, many of which Americans now take for granted, such as mesclun, and the advocacy of organic food— that is, ingredients produced and harvested in an ecologically sound way. She's also had quite a few outstanding cooks work in her kitchen—Jonathan Waxman, Joyce Goldstein, and Mark Miller included.

By 1984, when Pforzheimer was looking for work, Tower had just hung up his shingle at a restaurant across the bay from Chez Panisse, the much beloved Stars in San Francisco. Pforzheimer tried to approach Tower directly about a job, but he got the runaround: he'd make an appointment with Tower and turn up at the appointed hour only to be told that Tower wasn't available. Pforzheimer finally gave the person in the front room his résumé and told him to take it to whoever was in charge in the kitchen. "Sufficiently intrigued," perhaps by the Harvard connection, Tower emerged. Since he was getting rave reviews that kept the crowds coming, Tower actually needed additional help in the kitchen. Pforzheimer's persistence had paid off.

Tower's reputation from his days at Chez Panisse and Santa Fe Bar & Grill, along with the good press that accompanied the opening of Stars, drew a kitchen full of the country's most skilled cooks, many of whom had left sous chef and head chef positions for an opportunity to work with Tower and learn from him. Consequently, Pforzheimer's colleagues included Brendan Walsh, who came from Gotham Bar and Grill in New York; the chef de cuisine Mark Franz (who now heads his own restaurant, Farralon in San Francisco); and Jerry Comfort and Bob Hurley, both of whom had worked at Masa's—one of San Francisco's most exceptional restaurants. (Hurley is now the executive chef at Napa Valley Grille.) "They had all been head chefs, except for one other guy who had been a line cook for a long time. And then there was me. It was *amazing*."

This would prove to be his most formative learning experience, because it's as a line cook, Pforzheimer contends, that you learn the basic skills you will draw from throughout your career:

> As a sous chef, you learn management skills; and once you're a chef, you're on your own—you learn from books, you learn from stealing other people's stuff, or you learn from having a dream at night. But when it comes to actually acquiring hands-on skills, it's line cooking.

As he worked side by side with these heavyweights, including Tower himself, Pforzheimer observed how each of them did things, and he got advice from them throughout each night. One minute the chef on his left would advise him, "Wait another thirty seconds before you put the scallops in the oil because your oil is not hot enough." The next minute, he'd turn to the chef on his right and say, "I just did this and it came out great. Now, it looks like crap. What did I do?" Day in and day out, he'd bombard them with questions. But he learned that, beyond cooking skills, a good cook also has to have a sharp sense of timing.

With 400 covers—customer orders—per night, the energy in the Stars kitchen was extremely hectic and fast-paced. At any given moment Pforzheimer might be working on orders for a duck, a lobster, six steaks, two pastas, and a swordfish, with each dish only a single component of a table's order; and since he was a cook, it was his responsibility to manage in what order and how fast to cook each item. Though it's the job of expediter (the person who calls out the orders) to help cooks get the different components of the meals out in the right sequence and at the same time, any miscalculation on the line cook's part can throw off the timing of a cook in another area of the kitchen, and cause the other cooks to lose their cool. As a beginner, Pforzheimer says:

> You become acutely aware of timing. Somebody will say to you, how long for the pasta, and you know they need it badly. The temptation is to say, it's a minute. But it's not, it's six minutes. You just have to deal with the guy yelling and throwing something at you because you're not telling him what he wants to hear, because if you say anything but the truth, you've completely screwed up everyone else in the kitchen. And you'll get your head handed to you over and over again until a minute is actually a minute.

The pressure to get everything just right was intense.

As an escape from this pressure, Pforzheimer used to hang out with his college buddies in Los Angeles whenever he got a couple of days off. "I'd drive down to southern California, arrive at six A.M., maybe catch a nap, party for two days solid, get back into the car at 6 A.M. on the day I had to be back at work, and pull into downtown San Francisco by fifteen minutes before my two P.M. shift. I'd hop out of the convertible with my hair standing straight up from all the dust and bugs in my hair. I looked like Don King." He did that week after week, until finally, after a year and a half at Stars and going up and down the coast, he moved to Los Angeles, where he embarked on a career in which he would change jobs and move around quite frequently.

Yet this job mobility shouldn't be interpreted as a sign of flakiness. With a constant need to learn something new and plenty of opportunities to do so, cooks just starting out typically stay for no more than two years in one kitchen, rotating through as many positions as possible before moving elsewhere. Job changes are so frequent that, according to the Bureau of Labor Statistics, chefs switch jobs "at nearly double the rate for other professions."[3]

In Los Angeles, Pforzheimer started working with Patrick Healy, a former apprentice of Roger Vergé of Le Moulin de Mougins. Pforzheimer joined Healy at Colette, a "jewel-box" restaurant in a Beverly Hills hotel. "Jewel-box restaurants are almost always staffed by a kitchen full of immigrants—Chinese, Mexican, and Guatemalan guys—and they make some of the most amazing food I've ever had." In Pforzheimer's experience, immigrants, as opposed to native-born Americans, tend to work well with a really imposing central figure who wants the food done his or her way and no other way. "The problem with Americans, particularly Americans who went to cooking school, is that they don't want to take direction. They want to do their riff here and maybe a little bit of embellishment over there. And the classic French-trained chef doesn't want anyone touching his food like that." Colette contrasted pointedly with Stars, where chefs were given more freedom, albeit under Tower's watchful eye.

After Pforzheimer had spent six months at Colette, a friend put him touch with Peter Morton, who gave him an opportunity to be a consulting chef for the very first Hard Rock Café in the United States (in Los Angeles). Not only was the job glamorous, but as a consultant, Pforzheimer could make his own schedule, which allowed him to cultivate a long-distance relationship he was trying to sustain. There were other perks. "I could leave my car parked right in front of the Hard Rock, walk past this huge line of people every day, and just walk right in." And once inside, he could make whatever he wanted in the kitchen, bring it out into the dining room, go up to a table of six girls, and say, "'Hey, here is something we're trying out; I'd like you to try it.' It was the greatest job."

Great as it was, however, he was discovering some hard truths about the business. To its credit, he found that this is an industry that rewards talent. Unlike other businesses, where everything can depend on who you know, in cooking you rise or fall on your own merits. As a result, there is relatively little politics in the kitchen. For Pforzheimer this is because of the cultural diversity: "If you don't speak the language and know the cultural nuances, it's hard to be politic." But the flip side of this culturally diverse, multilingual environment is that there is no socializing either. "One of the hells of being in this business is spending your entire life surrounded by people with whom you have nothing to talk about. It's very tough." (For a different take on camaraderie, see Anthony Bourdain, page 28.) This lack of camaraderie may have been one of the reasons Pforzheimer was willing to uproot himself in 1986, when he moved yet again. This time he left the Hard Rock and Los Angeles for New York City. Since "both Jeremiah Tower and Peter Morton, who ate out all the time, had said at different times that the best restaurant they knew of in the country was Arcadia," that's the first place Pforzheimer went to seek work.

As he had at Stars, Pforzheimer walked right into Arcadia looking for a job. Anne Rosenzweig, the executive chef and co-owner, was sitting up front, and he asked her to take his résumé to the executive chef, not realizing that he was already talking to her. Pforzheimer recovered from his *faux pas* as Chef Rosenzweig and her partner Ken Aretsky passed his résumé back and forth. "They started giggling about it, and I think Ken's exact words were, 'Oh, no, not another Ivy-League-educated chef.'" Once again, Pforzheimer's timing was right. Rosenzweig happened to be looking for a right-hand person.

Pforzheimer was hired as Rosenzweig's personal assistant and was assigned to work on a variety of projects. He cooked at a restaurant she was a consultant to, and he responded to various media and publicity events that followed in the wake of her success at Arcadia. He found in Rosenzweig, a graduate of Columbia University who had also started her career as an apprentice, someone he could really admire. "Anne was pretty much self-taught, which is hard in this business. But she is smart and she's tough. At the same time, it was fun doing things with her, because she is very open to new ideas."

When she was hired to revitalize the '21' Club, Pforzheimer got to work on two memorable projects. One was the origination of a "big, classic American breakfast à la some inn in Vermont," which Rosenzweig revamped for patrons seeking the ultimate power breakfast. Following that, Pforzheimer was asked to develop the '21' Burger, a burger that would befit such a vital New York institution:

> I ended up copying this idea from a James Beard cookbook, where he put a knob of butter inside a hamburger. Anne changed it to herb butter, but basically the manufacture of the burger was the way we had done it at Stars. Plus, when I had been at the Hard Rock, we used to serve seven hundred hamburgers a day, and we had this way of churning out patties without ever touching them with our hands. And I put all these things together and, in 1987, it turned out to be a cover story in the New York Times Sunday Magazine. It was the most famous burger in the world.

The article on the '21' Club burger was not his first brush with the media. At both Stars and Arcadia, television crews and food writers frequently showed up to do stories. But this was one of the first times that his creation was a feature story. Other stories would follow.

Despite the press, Pforzheimer burned out at '21' Club. After traveling to Spain and Morocco, he came back to New York to work with the restaurateur Brian McNally (whose latest restaurant is Balthazar). And since he was a year short of turning thirty, he also took stock of his life. According to the blueprint for his career, he was supposed to have his own restaurant within a year. Yet owning a restaurant seemed like torture. By this time he was married and his wife was expecting a child, and he knew he didn't want to spend as much time away from home as a restaurant would demand. Something a bit more corporate—something with steady hours, insurance, and other benefits—started to look increasingly attractive. Then he heard that Martha Stewart was just about to launch a new magazine. While he was beyond begging and pleading at this point in his career, he knew he'd have to cleverly finagle his way into a job. He invited Stewart to the restaurant where he was cooking while he figured out what he wanted to do with his life. It must have been quite a meal, because she offered Pforzheimer the food editor's job. Without a moment's hesitation, Pforzheimer moved to Connecticut to begin his new life.

But the romance with offices, even one as dynamic and full of expectancy as *Martha Stewart Living*, was short-lived. He desperately missed the kitchen—its inexorable energy, its crazy ethos. More than that, he didn't take well to an office environment. "In the kitchen, you work straight through. You don't sit down and have a cup of coffee. You don't even talk to anyone unless it's specifically related to what you are doing." In contrast to an office environment,

> *in a kitchen, eight hours of work means eight hours of work. It doesn't mean get to something, go outside and take a smoke, get to something else. It means eight straight hours of work. It's a reason why you always find a lot of chef-waiter friction. We can't stand to see someone who is working half the time they are on the clock. It just drives us crazy.*

To illustrate how busy a line cook is, Pforzheimer recalls a day when he was just starting out as a line cook and he asked a waiter for a Coke with ice. He put the drink on a little shelf, a few feet away from the blistering heat of his station. Too busy to take a sip, even as the ice began to melt, he watched the drink out of the corner of his eye. "Two hours went by where I could see it and I really wanted it, but I couldn't actually reach my hand out and get it. Imagine being that thirsty and three feet away from a cold glass of something and not having the *time* to reach out and grab it and have a sip." It was this focus and intensity that he missed when he was working in the office. And he would seek this intensity again, though somewhat indirectly, in his next career move.

With a basic understanding of the business and an ability to do computer spreadsheets, Pforzheimer decided, after he left *Living,* to become a consultant. Ideally, he planned on advising clients who wanted to open up new restaurants or expand their existing restaurant base. One of his first clients wanted to open up a tapas bar. All the cooking would be completed by 6 P.M., at which point the chefs would leave and bartenders would take over. The owners wouldn't even have to hire waiters. As he wrote the business plan, he became so excited by the way it fit with his own personal needs that he decided to go in as co-owner.

In 1996, on a site directly across the corner from a movie theater in Norwalk, Connecticut, Pforzheimer and his partner opened their restaurant. They put a tapas bar, Barcelona, on one side and a hamburger joint on the other. After all, with his Hard Rock and '21' Club experience behind him, Pforzheimer knew how to make a better-than-decent burger. But the tapas bar became so popular that it overtook the space dedicated to burgers. "The restaurant grew and grew, and then we added a patio. We now have one hundred thirty seats, and there is *still* a ninety-minute wait on weekends." Eventually, they added a selection of full appetizers and entrées to the tapas menu, which includes scallop ceviche, grilled chorizo in polenta, and anise-flavored beets.

A big restaurant with a full menu and a high tab per check is not what he had planned. Indeed, he had specifically gone into consulting because he didn't want the onus of ownership. But good luck, a great location, and a smart menu at the right time led to what Pforzheimer calls "accidental success." Though he spent the first year at Barcelona back in the kitchen working as the executive chef, he and his partner soon hired and trained a chef with whom they were delighted. During his good weeks, Pforzheimer even gets to work quasi-regular work hours.

Now Pforzheimer is learning a new skill, one that he never anticipated, even when he was a Harvard student who thought he had it all figured out—how to operate *multiple* restaurants. He is opening two new restaurants, one in Westport and the other in Greenwich, Connecticut. One will be upscale Italian, a bow to his formal European training. And the other, in a nod to his more humble roots—Paco's Tacos and the Hard Rock Café—will be a hamburger joint. Though he wasn't a consultant for very long, it appears that he can still spot a smart business opportunity when he sees one. After all, he figures, if Americans eat, on average, three hamburgers a week, and hamburger has been an American favorite for over fifty years, his burger joint will be around long enough to give more than one aspiring cook an opportunity to break in and, if inspired, to move up.

Note: In June of 1998, as the stock market rose higher and higher, Arcadia, the beloved creation of Pforzheimer's mentor Anne Rosenzweig, closed its doors. The same economy that allowed people the luxury of eating in three- and four-star restaurants had also increased the rent prohibitively. After fourteen years, she served her last meal at Arcadia on a sultry New York evening. Meanwhile, though, her restaurant Lobster Club continues to draw loyal customers from around the city.

Andrew Pforzheimer's

Sautéed Shrimp with Garlic and Sherry Sauce

Chef's note: *This was one of our first tapas, and it is still our most-requested dish. We serve it on little red-hot cast-iron plates, and we pour the sauce in while it is still rather "loose," meaning that the butter has not quite melted. The resulting fajita-like explosion when it hits the cast iron not only finishes the sauce but leaves a fabulous-smelling vapor trail as the dish is carried through the dining room. After one is served, we tend to get orders right away for three or four more. Using fresh—as in "never frozen"—white or pink shrimp makes a huge difference.*

(Serves 6)
28 to 30 medium (21 to 25 large) shrimp, about 1¼ pounds
Salt and pepper to taste
¼ cup olive oil
10 garlic cloves, peeled and sliced
¼ teaspoon crushed red pepper flakes
1 cup medium-bodied sherry
1 teaspoon fresh thyme leaves
4 tablespoons sweet butter
2 tablespoons coarsely chopped parsley

Special equipment: cast iron serving plate

1. Peel the shrimp, leaving the tip of the tail shell on. Salt and pepper lightly and set aside.

2. Put a heavy cast-iron serving piece on a medium flame to heat.

3. Heat the olive oil in a heavy sauté pan over high heat. Add the sliced garlic and cook, stirring, until the garlic begins to brown. Add the shrimp and sauté quickly. Add the red pepper flakes and cook until the shrimp starts to turn pink.

4. Add the sherry off the flame, and then cook over the highest heat. (If using a weak burner, remove shrimp now and return them to the pan when the sherry is reduced.) Add the fresh thyme.

5. When the sherry is reduced by three-quarters, swirl in the butter and add the parsley. Remove from heat, pour into the sizzling-hot cast-iron pan, and serve immediately.

* JOB DESCRIPTIONS* *

Master Chef / Master Pastry Chef

The master chef or master pastry chef is an individual who possesses the highest degree of professional knowledge and skill. These chefs teach and supervise their entire crew as well as providing leadership and serving as role models for the ACFEI apprentices.

Executive Chef

A full-time chef who is the department head responsible for all culinary units in a restaurant, hotel, club, or other food-service establishment. He or she might also be the owner of a food-service operation. The person in this position must supervise a minimum of five full-time people in the production of food.

Executive Pastry Chef

A pastry chef who is a department head; usually responsible to the executive chef of a food operation or the management of his/her employing research or pastry firm.

Chef de Cuisine

A chef who is the supervisor in charge of food production in a food-service operation. This could be a single-unit or a multi-unit operation, or a freestanding operation. He or she is in essence the chef of this operation, with final decision-making power over culinary operations. The person in this position must supervise a minimum of three full-time people in the production of food.

Working Pastry Chef

A pastry chef responsible for the pastry section or shift within a food-service operation.

Sous Chef

A chef who is the supervisor of a shift, station, or stations in a food-service operation. A sous chef must supervise a minimum of two full-time people in the preparation of food.

Culinarian

A person positioned in any one station in a food-service operation, responsible for preparing and cooking sauces, cold foods (also called **garde manger**), fish, soups and stocks, meats, vegetables, eggs, and other food items.

Pastry Culinarian

A person positioned in any one station in a food-service operation, responsible for preparing and cooking pies, cookies, cakes, breads, rolls, or other baked goods and dessert items.

Rounds Cook

This person relieves various cooks on their days off, and therefore must be adept at a number of stations.

Prep Cook/Pastry Prep

From straining stocks to dicing onions, from slicing apples to glazing danishes, prep cooks perform the groundwork for all kitchens.

Expediter

The expediter serves as a liaison between the customers in the dining room and the line cooks, and makes sure that the food gets to the wait staff in a timely fashion, so that everyone sitting at a particular table is served simultaneously.

*The first eight definitions were provided courtesy of the American Culinary Federation.

Anthony Bourdain

A PORTRAIT OF THE CHEF
AS A YOUNG REBEL

Not many writers can claim to have written a New York Times Notable Book. *Fewer still can claim to have written it while they were pursuing a full-time career that demands nothing less than fifteen hours of standing a day, a willingness to suffer second-degree burns without complaint, and an uncanny ability to communicate—sometimes in words, sometimes in body language—with coworkers who hail from around the world. But Anthony Bourdain, a chef who has worked in the business for over twenty years, did just that with the publication of his first book,* Bone in the Throat. *Sharp-tongued and discerning, he humorously exposes the macho and fraternal world of the restaurant scene.*

What makes a good chef? Is it a fine-tuned, almost alchemical sense of taste, or is it an apprenticeship with Alain Ducasse? Must one be able to claim French ancestry, or will any old Mediterranean relative do? Just what, exactly, guarantees entry into the James Beard Hall of Fame? Alice Waters of Chez Panisse thinks that "being a really good cook has to do with having a point of view."[4] If that's true, if having an opinion is the elixir, then Anthony Bourdain is by all accounts a cook without parallel. For before he was a full-fledged teenager, Anthony had a point of view, some might even say an attitude.

Bourdain was indulged by his parents, and there was hardly a class that he wasn't offered—and nary a class that interested him. Music and still-life drawing classes bored him; tennis and riding lessons only exacerbated his ennui. When his parents suggested fox-trot lessons, he thanked them kindly but decided that the bourgeois lifestyle was not for him. So by the time he was fifteen, Bourdain and a bunch of buddies would regularly leave the hot, humid New Jersey summer behind and head north to Cape Cod's Provincetown, where they would pursue sun, fun, and the means by which to enjoy it all—a job. Because restaurant jobs were a dime a dozen, especially in the summer, Provincetown's busiest season, Bourdain easily got a job washing dishes at Flagship, a local restaurant.

While dishwashing is not the most glamorous position in the kitchen, a legion of other celebrated chefs and restaurateurs have started their careers either busing or washing dishes. Emeril Lagasse—the chef known for his bestselling books, his television show, *Emeril Live,* and for his restaurants, Emeril's and Nola in New Orleans—began his career washing pots and pans at a bakery. Norman Van Aken, executive chef and owner of Norman's in Coral Gables, Florida, started out washing dishes at a Holiday Inn. Like them, Bourdain was not content to just wash dishes. He had his eye on the chef's station, for of all the people Bourdain had encountered in his bourgeois world, chefs were most worthy of emulation. They hovered somewhere between princes, with their worldliness, and pirates, with their swashbuckling air: "Chefs had better sex and more money, drugs, and credit than anyone else I knew at the time." To Bourdain, a self-described clueless brat with no values at all, the lifestyle was appealing. And if his friends and family thought his interest in cooking and restaurants was something he would outgrow, something he could discard as he did all those many recreational activities—music, tennis, the like—they were mistaken. The restaurant business had seeped into his system.

Bourdain's immersion into the business was more elliptical than linear. During high school, he worked first as a dishwasher and later as a line cook. After graduation, he enrolled at Vassar, where he encountered the lifestyle he had rejected as a kid. Bored once again, he found himself refusing almost everything Vassar had to offer. There were two exceptions, though: women and drugs. The latter ended in drug abuse. "I wanted to get higher than anybody else, drink more than anybody else, and be more of a bad boy than anyone else. I was completely obnoxious."

Bourdain dropped out of college and went back to the Flagship. What drew him back to the restaurant scene? The money certainly helped to finance his accumulating vices. But far more important, in a restaurant kitchen Bourdain found a set of values he could respect: *order, hierarchy,* and *discipline.* Order is paramount in a professional kitchen, for on any given day, dozens of cooks and dishwashers smoothly execute hundreds of orders without burning or cutting themselves or one another, a feat which Bourdain finds almost balletic. To maintain order, a certain hierarchy must be adhered to, a hierarchy that is as steadfast as any in the military. Certain centuries-old rules apply. No one, for example, gets to advance up the "career ladder" before debearding a thousand mussels, washing a ton of spinach, or peeling a truckload of potatoes. And, finally, chefs are disciplined. Perhaps it was this quality, more than the others, that prevented Bourdain from giving himself over entirely to drugs. "In this business, it doesn't matter if you are a fire-starter, bed-wetter, drug addict, or psychopath, as long as you show up at work on time." If he worked as a cook, he could push his vices only so far.

Once in Provincetown, Bourdain thought he could just go back to the Flagship and pick up where he had left off. But the restaurant where he had cut his teeth had been sold to a new owner and was under new management, with an entirely different crew in the kitchen. The dinner crowds had doubled. Young and fearless, Bourdain swaggered into the kitchen and started bragging about his experience, assuring the management that he could handle just about anything. Flagship gave him the job, put him on the line, and let him self-immolate. "I had never seen so much business in my life." In a particularly humiliating moment, he lost it—orders were backing up, waitresses were yelling at him, everything was going awry. Then all hell broke loose. He burned himself on a sizzle platter. Reeling with pain, he asked the broiler man with whom he had been trailing if he had any ointment. The response was sheer unnerving sarcasm. "The whole kitchen went dead silent, and the broiler man held up his hands, which were covered with the most hideous scars and water-filled blisters. Smiling, without flinching or moving his eyes at all, he reached under the broiler, picked up a red-hot sizzle platter with his bare hands, and put it on the board in front of me and said something like, 'The kid wants a Band-Aid.'" Bourdain was instantly demoted to the prep crew, where he once again started peeling squid, picking scallops, and debearding mussels.

While he was knee-deep in the detritus of the kitchen, his mind was free to devise a plan that he thought would safeguard him against future humiliation. He'd go to the **Culinary Institute of America (CIA).** Ever arrogant, he figured that with a degree and formal training, he'd outperform "all those blue-collar slugs" who had never been rigorously trained. His plan paid off. He had no problem getting a job.

According to Bourdain, though the CIA did give him the competitive edge he sought, the now august and influential institution was then, in the early 1970s, not quite as prestigious an institution as it is today. According to Mark Ruhlman, author of *The Making of a Chef*, the CIA was conceived in New Haven, Connecticut, in 1944, when a group of concerned restaurateurs had become worried that with all the men at war, they'd soon have no skilled cooks. They hired Frances Roth, the first woman to be admitted to the Connecticut Bar, to open a cooking school for returning veterans. The school opened two years later. By the time Bourdain enrolled, in the 1970s, the school had moved from New Haven to its present site, a former Jesuit seminary overlooking the cliffs at Hyde Park, New York. As Bourdain recalls that time in the CIA's history, its student body—with such notable exceptions as Charlie Palmer of Aureole, Larry Forgione of An American Place, Roy Yamaguchi of Hawaii's Roy's Restaurant, and Susan Feniger of Border Grill—consisted of "marginals, for the most part, who chose cooking school over community college or who went to the CIA on the GI bill."

Since Bourdain's day, the school's student body has evolved considerably. Today the school has some of the country's top students, many of whom opt for a degree from the prestigious culinary academy (at an estimated cost of just under $33,000 for an associate degree) over one from an Ivy League college. Or they come from the corporate world, leaving behind lucrative but soulless jobs for an opportunity to pursue their dream of working in the food business. And of course, they come from the restaurant industry itself. Almost all students have at least six months of kitchen experience, and many have years more. Also, the curriculum was expanded in 1994, giving students the option of pursuing a bachelor of professional studies degree in addition to an associate degree in occupational studies. In essence, over the last twenty years, the CIA has evolved into the most prestigious cooking school in the country, perhaps in the world. As Ruhlman says in *The Making of a Chef,* his account of a year spent at the CIA, it's "the oldest, biggest, best-known, and most influential cooking school in America, the only residential college in the United States devoted solely to the study of the culinary arts."[5]

The changes that would eventually transform the CIA into the outstanding culinary educational center it is today were still some years out on the horizon, but this didn't stop Bourdain and his classmates from getting good jobs. In 1978, right out of school, Bourdain worked at the Rainbow Room, one of Manhattan's most exclusive establishments. Though Bourdain enjoyed the job, he confesses that even with his training he was overwhelmed by the volume and the level of perfection required by the crew. Nor was he prepared for the excessive machismo, the high testosterone levels that seem a by-product of an environment where thirty men work together for fifteen hours at a time. This was more than just the usual "dozens"—a game in which chefs try to outwit and humiliate each other with unsavory and scabrous remarks. He remembers one place where, on the most casual level, men would regularly have conversations "with one hand lodged next to the testicles of the other." He also recalls "a lot of grab-ass." Innocent though it was, the degree of play bothered this James Dean of the kitchen, this man who became a chef in part because he felt that owning a set of chef's whites would legitimize his own macho swagger, his rebellious air. So when the chef steward, a big Puerto Rican named Modesto, came after him one time too many, it was time to duel:

> One time I was working a tilting brazier, and I had a big meat fork that I was using to stir the turkey-chicken-tongue-mushroom-béchamel filling for Crespella toscanna, a kind of crepe, when out of the side of my eye I saw Modesto coming toward me. I knew he was going to go for my ass. Making sure it looked like an accident, I turned the fork around and I came down with it at the same time as he came in with his hand. It was one of those big, curved Dexter meat forks. It caught him right between the knuckles. The tines went all the way in, and he let out an incredible scream. The whole kitchen cracked up. That was my coming of age.

The incident earned Bourdain instant respect. From the Rainbow Room, he went on to work over the next ten years at a variety of restaurants in Manhattan, about twenty in all, including the Supper Club and Pino Luongo's Coco Pazzo Teatro. (Luongo is another restaurateur who started out as a busboy.)

Over the years, Bourdain developed a patchwork philosophy of food that bears the imprint not only of various food professionals but also of his childhood experiences. As a kid, he would regularly summer in France with his French parents. Though food wasn't the centerpiece of these trips, the culinary experiences were certainly not lost on Bourdain. Nor were the annual family pilgrimages to Lutèce in Manhattan. "Since I was so young, I often took the food for granted." But watching his parents speak with Madame Soltner and eating the food, Bourdain couldn't help but be affected by "their expression of almost religious expectation, of rapture. Going to Lutèce was like going to church."

Beyond his family and the chefs with whom he's worked directly, he's also been influenced by those he's only admired from afar. One such chef is Paul Bocuse. One of the first celebrity chefs, Bocuse was named to the Legion d'Honneur in 1975 by President Valéry Giscard d'Estaing of France, and in that same year made the cover of *Newsweek*. For Bourdain, Bocuse represented "money, power, and, in a sense, movie stardom." Bourdain, an adamant believer in presentation—"the ability to create beautiful designs is what separates us from the animals"—is also impressed by Marco Pierre White of London; and when it comes to the flavor contained in a beautifully designed plate, he is inspired by Roger Vergé, "an early advocate of a Mediterranean and sun-nouvelle cuisine."

Having worked in a number of different restaurants, Bourdain is comfortable serving a variety of cuisines, though he prefers anything Mediterranean. While he gets excited about his signature bouillabaisse and a fiery-hot Portuguese seafood stew he picked up in Rhode Island, he's just as excited when describing the kinds of dining requests that drive him mad. He's not a fan of low-fat food, and he thinks that most "lite" menus disguise many a fat- and butter-enriched meal. Vegetables and hamburgers get low marks as well. "Vegetarians bore most chefs. To make a plate of all vegetables is maddening; and on the other end, burgers are also frustrating because there is no way to really present a burger as anything other than what it is. Every time you flip one, it's soul-destroying in a small way." But there is a payback, which anyone foolish enough to order a well-done piece of meat will experience firsthand. "At the end of every shell steak there are two nervy, nasty pieces of meat, riddled with nerve and tendon, that you've got to get rid of somehow. It's in the back of the drawer, wrapped up, and it's two weeks older than every other piece of meat." But that's the one "chefs everywhere in the world give to the knucklehead who comes along and wants meat well done."

As for his own preferences, he'll take French bistro. Give him coq au vin, beef Bourguignon, a nice daube of beef Provençale, oysters, or plain old-fashioned steak frites over lemongrass chicken with coconut milk any day. Bourdain insists that the preference for bistro fare is universal among chefs trained in the French tradition: "We could be neck-deep in oysters all night long." He recalls one gala event at Grand Central Station in New York City, in celebration of the twentieth anniversary of D'Artagnan (a purveyor of foie gras and wild game). Afterward, a friend invited Bourdain to join him and a bunch of the European, primarily, French chefs, who had flown in especially for the event, for cocktails at Manhattan's Brasserie. "It was around two in the morning, and my friend is sitting at the head of the table with twenty of the greatest chefs in the world. Jean-Louis Palladin; Gray Kunz, formerly of Lespinasse; Daniel Boulud; everybody was there. When they came to take the order, every single one of them had steak frites. Every single one. I had the oysters."

It wasn't long after this dinner that Bourdain got a call about an opening at Sullivan's, a posh split-level restaurant and bar at the site of the former Ed Sullivan Theater on Broadway in Manhattan, where jazz musicians and singers re-create the rhythms of a lost era. He was hired on as the executive chef, with the responsibility for revamping a menu that had failed to draw customers. He came up with a menu that could be characterized as international retro food. Maryland crab cakes were served alongside Chinese vegetable dumplings; classic Caesar salad complemented Cuban black bean soup; and ever present were the sides of mashed potatoes that could brighten up any blue funk as well as go with just about everything, from the flame-grilled sirloin to the rosemary-infused lamb chops. While Bourdain would describe the food as comfort food, he also made sure it was sophisticated, because in the twenty years that he's been in the business, the American palate has become increasingly attuned to nuances in flavor and texture. There has been a revolution of expectations among people who dine out frequently in restaurants. "People are much better informed about food and wine. There's a more voracious appetite for new stuff. They'll take risks and eat things they wouldn't have eaten a few years ago."

As executive chef at Sullivan's, Bourdain had other obligations beyond redesigning a menu. He was responsible for ensuring that the staff correctly implemented the menu;

he ordered all the food, set the tone in the kitchen, and sought out the most dependable staff available. No matter where he's working, his rules for hiring are simple: you can play as hard as you like when you're off duty, but when you're on duty, you must first and foremost be *reliable*. Whether or not you're trustworthy is more important than where or even if you went to cooking school, though Bourdain would advise aspiring chefs to go to culinary school. "A graduate of a cooking program benefits from understanding the vocabulary and knowing how to use the tools of the trade, because on a busy night, no one has time to explain a mirepoix."

Bourdain also thinks it's critical for all chefs to apprentice in the best kitchens their city or town has to offer, and to do this as soon as they can. One of Bourdain's major regrets is that he hit the jackpot, in terms of salary and responsibility, too quickly. Consequently, he could never afford to apprentice in the kitchen of someone like Eric Ripert of Le Bernardin or Daniel Boulud of Restaurant Daniel.

If you want a job in this industry, "go bang on the door, and keep banging on the door of the kitchens of great chefs like Gray Kunz (formerly of Lespinasse) or Alfred Portale of Gotham Bar and Grill. Beg, beg, beg. Work for free or for next to nothing. Tell them you will do anything, mop their brow, sweep their floor. Whatever it takes." With that experience in hand, finding a job should be easy. "If you come to me cold off the street, and you've managed to endure six months at Le Bernardin or Gotham, the interview is pretty much over. Unless you have an X tattooed on your forehead, I'm going to hire you right there."

Bourdain has more advice for any aspiring chefs: kiss your ego goodbye, at least temporarily. For the first year or two, a new hire doesn't really exist as a person. "You have to get rid of any preconceptions about how you should be treated as a man, as a woman, as a human being, because you will be asked to do unreasonable and demeaning things." Bourdain calls it the hierarchy of humiliation. In the first couple of weeks, you're being tested. Though your colleagues may appear indifferent to your presence, they're really watching you to see if you can endure without complaint. They want to know if you get your back up when you are treated as less than an individual with a mind and abilities of your own. "You come in, take your orders, go into your corner, and do it. End of story. We don't want a lot of questions or suggestions. We don't want 'Oh, could we do it this way?' Or, 'This is how I saw it done.' Right or wrong, nothing short of fanatical, blind obedience and loyalty will do." Then, after months of obedience, you may just find acceptance:

It's lonely in the beginning, because not only is the chef a monster—or he appears to be one—but the person you've been assigned to work with is incredibly annoyed at having to take time out of a really busy schedule to show you where everything is. Because it's very exhausting and really irritating for him, chances are he's going to make your life a living hell. The people above him probably look down on him. So imagine how they are going to look at you when you are in that position.

The upside is that if you make it through six months, you're in solid. You won't even know when it happens. "You will all go out and get drunk and suddenly people will realize, 'Hey, this guy isn't going away; he's in it for the long haul. And not only that, we haven't had any problems over there. We may even grow to love this guy." Bourdain's use of the "this guy" may not be politically correct, but it reflects his experiences. "I am guilty of the same prejudices that guide my peers—only I'll cop to it. Women are assumed to be good pâtissières and lousy line cooks until proven otherwise. I have, of course, worked with plenty of positively heroic female line cooks who utterly disprove any assertions of female inferiority or 'weakness' in line cooking—they are glorious and revered exceptions, and I consider myself privileged to be able to work with them. But if I'm looking for a replacement for my very busy saucier, I'll go for the Hispanic ex-dishwasher every time." (For a woman's perspective, see Patricia Williams, Anne Kearney, or Linda Rodriguez.)

Once new cooks—male or female—are accepted, they have to prove that they can cook. But, again, even that is secondary to demonstrating reliability. An executive chef like Bourdain needs to know that no matter what his crew did the night before, they will show up at work ahead of time so that their *mise en place* is ready before their shift begins. No exceptions, no excuses. Because trust is so essential, the first thing Bourdain does when he moves from one restaurant to another is ask the sous chef to come with him. His sous chef may bring a line cook, who may bring a sauté man, and so on. Consequently, in most kitchens, it's not uncommon to find that at least half the staff have worked together before, and they're remarkably loyal to one another.

All this talk of trust and loyalty notwithstanding, cooks are not without their petty side. While there is cohesion within a crew, cooks at competing restaurants can sometimes regard each other with extreme jealousy. If a restaurant or chef is going through a difficult time, gossip spreads quickly. "It's great if someone is missing payroll or the food has gone downhill, or someone gets a bad review. When that happens, you know your friends are going to put it up on the board and have a good laugh over it."

Petty jealousies aside, chefs tend to hang together, almost exclusively. This may be because deep down they sincerely enjoy one another's company. But it may also be that there's a lack of other options. Chefs typically get off after midnight, work when the rest of the world prepares to play, on Friday and Saturday nights, and as a result hang out with a lot of other denizens of the night—chefs, cooks, bartenders, and wait people included. "There's plenty of opportunity to drink too much, go out too late, and sleep with people to whom you've not been properly introduced." There is also plenty of opportunity for alcohol and substance abuse.

In the early 1980s, Bourdain and his colleagues would party until they had closed down the bar at whichever Greenwich Village restaurant he was working in at the time. "Here we are, on $150 a week, drinking Cristal Champagne every night and snorting rails of coke that we'd run from one end of the bar to the other." They'd also regularly hit the rock clubs. "Any time a new club would open up, we'd send the salad man down in the middle of the shift to introduce the crew. He'd take a load of sandwiches for all the security guys. We'd show up later, get in free, and lord it over the joint like we owned the place." Bourdain and several other chefs were also regular members of what he calls the "beach club," a tanning competition among chefs that would surely surprise the industry's more conservative members:

> After working twelve hours a day, and knocking off around one A.M., we'd go out to the rock-and-roll clubs till around two or three in the morning, before going to some after-hours club. We'd stay out until six-thirty A.M. or so, completely wasted, before getting on the seven-thirty A.M. train to Long Beach, where we'd all pass out on the sand. When one chef would wake up, he'd roll over the chef lying next to him, that person would reach over and roll over the next guy, until the end of the line. We'd all head back to the city at around two in the afternoon. Glowing with health, we were lepers on the inside.

It was everything Bourdain thought he wanted. "Everything, I think, just about all of us thought we wanted at age nineteen and twenty." So becoming a chef had not so much extinguished the fire within, the tendency to rebel, as it had confined it.

With hindsight, Bourdain realizes just how destructive drugs are, especially co-caine. But in the world of chefs, the temptation is there. Given how well-known the per-nicious effects of cocaine abuse are, Bourdain is surprised at the number of people in the industry who still use drugs. And it's not just the cooks. He knows plenty of dish-washers and porters with beepers who are pulling down a couple grand a week extra dealing coke to the cooks.

Unlike some of his peers, Bourdain has managed to trade in his drug vice for a writer's life, often getting up at six in the morning to work on his novels. His efforts have paid off. His first book, *Bone in the Throat*, was a *New York Times* Notable Book the year it was published, and a script based on the book is now in development in Hollywood. His sec-ond book, *Gone Bamboo*, a thriller about a lovable homicidal couple in the Caribbean, was published in 1997. How does he reconcile these two sides of his life? He doesn't. Nor does his crew. As a cook, "you're judged by what you do in the kitchen," nothing else.

Still, as much as Bourdain enjoys both writing and cooking, he can't see himself cooking forever. He feels that standing on his feet all day would be an undignified way to grow old, a sentiment shared by many of his colleagues. And unlike a host of other chefs, Bourdain has no desire to open his own restaurant. He's put off by the odds against fi-nancial success: "You stand a much better chance of a return on your investment at the track." But more than this, he thinks that the amount of time and energy you have to use scrutinizing your employees, and the obsessive drill of worrying about insurance, cus-tomers, taxes, and reviews, would gradually destroy his humanity:

> I know plenty of chefs who want to own their own empire and profit from their
> own sweat, but they have to be at their place always, or control it with an iron
> fist. That's a very unpalatable option. I would never want to do that. I feel much
> more comfortable coming in and working for an honest dollar and then going
> home at the end of the night without worries.

So for him, a writer's life would be a much more spiritual, albeit solitary way to retire. Yes, he would miss the energy and drama of the kitchen. And more than anything else he'd miss the camaraderie he establishes with his crews—the other cooks, the dish-washers, the prep staff with whom he works. He's not just their colleague; he's also their "drill sergeant, father confessor, psychiatrist, inquisitor, and best friend." As a result, he is able to extract their loyalty and their best work. In return, they get something out of him. They penetrate his tough exterior; they get inside. Though they come from all over the world and speak several different languages, they form one family. And it is this he'd miss most: "everybody I know and really have loyalty and affection for—the people with whom I am most comfortable, my crew."

If the world Bourdain has described seems different from a chef's life as it is depicted on the TV Food Network or on your favorite morning show, it is the world that some chefs know well. It's a virtuous life, an occupation that centers on making people happy, but it's also rife with temptations like drugs, alcohol, and exhausting partying. It is a world as chaotic as it is predictable. After all, no matter what goes on during the wee hours of the night, the show must go on the following day. For Bourdain, that is part of the thrill. He acknowledges that most foodies—people for whom preparing a multi-course meal or eating out at a fine restaurant beats a night at the theater—are quixotic in the way they regard the industry. But he wants them to dig deeper, to see the pathos and pain, fun and scandal beyond the romance. "I can deal with seeing a chef passed out on a sack of flour, cigarette butt in hand, at the end of the evening. I find that interesting. But I really don't think that would play too well with the crowd."

Perhaps he's selling the crowd short. Maybe they can stand the heat after all.

A Portrait of the Chef as a Young Rebel

Anthony Bourdain's

✕

Portuguese Seafood Stew

Chef's note: *Inspired by a classic yet humble stew made by Portuguese fishermen in the off-season in Cape Cod's Provincetown, this seafood stew is a great cold-weather dish and perfect for a casual dinner party. I think it's best served with many cold Narragansett beers and reheated after sitting overnight in the fridge, where the flavors marry up and the cumin mellows. I prefer this dish fire-hot and heavy on the cumin so that it induces a full flop-sweat. For a more intense taste, double the amount of hot sauce. For a more picturesque account of the preparation, check out the book* Bone in the Throat.

(Serves 8)

⅓ cup olive oil

2 tablespoons chopped garlic

2 onions, finely diced

2 to 3 finely diced jalapeño chile peppers, seeds removed

2 red bell peppers, diced

2 green bell peppers, diced

3½ tablespoons ground cumin

2 fresh bay leaves

1 tablespoon chopped fresh thyme

1 tablespoon chopped fresh oregano

2½ pounds cleaned fresh squid, tails cut in rings, head trimmed,
    ink sac removed

1 quart red wine, preferably Burgundy

One 8-ounce can crushed tomatoes

1 cup tomato paste

3 quarts fish stock or clam juice

2 pounds codfish filet, cut into 1-inch chunks

6 Idaho potatoes, medium-diced

¼ cup Frank's Red Hot Sauce

Salt and pepper to taste

1 pound medium shrimps, head on, peeled

About ¼ cup of roux (equal parts fat—oil or butter—and flour) or cornstarch-water mix to thicken. If making a roux, melt the butter and add the flour. Cook for 3 to 5 minutes or until the flour and butter are smooth and evenly mixed.

1. In a heavy stockpot heat the olive oil and sauté the garlic and onions until clear. Add the chiles, bell peppers, cumin, bay leaves, thyme, and oregano. Add the squid and sauté for 5 minutes. Add the red wine, tomatoes and paste, and fish stock. Simmer for 25 minutes on low heat.

2. Add the codfish to the simmering liquid and continue simmering for 5 minutes. Add the potatoes and continue cooking until tender. Add the hot sauce, the salt and pepper, and finally the shrimp, being careful not to break the heads (they look cool). Cook another 2 or 3 minutes, after adjusting thickness by slowly adding the roux. Remove the bay leaves. Allow the stew to sit overnight, refrigerated, if possible, before letting it come to room temperature and reheating.

Note: If you're worried about overcooking or breaking the shrimp, you can complete the stew without them. Then just before serving, steam them separately in water or white wine and simply use them to garnish the finished dish.

✳ THE TEN ✳
CULINARY SCHOOLS
WITH THE HIGHEST ENROLLMENT

The culinary schools with the highest enrollment are listed below. Of course, this number falls short of the total number of professional schools that exist in this country, and by no means claims to be a *top*-ten list. In the ten years from 1988 to 1998, the number of culinary schools has more than doubled, from 150 to 358. These institutions alone educate over 50,000 students per year. In addition to the professional programs, there are also vocational courses, community college programs, and food-oriented vacations for "foodies" (for more information on these culinary vacations see page 54 and Appendix C), bringing the total number of cooking school programs to 881.

For a comprehensive guide to all schools, both professional and recreational (location, tuition, faculty and student profile, and so on), consult *The Guide to Cooking Schools*, published annually by Shaw Guides and unabridged on the Internet at http://www.shawguides.com. For information on scholarships to culinary and hospitality schools, see Appendix B.

Baltimore International College
Baltimore, Maryland
800 students

California Culinary Academy
San Francisco, California
700 students

Career Education Corp.
Hoffman Estates, Illinois
1,400 students

Cooking and Hospitality Institute of Chicago
Chicago, Illinois
650 students

Culinary Institute of America
Hyde Park, New York
2,000 students

Johnson & Wales University
Providence, Rhode Island
4,500 students (includes all five campuses)

New England Culinary Institute
Montpelier, Vermont
625 students

New York City Technical College
Brooklyn, New York
800 students

Pennsylvania Culinary
Pittsburgh, Pennsylvania
1,100 students

**School of Culinary Arts
of the Arts Institute International**
Pittsburgh, Pennsylvania
2,700 students (includes all ten campuses)

(For information on contacting any of the culinary schools listed above, see Appendix A.)

Marc Jolis

COOKING AS A SECOND
OR THIRD CAREER

According to one survey of executive chefs, 25 percent switched into cooking after trying their hand at something else, which means that Marc Jolis joins the one in four who came into cooking having done something different first—from architecture to banking, from raising children to writing advertising copy.[6] Cooking wasn't his first career choice. In fact, it wasn't even his second. But he didn't let that stop him from putting his mark on Atlanta's food map. Though not a vegetarian himself, he learned how to coax flavor out of vegetables for patrons of Café Sunflower, a vegetarian restaurant in a strip mall just outside downtown Atlanta. While only an estimated 12 million to 16 million Americans consider themselves vegetarians, anyone who wants to incorporate more vegetables into his or her menus will find inspiration in Jolis, who in turn found inspiration in the history of the spice trade.

Some people know from an early age exactly what they want to do in life. Many of the chefs and restaurateurs in this book knew even as preadolescents that they wanted to cook. Not so Marc Jolis. His entrée into the world of professional cooking came quite unexpectedly, and late in life compared with the entrées of those who go into cooking just out of high school or college.

Though Jolis's earliest memories of food are fond ones, it never occurred to him to cook professionally. Right out of prep school, he got married and then trained to become a respiratory therapist. But when his marriage began to dissolve, his father urged him to get a divorce and relocate from southeastern New York to the Florida Keys. Once there, he learned very quickly that jobs for respiratory therapists were scarce, and before he had a chance to do more than even dabble in his first vocation, he was already looking for something new.

To make ends meet, Jolis started working with hotshot recreational fishing professionals competing in catch-and-release tournaments, where the prizewinning boat could take home $50,000. Initially, earning $25 a day, he worked as a third deckhand, doing whatever was necessary—painting, scraping, and cleaning—to learn the trade. He worked his way up from a deckhand to bona fide fishing pro, and what was supposed to be a transitional career lasted twenty years. Like the rabbit hole in Alice's wonderland, Florida's coast led Jolis to sights he had hitherto never even imagined. Fishing professionally, nine months out of every year, he traveled to three continents and eleven countries, including Australia, the Virgin Islands, Cuba, Mexico, Venezuela, Aruba, and Bonaire.

Twelve hundred miles from his home port—Islamorada in the Florida Keys—Jolis and his fellow crew members would typically stay three months at a time, and it was there among the beautiful, multicolored parrot fish and barracudas that Jolis's interest in food began to take off. With each offshore visit, he would enjoy the foods of the Caribbean islands with the attention of a scholar, reveling in all their differences, finding comfort in their similarities. He discovered that there was an almost universal appreciation for fish, conch stews, and condiments made from some of the hottest chile peppers in the world (the scotch bonnet, which is used throughout the Caribbean, is 50 percent hotter than the jalapeño). Yet the cuisines were refreshingly varied. Pepperpots—meat stews made using cassareep, a juice made from boiled-down grated cassava—are common to the English-speaking islands, while Curaçao in the

Netherlands Antilles is almost unique in its love for fried fish served with funchi, which is a kind of bread made out of cornmeal. And while arroz con pollo is popular throughout the Caribbean, nowhere, perhaps, is this chicken dish seasoned with saffron and nutmeg, bell peppers and pimientos more treasured than in Cuba.

As Jolis traveled throughout the Caribbean, observing a kaleidoscope of cultures, he learned that there was a history embedded in each dish. If the food of this region could talk, there would be stories of the spice trade and slave rebellions, of peanut seeds and gunga peas carried across the Atlantic by Africans stolen from their homelands to work the sugarcane fields of the New World. There would also be tales to explain how ginger, curry, and colombo powders made their way to the New World on the backs of the Chinese, Indian and Bengalese Hindus, and other indentured laborers brought over to replace the Africans. And in the desserts lay a legacy of wars fought over cocoa and vanilla beans, cinnamon and nutmeg, once the most precious commodities in the world.

Though it would be a while before Jolis would learn this history in a formal classroom setting, his curiosity about both the historical and the cultural aspects of food had been aroused. In the meantime, he went on fishing professionally, and he might have continued doing so had he not met and fallen in love with Ina, a woman who lived stateside. They met in Harbor Island in Eleuthera, a small island just a half-day's trip from Nassau by boat. For their first date, he took her to "a beautiful African lady's restaurant called Deanna's Starfish. It was absolutely wonderful." Somehow it's fitting that their relationship began with food, because Ina was later instrumental in getting Jolis to make the transition from professional fishing to cooking. But that didn't happen until after he began experiencing some business problems. According to Jolis, "There was no growth in the fishing industry. A lot of people were coming into the business, splitting it up into minuscule portions," which made it difficult to earn a living. So when the time came to walk away from the sport and the lifestyle of the Keys, he did so with few regrets.

With only a few years of respiratory therapy and twenty years of sports fishing under his belt, Jolis was tentative about taking the next step. Given his growing love for food, in 1991 he called the **Florida Culinary Institute (FCI)** in West Palm Beach, where he and Ina had decided to relocate. Though he was inspired by the initial phone call, he hesitated. Did he really want to go back to school at the age of forty-two? Was he ready to earn an entry-level salary once he got out of school? Finally, it was Ina who pushed him to take a leap of faith. One day, she simply told him to get in the car. She didn't say where they were going or whom they were to meet. Unbeknownst to Jolis, she had arranged an interview for him with Terrel Murphy, the chairman of the school. One look at the facilities, particularly the kitchens, and the energy of the students, and Jolis was an instant convert—as Ina had known he would be.

Within his first twelve weeks at Florida Culinary, Jolis distinguished himself, and ultimately he graduated with honors. He attributes his performance to the fact that he was focused, "probably for the first time in my life." According to Brendan Keenan, the programs director at the **New York Restaurant School** (which is part of the Arts Institutes International, a national technical school with campuses in more than fifteen cities), where a number of students pursuing cooking as a second career go for an education, it wasn't just focus. It was experience and maturity as well, traits common to many people who turn to cooking as a second career:

> *Most career changers are highly driven for a couple of reasons. First, it usually takes effort and planning, for people with a full life, perhaps even a family, to get to school in the first place. And if they have a family, they're usually concerned about being able to contribute income as soon as possible. So they're highly motivated. In addition, because they have work experience, they have some sense of workplace dynamics, and a work ethic. They know they'll have to start at the bottom before moving up, whereas the typical high school student gets more carried away with the romance of being a chef.*

Like the students Keenan refers to above, Jolis had some sense of the work ethic, albeit an ethic he picked up on a boat. And by this time, he was engaged to Ina, so he also had to consider his family. As a result, Jolis was determined to seize every opportunity presented to him.

One such opportunity was an invitation by Murphy to work with another student to assist in running the school's central purchasing and requisitioning department. Only twelve weeks into the program, Jolis assisted in purchasing enough food to operate a culinary school with over 450 students. The experience provided him with income to offset his tuition fees, and it enabled him to become intimately involved with every product purchased by the school, which expanded his knowledge of different kinds of produce, meat, and fish.

After Jolis completed his culinary studies, he parlayed his performance at school as well as his experience with requisitioning into a position as dinner sous chef at the school's Café Protégé, an upscale dining room, which had seven new kitchens, including a state-of-the-art theater kitchen. It was a particular treat for Jolis, whose primary cooking experience had been on Lilliputian boat stoves, where the only thing preventing his skin from a series of second-degree burns was a thin metal ring.

After he left the Florida Culinary Institute, Jolis landed his first job as a "first cook," serving traditional continental cuisine at the posh Frenchman's Creek Country Club in West Palm Beach. It was a nice job to land early on, but—like most positions in resort towns—it was only temporary. After Mother's Day, the end of the tourist season in many tropical resorts, it's not unusual for an executive chef to lay off half his or her staff. That's great if you're single and carefree. You finish in one place and head to somewhere like Martha's Vineyard, Fire Island, or Montauk—where jobs are plentiful—to cook and cool off for the summer. But for Jolis, who was about to get married, transience was a problem. So, he talked his way into staying. "I went back and told them, 'There's no way. I'm not going to let you lay me off; I'm going to work harder than anybody else, and I'm going to keep the gig.'" True to his word, he stayed on.

Because the Olympics were coming to Atlanta, and Ina had property there, they decided, in 1994, to move to Atlanta, where "there are as many certified master chefs and pastry chefs in the greater metropolitan area as anywhere in the country." Determined to do business there, Jolis sought work at a restaurant serving Mediterranean, Floribbean (an amalgamation of Caribbean, Floridian, and southern cooking), and American food. When Jolis interviewed for the job, he was asked by the executive chef, Jesse Gislason, to audition—to cook something on the menu without instruction. He knew he could technically execute the dish, but he wanted to do more than that—wanted to bewitch Gislason's eye. "I love beautiful presentations. I call it food foreplay. You've got to dig it first before you eat it. When it comes to the table, it's got to make you jump back and take notice." Over time, Gislason and Jolis developed a perfect working relationship, but they had problems with the four partners who owned the restaurant. The owners were more interested in "drinking up all the profits and giving what was left to their hotshot friends" than in running a viable, venerable restaurant. (For a story about a successful partnership, see Bobby Flay.) "We were not getting paid. We had to hang around until three A.M. to see if there was enough money in the register. It was a big hassle. We even had to go to court."

Gislason left to seek his fortune elsewhere. But Jolis's pending marriage prevented him from doing the same. "I couldn't go and try to get another job and say, 'Listen, I need to take off for my wedding.'" Fortunately—as Anthony Bourdain indicated is customary (see page 28)—Gislason kept his eye out for Jolis, and one week after he got married, Gislason brought him over to the Café Sunflower, a vegetarian restaurant where he himself had landed. Initially, Jolis's new position was less than ideal. Over forty years of age, and with professional credentials that had cost him over $20,000, he started out as a line cook, making only $8 an hour. But in less than a year, Gislason left, followed by the chef de cuisine, leaving the top vacancy to Jolis.

The primary job Jolis faced as the new chef de cuisine—his first managerial chef position—was figuring out how to coax flavors out of vegetables following strictly vegetarian and, for the most part, vegan restrictions. He was told he couldn't use virtually anything that came from an animal. Most cooks would be lost if they couldn't use liberal amounts of olive oil, to say nothing of butter, when preparing dishes. Jolis could use butter only in small proportions; likewise, he could use olive oil only if it was mixed with canola (80 percent canola and 20 percent olive). But far from being discouraged, he took these vegetarian dietary restrictions as a culinary challenge.

For ideas, he once again drew on what he knew best. First, he went back to recipes his mother, an excellent home cook who used lots of vegetables, gave him. Then he turned to the books. From the history books that he had read at the Florida Culinary Institute, he recalled that "Christopher Columbus brought pigs and cows with him to the New World. But it's what he took back to Europe that interested me—chocolate, chiles, corn, tomatoes, bananas, vanilla beans," all wonderful things that Jolis could use as a chef in a vegetarian restaurant. He added to those ingredients the foods that the slaves and indentured laborers brought with them: calaloo, okra, yams, and peanuts, for the Africans; ginger, curries, Asian-style pickles, satays, and peanut sauces from the Chinese, Indians, Bengalis, and other Asians. Thus his pantry was unusually broad. And he quickly realized that he didn't have to stop with the Caribbean. As with the Tunisian vegetarian stew he added to the Sunflower's repertoire, he began to draw on herbs and legumes, roots and grains, found in every corner of the globe.

To these world influences and ingredients Jolis added his own signature touches. Sometimes it was a vegetarian barbecue sauce that he created not for big slabs of ribs, but rather as a moistening and flavor agent for everything from baked heirloom beans that have been sautéed in onions to seitan, a form of wheat gluten that is quite popular at vegetarian restaurants because it's high in protein and low in fat and can be used to make a variety of mock meat and poultry dishes. At other times he added the almond-, sage-, or roasted garlic-infused oils that he always keeps close at hand. And he's also known to have a penchant for spices, particularly allspice from Jamaica. "It's peppery and sweet, and it jazzes up the food. I used it in *everything* here, particularly if I needed a sweetener, because I don't like to use refined sugar, which is not a naturally occurring product. Instead, I prefer to use natural sugars such as honey, sorghum, and molasses. But that's not as easy as it sounds, because most recipes call for white sugar. So, as chef de cuisine, it was my responsibility and challenge to modify the recipes to achieve the desired results."

While he got around dietary restrictions by adjusting recipes and calling upon different cultural traditions for inspiration, he had another constraint: price limitations. "Our price structure was not very high. Our most expensive lunch item was $6.95; our most expensive dinner item was $12.95. The philosophy of my owners was to sell it cheap, get the people in, do the numbers." If the average ratio of food cost to food revenue is 25 percent to 33 percent (see page 254), then a meal that sells for $6.95 can cost no more than $1.74 to $2.32 to make.

Within these price and dietary restrictions, Jolis worked on the menu standards and came up with six specials a week, about three hundred a year. He's especially fond of a summer dish that he came up with one July, a "far-out pasta with a hot-and-sour lemongrass sauce, dried apricots, and fresh strawberries." Fortunately, he served it on the day a food critic from the *Atlanta Journal-Constitution* and her dinner companion, the cookbook author Mollie Katzen, were eating lunch at Café Sunflower. As he recalls their enthusiasm, and the eagerness with which they interrogated him about the ingredients, a grin displaces his otherwise understated smile.

That food critic was not the only pleased person to have reviewed Jolis. Within one year of his taking over the kitchen at Café Sunflower (and in the following two years), readers of *Atlanta* magazine voted it the city's best vegetarian restaurant, and Jolis was also featured in both *Creative Loafing* and *Vegetarian Times* magazine, as well as in the "Chefs of the South" column of the *Atlanta Journal-Constitution*.

If it is gratifying when both the media and the public recognize someone's hard work under any circumstances, just imagine how Jolis, a chef who took twenty years at sea and a career change or two to find his true muse, must feel.

Lucky Seven Vegetable Tunisian Stew

Chef's Note: *When I was first served this traditional dish, many years ago, it included lamb. Since then, I have learned more about blending spices and have been able to incorporate more vegetables into the mix. Nonvegetarians will find this a surprisingly hearty meal, while vegetarians looking for something new will find it a pleasant addition to their repertoire. This is a very adaptable recipe—you can also vary the vegetables, depending on the season.*

(Makes 10 cups)
1 tablespoon canola oil
2 large onions, cut into large dice
3 tablespoons minced garlic
1 tablespoon mild curry powder
1 tablespoon ground cinnamon
½ tablespoon turmeric
½ teaspoon sweet Hungarian paprika
½ teaspoon ground ginger
½ teaspoon cardamom
½ teaspoon ground coriander
Pinch cayenne pepper
Salt and pepper to taste
2 cups peeled and diced turnips
2 cups peeled and diced parsnips

2 cups peeled and diced carrots
1 cup peeled and diced potatoes
1 cup cauliflower florets
½ cup raisins
1 cup cooked chickpeas, drained and washed
5 cups strong vegetable stock
1 cup chopped parsley leaves
1 cup chopped cilantro leaves

1. Put oil, onions, and garlic in a large Dutch oven and cover. Over medium heat, cook for 3 to 5 minutes. Add the curry powder, cinnamon, tumeric, paprika, ginger, cardamom, coriander, cayenne, salt, and pepper and stir.

2. Add the turnips, parsnips, carrots, potatoes, cauliflower, raisins, chickpeas, and vegetable stock. Reduce heat to low and add the parsley. Cover and cook until the vegetables are cooked through, about 20 minutes. The broth will thicken.

3. Serve sprinkled with cilantro.

✳ COOKING ABROAD ✳

If you don't have the chutzpah to talk your way into a French kitchen as Andrew Pforzheimer did, or friends who can introduce you to truffle merchants and other food professionals as Patricia Williams had, do you have any chance of getting into a French kitchen? As it turns out, there are several educational culinary programs abroad that introduce eager students to cooking techniques and food professionals of a particular region. Though most of these "culinary vacations" are for food enthusiasts, not professionals, this might be a good way for the undecided to get their feet wet.

Some programs emphasize trips to the markets, demonstrations by visiting chefs, and hands-on cooking, while others stress relaxation with a little bit of cooking thrown in for variety. Some allow for both. Because they do vary so much and tend to be fairly expensive, make sure you know exactly what you're getting before you commit yourself financially.

France

Cooking with Friends in France
La Pitchoune-Domaine de Bramafam
06740 Châteauneuf de Grasse, France
Phone: 33 4 93 60 10 56
Fax: 33 4 93 60 05 56

or c/o Ms. Alex
Jackson and Company
29 Commonwealth Avenue
Boston, MA 02116
Phone: 617-350-3837
Fax: 617-247-6149
URL: http://www.cookingwithfriends.com

A six-day-long "cultural immersion" in Provence, which, in addition to classes on the basic techniques of traditional French cooking, includes trips to markets, village tours, restaurant visits, and free time to explore the French Riviera. Classes are given in English by French chefs. Classes are limited to no more than eight students per week. Some guests get to say in La Pitchoune, the house where Julia Child wrote and tested recipes for her television show *The French Chef* and began conceptualizing the second volume of *Mastering the Art of French Cooking*.

Le Cordon Bleu
404 Executive Airport Park
Nanuet, New York 10954
Phone: 800-457-CHEF, ext.130
URL: http://www.cordonbleu.net

While it's best known for its classic program that leads to a cuisine or Le Grande Diplôme, Le Cordon Bleu does offer the following shorter courses in Paris.

• 4-week catering seminar
• 3- and 5-week intensive basic courses in both pastry and cuisine
• 1- to 2-week professional chef continuing education program
• 4-day session based on the most representative themes of French regional cuisine—French bread, chocolates, and so forth
• 1-month session, "Initiation to French Cuisine and Pastry"

- 1-day in-depth look at French culinary culture through trips to Parisian markets, followed by demonstrations
- Daily 3-hour demonstrations

There is also a Cordon Bleu in London, and one in Tokyo. All classes are translated into English, with the exception of the practical lab portions of the intensive courses.

L'Ecole des Chefs
P.O. Box 183
Birchrunville, PA 19421
Phone: 610-469-2500
Fax: 610-469-0272
E-mail: info@leschefs.com
URL: http://www.leschefs.com

Designed to accommodate both the home chef and professionals, this program allows passionate cooks to intern with a chef at a two- or three-star restaurant in France. The program runs about six days and includes both kitchen work and trips to markets and kitchen supply stores. Participating restaurants include Restaurant Troigros in Roanne, La Côte Saint-Jacques in Burgundy, and Restaurant Guy Savoy in Paris. Note that the program costs more for a three-star restaurant than a two-star and more for the professional chef than the home cook.

A Taste of Provence
c/o Tricia Robinson
925 Vernal Avenue
Mill Valley, CA 94941
Phone: 415-383-9439
E-mail: info@tasteofprovence.com
URL: http://www.tasteofprovence.com

A weeklong seminar of cooking lessons and culinary adventures in a restored Provençal farmhouse. Every year, a guest chef from the region or an American cookbook author gives cooking demonstrations. In addition to spending a day at Roger Vergé's Ecole de Cuisine in Mougins, guests go to market with the school's director. The French countryside offers plenty of options for relaxation, from mountain hikes to swims or picnics.

For more information on culinary experiences in France, Italy, and Mexico, see Appendix C.

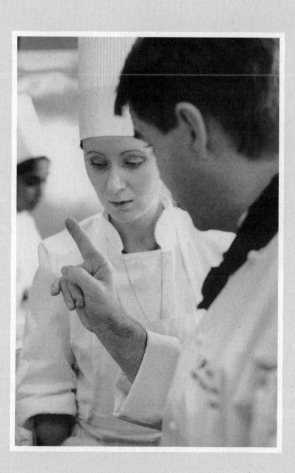

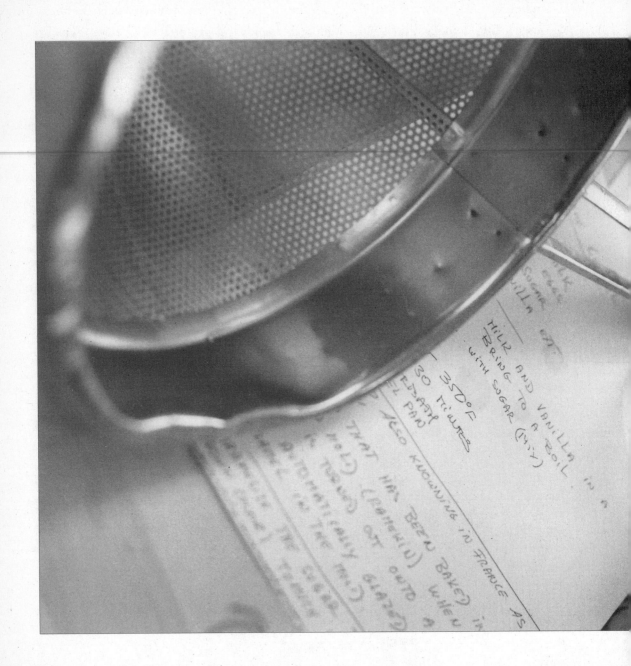

PART 2

A Taste of America's Regional Cuisines

Edna Lewis and Scott Peacock

SOUTHERN REVIVAL

Author of three now classic cookbooks, including A Taste of Country Cooking, *Edna Lewis is a repository of knowledge about the origins and authentic flavors of southern food. A pioneer, Lewis has been profiled in several magazines, including* Gourmet, Essence, Redbook, House and Garden, *and* American Visions. *In addition to her work in restaurants, she has catered, taught cooking, and sold her poached pears and cat's-tongue cookies through Dean & Deluca, the ultra-deluxe New York City gourmet store. Immediately before retiring in 1992, Lewis could be found at the four-star Brooklyn restaurant Gage & Tollner. Like any true culinary gatekeeper whose reputation is nearly legendary, she has her share of fans, one of whom is Scott Peacock, former chef of the acclaimed Horseradish Grill in Atlanta. Together, Lewis and Peacock exemplify the importance of the mentor-protégé relationship. Beyond that, they are wisely passionate about the primacy of southern food in our national culinary mosaic.*

Photo of Edna Lewis and Scott Peacock: © Carla Gahr

Most cooks, from the home cook to the professional, hold sacred at least one family recipe. "No one makes rugelach like my aunt" is one refrain. "This recipe for sweet-potato pie goes back three generations" is another. Professional cooks carry their family legacies around with them as well. For instance, take André Soltner's cookbook, based on his experiences at Lutèce. Before divulging the recipe for his cream of mussel soup with marrow dumplings, he notes that it is a "dish very close to the heart of the family," something his mother would prepare for his father. Beyond their family, professional chefs have an even larger well from which to draw: When they leave one job to pursue another, they automatically extend their repertoire by taking with them the recipes and techniques of the professionals they are leaving behind. Some chefs even insist that their assistants keep a *vade mecum* describing every single dish on the menu in great detail—from precise measurements to exact plating techniques. When they leave, this reference book often goes with them.

In addition to the people with whom they've worked, astute cooks will be influenced by chefs they've only read or heard about—chefs who are internationally recognized as groundbreakers. Any number of contemporary American cooks, for example, were influenced by Larry Forgione's modern interpretations of American food at An American Place or by seasonal organic foods at Chez Panisse.

Scott Peacock is an example of someone who was influenced by Alice Waters (for more on Waters see page 16), though he's never actually worked directly with her at Chez Panisse. But Edna Lewis's influence on Peacock has perhaps been even more profound. The two met in 1988, when Peacock was asked to assist Lewis with a benefit dinner she was hosting in Atlanta, where he lived. It was an unlikely pairing: He's white, she's black; he's in his thirties, she's more than twice his age. He was born in a former slaveholding state, while she was born and raised in Freetown, Virginia, a farming community settled by freed slaves, who included her grandmother. Despite their differences, however, they've become almost inseparable friends, bonded by their love of the pure, simple flavors of the South and, ultimately, by their love for each other.

Lewis was born just as the First World War ended, and she recalls her childhood as a time when everyone talked about three things: food, gardening, and the weather. But the love of food was supreme. For a community with limited capital resources, food guaranteed sustenance and independence. Another aspect of food—less practical but no less integral to their lifestyle—was that it marked celebrations and cemented friendships. "Food was *the* big thing among the freed slaves. Everybody was farming in their garden or on a piece of land that they'd rent outside of Freetown, where they'd grow corn or wheat," as well as a variety of other crops, including cymling—a white, nearly flat, circular squash with scalloped edges—butter beans, cabbage, tomatoes, eggplants, an array of lettuces and potatoes. Of all the crops, though, corn, a crop native to the Americas, was preeminent. In nearly every home, you'd find at least one corn dish on the stove, be it corn bread or corn pudding, hominy, or cornpone, a snack made of cornmeal, milk, water, and butter.

With all the crops, there was always work to be done on the farm. In due season, the corn had to be plowed, cut, dried, or shucked. While the adults did the bulk of the work, the kids contributed as well. Lewis recalls, "At night, all of us children would get around a big tub and shell the corn. My father would take it the next day and have it ground into meal, and then that night we would have it for supper." If the preliminary work was communal, with the kids helping the parents, then so too was the preparation. Both her mother and her father put supper on the table—this was a legacy the men carried with them from plantation to settlement, because "during slavery the men were also cooks" in plantation kitchens.

Once the work was done and before the food was put on the table, neighbors were invariably invited over to share meals. Lewis recalls that no matter the season, "if someone made something real delicious, they would bring it to my mother to taste. And at holiday time, *everybody* exchanged food. At Christmastime, they would kill hogs and make all kinds of different dishes from the hog killing." Like corn, pigs were a staple that no household was without. "Ham held the same rating as the basic black dress. If you had a ham in the meat house any situation could be faced. On short notice, it would be sliced and fried with special red gravy. Otherwise, it would be leisurely simmered, then defatted and browned." Lewis's recollections square with the historian John Egerton's assessment of the place both pigs and corn hold in the diet of the South. As he writes in *Southern Food,* "Pigs and corn . . . pork and pone. In combination, they have meant the difference between life and death for individuals, families, even entire communities. In the American South, no other edible substances have meant more to the populace in nearly four centuries of history than pork and corn."

Apart from pork and pone, there were other household mainstays, especially in Lewis's home. Spring brought lamb and lettuce-and-scallion salad; summer brought turtle soup, a delicacy made from the surfeit of turtles that came out during the storms, and a variety of ripe fruits, including melons and wild strawberries, which the family would eat with fresh cream from their own dairy cows. Game of all varieties—pheasants and guinea hens, rabbit and squirrel—graced the table in the fall. By wintertime, they were eating canned fruits and vegetables preserved from the summer bounty alongside meals cooked right in the hearth. One example is ashcakes, a savory made of fresh-ground cornmeal that was wrapped in cabbage leaves before being placed in the fireplace to bake; roast chicken is another. And except during the relentlessly humid summer, at the center of every table in town one could find butter, which the entire family made from scratch:

> We would spend a whole day skimming the cream from the top of a number of milk crocks. . . . The cream was poured in, and Grandpa usually did the churning, sitting on the front porch in warm weather or before the fireplace hearth in winter. Mother would spend hours washing the butter by kneading it with wooden paddles. . . . Then, after all the water was removed, the salt was worked in. [And] then the butter was pressed into . . . decorated prints. When the butter was pressed out of the mold it would be beautifully decorated on the top. We kept most of these butter prints in the well house and used them as needed, but sometimes when we had extra we would sell them to stores in town.[7]

In terms of all sorts of foods, from butter to wild game, Lewis's was a community which literally lived off the land, and which made most dishes by hand, be it biscuits, soup stock, or yeast rolls.

These early memories would stay with Lewis, as would the tradition of giving and exchanging food, even though she moved up North when she was only sixteen. After a brief stint in Washington, D.C., Lewis accompanied friends on a visit to New York City. They stayed a week; Lewis "stayed forever." To support herself she found work at a laundry ironing shirt collars. When she was all but fired for her lousy ironing, she found work in the mailroom of the Communist Party newspaper *The Daily Worker*, where she addressed envelopes and filed the "thousands of letters a day" from people who sent in money for the paper. It was a cause that, like many of her contemporaries, she really believed in. "At that time, there were places in New York that didn't hire blacks, even Bloomingdale's. I remember we picketed Bloomingdale's and, finally, they hired a black girl to do the cash register. So I went and congratulated her. It was a big and exciting time. There were rallies in Madison Square Garden, and Paul Robeson came and sang. His voice was simply beautiful."

During World War II, Lewis began assisting some friends who were working as window display artists. After the "good war," when people could actually enjoy the prosperity the war had brought, window-display work began to boom. Finally, Lewis was assigned a set of windows of her own to dress at Bonwit Teller. In just a few short years, Lewis had gone from picketing a major department store because it didn't have black employees to working as a window-display artist at one of Fifth Avenue's most hoity-toity.

It was about this time that Lewis began cohosting parties with her bohemian and political friends. Though Lewis recalls the food as being "awful," she was, in fact, gaining a reputation among her integrated set of friends as one of the best cooks. Though she hadn't considered cooking professionally, one of her window-display colleagues was wise enough to notice that Lewis possessed notable flair in the kitchen. He approached her with an irresistible offer: "I'm going to open a restaurant and you're going to be the chef." So in 1948, Café Nicholson opened up on 58th Street on New York City's East Side. (Initially, Lewis was to be the kitchen supervisor, and for her efforts she was to get one third of the profits.)

Café Nicholson was housed in an antiques shop, and its kitchen had only two burners and no oven. But what the place lacked in hardware, it more than made up for in atmosphere, which became all the more lovely by the addition of a garden. There was only one problem. The chef, a white man they had hired to cook under Lewis's supervision, quit when he found out that Lewis was black. Though he didn't write a letter of resignation, he did leave some words to be remembered by: "I'm not going to work where any black woman is going to be the supervisor." After he resigned, there was no one left to cook but Lewis. For someone with little experience in formal cooking, she had to learn volume very quickly.

Eventually, Lewis and her partner acquired a rudimentary oven, which they put over the burner. They served omelets, roast chicken, soups, and salads. For dessert, Lewis and her waitress perfected a chocolate soufflé. (Their secret: Take it out just before it's done and let it finish cooking in its own internal steam, so that by the time it reaches the table it has finished cooking but is not overcooked.) Of all Lewis's cooking experiences, Café Nicholson is the one that makes her eyes glimmer. In no small part, she attributes that to the clientele. Eleanor Roosevelt and Muriel Draper were patrons, as were Tennessee Williams and Greta Garbo. Café Nicholson also catered to the fashion industry. "We had all the fashion people"—models, illustrators, and photographers, including Richard Avedon.

After almost five years, Lewis left Café Nicholson. "I got tired of the restaurant, the glamour of it. It was too much." Her time there had been remarkable—not so much for the celebrated clientele, but because Lewis was one of the first black women to co-own an integrated restaurant in New York City, sixteen years before the passage of the Civil Rights Act. Notable too is that during Lewis's forty-plus years as a chef, the only time she recalls experiencing direct discrimination is when that chef stormed out of her kitchen.

Lewis was married by the time she left Café Nicholson, and she settled in New Jersey, where she tried her hand at raising pheasants on organic feed. This experience no doubt reminded her of her childhood, when she used to help her family raise the game they'd take to the city market. Complications with the chicks caused her to cast this hobby aside, but it did reinforce her interest in raising, cooking, and eating chemical-free foods—livestock, fish, or fruits and vegetables. After the pheasants, she began catering. While she didn't put particular emphasis on southern food, she did insist on making as much as possible from scratch; this was another habit cultivated from her early years, when she used to watch her parents cook. As her reputation began to grow, she was approached by an editor in New York City, who asked her to do a menu cookbook that would draw on her experience catering and at Café Nicholson. *The Edna Lewis Cookbook* was published in 1972.

With her first cookbook behind her, Lewis decided to return to the South. Her first stop was Fearrington House, a 600-acre farm near Chapel Hill, North Carolina. From there she moved to Middleton Place in Charleston, South Carolina, a historic preservation of a former plantation, where she worked as the head chef. At these two restaurants, she began to refocus on southern cuisine. Her menus included food rooted in the traditions of the South, such as she-crab and thirteen-bean soups. Eventually, she returned to New York City, where she was hired at Gage & Tollner, a renowned four-star fish and steak house in Brooklyn. Lewis instituted an entirely southern menu, which attracted people in the tristate area and beyond. Her success there heightened her already enviable reputation, causing people far and wide to come under her sway. Scott Peacock was one such person.

Scott Peacock had never intended to cross paths with Edna Lewis—or with any other chef, for that matter. Though he grew up cooking for his family and watching Julia Child on television, the idea of becoming a chef had simply never occurred to him. "It was sort of a neat idea, but who knew? Being from Hartford, Alabama, I knew people who became doctors, but not chefs." His first attempts at cooking for people outside his family were inspired by television. "I had two dinner parties in high school. They were wretched. I didn't know anything about how you had a dinner party except for what I had seen on television." Peacock took his cues from shows like *Family Affair,* where Uncle Bill would always go to dinner parties with glamorous dates; and *Bewitched,* where "Daren and Samantha were always going to the Tates' house for dinner." And since those fictitious hosts served seven courses at their parties, Peacock assumed that he had to do the same. He'd start off with "pressed meat and olives on crackers and doctored Campbell soup," because he didn't know how to make a proper soup. He would finish with his signature lavish dessert: baked Alaska made with Betty Crocker's devil's food cake. For the baked Alaska, "you took ice cream and you mixed in chocolate chips because this was before you could buy chocolate chip ice cream. The interesting thing was the meringue, which was made from brown sugar. I would put sparklers on it sometimes. It was really unpleasant, because as the sulfur would burn off, it would fall into the meringue. Real typical sixties and seventies." At one party, he served fudge and divinity as an hors d'oeuvres; at another he served spaghetti followed immediately by shrimp Creole, and then a standing crown roast of pork! Even then, he knew that he had a few things to learn about creating a menu and assembling flavors.

Peacock got his chance when, during his senior year at college in Tallahassee, he went to work at a French restaurant, where he began to realize that his interest in food was stronger than his interest in his first ambition, politics. Derailed by food, after graduation he pursued a tip he had heard about a chef's position at a hunting club outside Albany, Georgia. The hunting club, an old family plantation, was rented out by businessmen and lobbyists looking for an appropriately grand place to schmooze. After a day of meetings, clients would go out and hunt game. Peacock did all the cooking and the baking. "It was very hard. Three meals a day, plus cocktails and hors d'oeuvres. It was all home cooking, which I wasn't really interested in at all" as a type of food; but "it seemed *appropriate* for where we were." He'd serve quail, game, and big family-style breakfasts every morning and something different every night. "It was wonderful, because you'd finish your breakfast in this big dining room and then these mule wagons would pull out with your horses, all the attendants, and the dogs in the kennel underneath the wagons." When it came to preparing dinner, he was on less solid ground. But that did not stop him; he would assiduously consult cookbooks and friends. "I remember the first time I ever cooked a tenderloin. I was on the phone with my friend Jenny Herrera, who was the chef at the Florida governor's mansion at the time. And I'd ask, 'How do I do this?'" Though he was daunted, he still persevered, always trying to make things that "were compatible with the setting and the experience people would get."

Although Peacock was successful, the job at the club was seasonal. As the hunting season came to an end, one of the clients told him that the governor was looking for a chef to cook at the mansion in Atlanta. Peacock settled into the job and began cooking "southern-type food" for Governor Harris and his wife, though at the time Peacock didn't have any deep-seated passion for southern cuisine. Rather, it just seemed apropos for the governor's mansion, as it had been at the hunting club.

Peacock's initial indifference reflected a disregard for southern food shared by many people, even some southerners, until very recently. When the Democratic national convention was held in Atlanta in 1988, for example, the Harrises hosted a lunch for Michael Dukakis and all the Democratic governors in the country. Peacock had proposed a menu that used only Georgian ingredients: quail, Vidalia onions, snapper from the Savannah coast, and blackberry cobbler for dessert. But the governor did not want a southern menu. Defeated, Peacock served lobster and this "big flower salad with California lettuces." Only the dessert—homemade peach ice cream—had anything to do with Georgia.

The biggest obstacle to southern food was that it had this huge public relations problem. When people think about the South, they think about what television has fed us rather than this genius bank of writers and artists we have. They think of Gomer Pyle and the Beverly Hillbillies, rather than Tennessee Williams and William Faulkner, Truman Capote and Carson McCullers.

Peacock was limited in what he was allowed to serve at the governor's mansion, but he managed to derive some good from his tenure there. In 1988, Edna Lewis, who was by that time at Gage & Tollner in Brooklyn, was invited to Atlanta to cook for a benefit: the Southern Food Festival, sponsored by the **American Institute of Wine and Food (AIWF)**. Peacock was assigned to take her shopping. Their first meeting didn't make much of an impression on Lewis. But for Peacock, who had been a fan of Lewis's ever since reading her cookbook *In Pursuit of Flavor,* it was a memorable event. When they met a second time, at another benefit, Peacock was asked to help her make enough desserts and bread to feed over a hundred people. As they rolled pie dough together and prepared the filling for blackberry and rhubarb cobblers and pecan pies, their friendship began. The next day Peacock invited her to tea at the governor's mansion. Though she returned to New York City shortly thereafter, he pursued the friendship by telephone. In a casual conversation a few weeks later, Lewis suggested that he come to New York for a visit. Though New York is one of the country's food capitals, the idea of going there had never occurred to Peacock, as he had his sights set on Italy and Italian cuisine. Indeed, he had moved into a garage apartment in order to save money for a trip to Europe.

Enticed, nonetheless, by the invitation, Peacock arrived in Manhattan a month later. "We met outside Dean & DeLuca and had coffee for a few hours, then we went to Chez Josephine for drinks and Gotham Bar and Grill for dinner. And the next day, we went to Orso." At each place, they talked about their common ideas and interests—surprisingly, southern food was not one of them. Lewis kept trying to interject the topic into the conversation, but Peacock wasn't interested. "I remember thinking, 'I like her a lot, but I hope this isn't going to become a problem,' because I wasn't really interested in southern food. I was cooking southern-type food at the governor's mansion, but it was for the same reason that I had been cooking it at the plantation: It seemed appropriate."

Then, as he reflected on what Lewis was saying and on the philosophy behind her second cookbook, *A Taste of Country Cooking,* he had an epiphany of sorts. He realized that he "had this narrow image of southern food" and had never encountered many of the dishes she was writing about—blancmange, a rich dessert that her family and childhood neighbors on the settlement would make with surplus milk and heavy cream from the cows; black raspberry preserves; corn puddings; and the like. Seen through the prism of Lewis's experiences, southern food began to seem interesting and exotic.

The next day, before leaving Manhattan to return to Atlanta, Peacock went to say one last good-bye to this woman who had brought him East and given him so much food for thought. At Gage & Tollner, Lewis greeted him wearing an apron and a chef's coat and carrying "two bags, and a coffee cup with the same pattern as the one from Orso." She had also put "a thing of frozen gooseberries and frozen damson plums and a whole jar of sugared raspberries" into an insulated bag so that they would stay frozen until Peacock got back to Atlanta. Like her insistence on organic foods and making things from scratch, Lewis's custom of giving food was something she'd carried with her from Virginia, where the freed slaves often gave food to their friends and neighbors. Whether it was her generosity or her enthusiasm about southern culinary traditions, she somehow got to Peacock.

Back in Atlanta, Peacock continued to think about Lewis. He also started to think about Alice Waters and what she had done with Chez Panisse. "She started out having a French restaurant, but she finally realized she could get better food locally grown. And I thought, well, no one is doing that with southern food." So just as Waters turned to locally grown produce to make a California cuisine, Peacock decided that he wanted to emphasize southern food and, whenever possible, food grown in Georgia. The opportunity arose when investors he was approached by wanted to open an American restaurant with a southern twist, the Horseradish Grill.

"I made it really clear in negotiating with them that the only restaurant I could do was a truly southern one." Peacock was fairly adamant about what he wanted to serve, starters like southern flatbread with caramelized onions, fresh goat cheese and toasted pecans, or roasted Appalachicola oysters served with drawn butter; and entrées like roasted pork loin served with whipped sweet potatoes and southern greens. While Peacock got his way in some things, he found that to accommodate the owners he had to compromise on some others. For instance, there was a Caesar salad on the menu. This is not a southern dish, but the owners insisted that they couldn't have a restaurant without it. Compromise was difficult at first, because at the hunting plantation and at the governor's mansion Peacock had been completely in charge. Still, he soon learned that when you are working *for* other people, "you have to learn how to choose your battles real carefully, because otherwise it's not going to work."

By that time, Lewis had retired to Atlanta, and Peacock consulted her as he prepared to open the restaurant. She was right by his side to witness his success. From the moment it opened, the Horseradish Grill was widely reported as being one of the best restaurants in Atlanta. Before long, Peacock was appearing in magazines across the country, including *Esquire.* He was celebrated not only for turning out simple yet flavorful food—such as grilled trout wrapped in bacon and served with a mayonnaise sauce, and his famous macaroni and cheese—but also for making nearly everything from scratch, from the baking powder to the ice cream. "Cooking for me has always been just an innate thing. You know, some kids will take radios or things apart. I was interested in 'How did they make that?' 'How do you make an éclair?'" In this he was influenced, again, by Lewis, and also the lessons he learned at the **Beringer Vineyards' School for American Chefs,** a kind of "graduate school for chefs" that Madeleine Kamman, founder of the Modern Gourmet Cooking School in Newton, Massachusetts, and author of the classic book *The Making of a Cook,* helped to establish.

Relying on homemade products and the freshest ingredients meant that very little in the kitchen contained preservatives. Also, Peacock's kitchen had no freezer and very few canned goods. Though he was committed to breaking things down to the bare essentials, the management was not as enthusiastic. "It costs money to do things the right way, to get the best ingredients, not to open cans, not to have a freezer in the restaurant. There was always a battle going back and forth." Unlike the Caesar salad, however, fresh, homemade goods were a battle he was unwilling to lose.

In a sense, Peacock's approach to food can be thought of as a triptych. The use of local ingredients is one element; making as much as possible from scratch is the second; and the third is his preference for *simple* food. He trained his staff to focus on cooking things properly and seasoning them well, not on arranging things in "circles and haystacks." He thinks other restaurants put too much emphasis "on just how uniformly you can julienne a potato and not enough emphasis on where the food comes from, on how it's grown, or on what it really tastes like."

Despite the success of the Horseradish Grill, and in no small part because of the compromises one has to make while working for others, Peacock left after two years. "If I had felt that there was a lot more I could have accomplished, I would have stayed. But there wasn't much more I could do without total control." Suddenly he had free time on his hands, and he took advantage of it by volunteering to assist Lewis at the many cooking benefits she is invited to host across the country. They also began collaborating on a cookbook, *Coming Together to Cook*—her fourth, his first. It is a menu book that will draw on recipes from all over the South. The recipes emphasize the taste and flavors of the Old South, because Lewis and Peacock are interested in teaching people about how food *used* to be grown and cooked. The book also includes lists of the people who grow, raise, and distribute organic food, as well as advice on how to cook food for maximum flavor.

They also have their sights set on a 175-year-old Georgia farmhouse on 25 acres of land, which they hope to convert into an artists' colony of sorts. Ideally, artists from all disciplines would come and cultivate their craft—be it music, poetry, painting, or cooking. There would be two seatings at a dinner that everyone would have contributed to in some small way. Some people will harvest fresh food from the garden, while others will gather fruit from the orchards. Regardless of what skills an artist is there to pursue, he or she will learn about the food of the South: how to grow it, how to prepare it, how to preserve its legacy. After dinner, all participants will retire to their own individual cabins and swept yards and enjoy a sound night's sleep. They'll wake up to a cup of java on their porch, and they'll be able to peer down into rows of neatly cultivated vegetables. Both in the look and in the communal spirit, the farm will resemble the world Edna Lewis grew up in, nearly three-quarters of a century ago.

Roasted Salt-Brined Turkey

Chefs' note: *Soaking a turkey overnight in salted water produces an especially moist and well-flavored bird. Careful attention to basting, especially during the last hour of roasting, is also essential.*

(Serves 12)

Brining and Roasting

1 cup plus 2 tablespoons kosher salt
1 gallon cold water
One 12-pound free-range turkey—neck, wingtips, heart, and gizzard
    reserved for giblet gravy

6 tablespoons unsalted butter, softened
¼ cup fresh orange juice
2 tablespoons fresh lemon juice
1 tablespoon dried thyme
1 teaspoon kosher salt
¾ teaspoon freshly ground pepper
1 large onion, quartered
2 celery ribs, cut into 2-inch lengths
1 bunch of thyme sprigs (2 ounces)
4 sage sprigs

4 garlic cloves, unpeeled
3 bay leaves
6 thick slices of bacon
1 quart chicken stock or canned low-sodium chicken broth
Giblet gravy, for serving

1. *Brine the turkey:* In a large stockpot, dissolve the salt in the cold water. Add the turkey and refrigerate for 12 to 24 hours. Remove the turkey from the brine and pat dry inside and out with paper towels.

2. *Roast the turkey:* Preheat the oven to 325°F. In a small bowl, blend the butter with the orange juice, lemon juice, thyme, salt, and pepper. Rub the turkey inside and out with the butter mixture. Fill the cavity with the onion, celery, thyme sprigs, sage sprigs, garlic, and bay leaves. Truss the bird tightly and transfer it to a rack set in a roasting pan. Arrange the bacon slices over the breast and pour 2 cups of the stock into the roasting pan.

3. Roast the turkey in the oven for 45 minutes, then baste with 1 cup of the stock. Roast the turkey for 1½ hours longer, basting with the pan juices every 20 minutes. Add the remaining 1 cup of stock to the pan and roast the turkey for about 1 hour and 50 minutes longer, basting every 15 minutes with the pan juices. The turkey is done when an instant-read thermometer inserted into the thickest part of the thigh registers 170°F.; if the bacon is very dark, remove it from the breast. Transfer the turkey to a carving board, cover loosely with foil, and let rest for at least 20 minutes.

4. Pour the pan juices into a glass measure or bowl and skim off the fat. Reserve the juices, if desired, for a gravy. Carve the turkey and serve.

Sweet Potato Casserole

Chefs' note: *Sweet potatoes and pecans are major fall crops in the deep South, and this casserole is a staple on holiday tables there. Nonsoutherners might find it dessertlike, but this is an important illustration of the way southerners combine flavors: the sweetness is the perfect foil for the savoriness of the turkey.*

(Serves 12)
Sweet Potatoes

5 pounds sweet potatoes (about 10)
1 stick (4 ounces) unsalted butter, cut into pieces
⅔ cup granulated sugar
½ cup light brown sugar, packed
½ cup honey
2 teaspoons pure vanilla extract
1¾ teaspoons salt
¾ teaspoon freshly grated nutmeg
3 large eggs, lightly beaten
2½ cups hot milk

Topping

1 cup all-purpose flour
1 cup light brown sugar, packed
½ teaspoon cinnamon
½ teaspoon freshly grated nutmeg
¼ teaspoon salt
1 stick (4 ounces) unsalted butter, cut into ½-inch dice and chilled
1 cup (4 ounces) coarsely chopped pecans

1. *Make the sweet potatoes:* Preheat the oven to 350°F. Spread the sweet potatoes on a rimmed baking sheet and bake for about 1½ hours, or until tender. Let cool slightly, about 10 minutes, and then peel.

2. In a large bowl, beat the hot sweet potatoes at low speed. Beat in the butter. Add the granulated sugar, brown sugar, honey, vanilla, salt, and nutmeg and beat until blended. Add the eggs and beat at medium speed for 2 minutes. Reduce the speed to low again and gradually add the hot milk.

3. Preheat the oven to 375°F. Butter a 13- by 9- by 2-inch baking dish and pour in the sweet potatoes; spread in an even layer.

4. *Make the topping:* In a bowl, rub together the flour, brown sugar, cinnamon, nutmeg, and salt. Add the butter and rub or cut it in until the mixture resembles coarse meal. Stir in the pecans.

5. Sprinkle the topping evenly over the potatoes and bake for 1 to 1¼ hours, until the topping is golden brown and crisp. If the topping browns too quickly around the edges before the center is crisped, cut a large hole in the center of a sheet of foil and rest the foil on the dish while it finishes baking. Serve hot.

Advance preparation: The pureed sweet potato mixture and the topping can be refrigerated separately for up to 1 day. Bring to room temperature before proceeding.

Roasted Beets in Gingered Syrup

Chefs' note: *Baking the beets rather than boiling them intensifies their flavor. The beets must marinate overnight, so plan accordingly.*

(Serves 12)

2 pounds medium-size beets

2 tablespoons vegetable oil

Freshly ground pepper

2 cups cider vinegar

2 cups sugar

One 2-inch piece of fresh ginger, peeled and thinly sliced

4 whole cloves

1 bay leaf

½ teaspoon salt

1. Preheat the oven to 325°F. Put the beets in a large roasting pan. Drizzle with the oil and sprinkle with pepper. Cover with a sheet of baking parchment and then with a double thickness of foil, sealing tightly. Bake for 1 to 1½ hours, or until the beets are tender when pierced. Remove from the oven and let cool, covered.

2. Meanwhile, in a medium stainless-steel saucepan, combine the vinegar, sugar, ginger, cloves, bay leaf, and salt. Simmer over low heat until syrupy, about 20 minutes. Strain the syrup and let cool to room temperature.

3. Peel the beets. Slice them thickly or cut into ½-inch wedges. Transfer the beets to a large bowl and pour the syrup on top. Cover and refrigerate overnight. Serve chilled or warm, in the syrup.

Advance preparation: The beets can be refrigerated in their syrup for up to 1 week.

Edna Lewis's

Corn Pudding

Chef's Note: *Corn pudding was one of the great delicacies of summer and the first corn dish of the season. After helping to thin out the corn and weed it, we watched eagerly for the day when Mother made her rich, aromatic, golden-brown corn pudding. It was always served with a sweet potato casserole made from fresh-dug sweet potatoes. The sauce from both dishes mingled together in the plate and combined in a flavor that was memorable. The richness of the dishes reflected the season of the year—a time when there was a plentiful supply of milk, butter, and eggs.*

(Serves 6 to 8)*
2 cups corn, cut from the cob
⅓ cup sugar
1 teaspoon salt
2 eggs, beaten
2 cups half-and-half
3 tablespoons butter, melted
½ teaspoon freshly grated nutmeg

One 1½-quart casserole

*To feed twelve, double the recipe.

1. Cut the corn from the cob into a mixing bowl by slicing from the top of the ear downward. Don't go too close to the cob—cut only half the kernel. This gives a better texture to the pudding.

2. Sprinkle in the sugar and salt and stir well. Mix the beaten eggs and half-and-half together, and pour the mixture into the corn.

3. Add the melted butter. Mix thoroughly and spoon the mixture into a well-buttered casserole. Sprinkle the nutmeg over the top.

4. Set the casserole in a pan of hot water and place this in a preheated 350°F. oven for 35 to 40 minutes or until set. Test by inserting a clean knife into the center of the pudding. If it comes out clean, the pudding is done.

Note: An ingenious way we had to retain the freshness of corn was to stand the ear in a tub of water about 2½ inches deep. When the ear is severed from the stalk, its source of moisture is cut off, but if the corn stands in a dish of clean water, the cob continues to absorb moisture. Refrigeration, of course, helps, but how many ears will your refrigerator hold?

Lane Cake

Chefs' note: *A certain Mrs. Lane created her rich and delicious raisin, pecan, and coconut confection in Alabama in the late nineteenth century. It has been Scott Peacock's birthday cake since he was a child. The flavor improves if you assemble the cake a week ahead.*

(Serves 12 to 16)
Cake

3½ cups cake flour
2 teaspoons cream of tartar
2 teaspoons baking soda
¼ teaspoon salt
1 cup milk, at room temperature
1 teaspoon pure vanilla extract
2 sticks (½ pound) unsalted butter, softened
2 cups sugar
8 large egg whites, at room temperature

Filling

12 large egg yolks
1½ cups sugar

1½ sticks (6 ounces) unsalted butter, melted and allowed to cool

1½ cups (6 ounces) finely chopped pecans

1½ cups (10½ ounces) finely chopped raisins

1½ cups freshly grated coconut

½ cup bourbon

1½ teaspoons pure vanilla extract

¼ teaspoon salt

1. *Make the cake:* Preheat the oven to 325°F. Butter three 9-inch round cake pans and line the bottoms with baking parchment. Butter the paper and dust with flour, tapping out the excess.

2. Sift the flour, cream of tartar, baking soda, and salt into a medium bowl. In a small pitcher, combine the milk and vanilla. In a large bowl, beat the butter at medium speed until creamy. Slowly add the sugar and beat until light and fluffy, scraping down the sides of the bowl. At low speed, add the dry ingredients and the milk mixture alternately in 3 batches. Beat the batter until smooth, scraping down the sides of the bowl as necessary.

3. In another bowl, using clean beaters, beat the egg whites until they form soft peaks. Stir one-third of the egg whites into the cake batter to lighten it. Using a rubber spatula, fold the batter into the remaining egg whites until no white streaks remain.

4. Pour the batter into the cake pans and smooth the tops. Tap the pans lightly on a work surface to release any air bubbles. Bake the cakes on the middle and lower racks of the oven for about 30 minutes, reversing the positions of the pans halfway through, until the tops spring back when pressed lightly and a toothpick inserted in the center comes out with a few moist crumbs attached. Let cool in the pans for 5 minutes, then invert the cakes onto a wire rack to cool completely. Peel off the paper.

5. *Make the filling:* In a large saucepan, combine the egg yolks and sugar and stir until smooth. Add the melted butter and cook over moderate heat, stirring, until thick enough to coat the back of a spoon, about 6 minutes; do not let it boil. Stir in the pecans, raisins, and coconut and cook for about 1 minute. Add the bourbon, vanilla, and salt and let cool to lukewarm.

6. Place a cake layer on a serving plate, right side up, and spread with 1¼ cups of the filling. Repeat with a second cake layer and another 1¼ cups of filling. Top with the last cake layer and frost the cake with the remaining filling. Let the filling cool completely before serving.

Advance preparation: Refrigerate the cake in a tightly covered container for up to 1 week. Serve at room temperature.

Michael McCarty

CALIFORNIA DREAMING

Michael McCarty didn't set out to be a chef; he set out to be a restaurateur. By the time he was twenty-five, he was both. In addition to his pioneering work at Michael's in Santa Monica, where he was one of the first to serve what is commonly called "California cuisine," McCarty worked alongside Julia Child, Robert Mondavi, and Richard Graff to establish the American Institute of Wine and Food. When the history of modern American cuisine is written, McCarty, creator of Michael's Cookbook, will have a place at the table. To paraphrase one critic, you can't talk about California cuisine without talking about Michael McCarty. McCarty was trained in France during the rise of nouvelle cuisine; here he describes the importance of this training and the blossoming of California cuisine.

For the very first restaurant ever (circa A.D. 750), we have the Chinese to thank. For the art of the restaurateur, we turn to France—where, after the Revolution, "numerous chefs who had once served the aristocracy opened eating places for the common people."[8] Given that the Chinese started restaurants and the French made them an art, it should come as no surprise that chef Alan Wong (see page 115), believes that the two best cuisines in the world are Chinese and French. But it was the French way of the restaurateur, combined with a few things he picked up at his parents' home, that most appealed to Michael McCarty.

In 1969, at age fifteen, McCarty had his first memorable restaurant experience. Till then, he had done most of his eating at his home in Briarcliff Manor, New York, where his parents would often entertain al fresco. While his parents' friends were enthusiastic diners, their gatherings weren't "what we would know today, where people studied cookbooks or they sat around a table and talked about food and wines. They were more interested in life and people, art and literature, history and themselves. It was more about *joie de vivre* and *entertaining*." There were, however, certain unspoken rules: regardless of the mood, there was always good food and good drink, something both his father and his mother worked to ensure. From his perspective as a young child, entertaining was something his parents did together in the home, after his father returned from the "business world." McCarty never thought that the worlds of business and entertaining could intersect. And he held on to that impression until a trip to New York City before his junior year in France forced him to reconsider.

To kick off his departure for this year abroad, his parents and their best friends took McCarty out to a fancy French restaurant in Manhattan. It is not surprising that the restaurant they chose was French since, at the time, as George Lang writes in his memoir *Nobody Knows the Truffles I've Seen,* in New York, "only traditional French cuisine bore the upper-class stamp of approval [for] . . . those who liked food and wine." McCarty can still recall that first memorable restaurant experience—the feel of the fine china, the wonderfully cryptic sounds the French waiters made as they wound their tongues around the English language, and the elegance of the waiters in their tuxedos. In that torrent of stimuli, McCarty had a revelation. "The owner of the restaurant walked in, and the electricity level of the room just ratcheted up." But the real moment came at the end of the meal, when the check was presented. "My father and his colleague argued over the bill. And it just clicked. The quality of the service and the food, the way the whole place looked, the money changing hands, the *business* aspect of it. It totally made sense." As it had never done before in his life, the meaning of the word "commerce" came alive for him, and he began to understand the art of entertaining.

McCarty's year in Europe reaffirmed the magic of that night. The aristocratic family with whom he stayed in Brittany had lost everything in World War II except the country château. "The roof was leaking and their silverware had been buried outside somewhere during the war. They did such a good job hiding it that no one knows where it is even today. But they still had their chicken, vegetable, and dairy farms." The rest of the food, like wild oysters and the local lobster they got from the sea. He watched his "family" consume this hearty fare in abundance—at weddings, on vacations, and at Celtic parties, which were given for any and all reasons. And at celebrations everywhere, he found Breton favorites such as crepes, cotriade, a local variation of bouillabaisse, and white beans served in a dozen ways—whole, as an accompaniment to a main course, or thinned out in a soup or sauce.

The Breton family's emphasis on quality stayed with McCarty throughout his life. But it wasn't the only thing he would take home. His family had told him about traditional French cooking schools. Back in the States, he considered going to college, but his heart wasn't in it. Instead, he wanted to create an environment that brought art and commerce together. He applied to and was accepted by the **Ecole Hôtelière de Paris**, a hotel and restaurant school, **Le Cordon Bleu,** and **L'Académie du Vin** (Wine Academy). Then eighteen, McCarty was a few years older than the average student (such schools are typically attended by French teenagers, from fourteen to sixteen years old, who do not pursue a university degree), but he decided to enroll in 1972 anyway.

By attending all three schools at once, McCarty could count on two things—a busy schedule and a complete and diverse education. "I was one of sixty kids in my class at the Ecole Hôtelière, and we had to do things in a very regimented way. At the Cordon Bleu, I was one of five kids, and if I wanted to make pâte feuilletée a hundred times, I made it a hundred times. I had a mentor there and a chef, who was the last apprentice of Pellaprat, who was the last apprentice of Escoffier," the famous chef and author of *Guide Culinaire* (1903) and *Ma Cuisine* (1934). Complementary to that, at the hotel and restaurant school, he learned the Escoffier classic method of cooking, which he credits with being the basis of everything you need to know in the kitchen. "It's phenomenal to have that education. It's like learning Latin. A lot of chefs today don't have it, and they cook for the worse because of it."

McCarty was also taught the classic mode of service and the fundamentals of the business side—subjects like how to manage your labor and food costs. He's particularly grateful to have learned this at a young age, because it now forms an integral part of his approach to being a restaurateur. "If you want to be a great restaurateur, you can never, ever be at the mercy of the people in the kitchen. They'll hold you for ransom. And you can never be at the mercy of the person in the bookkeeping office or at the mercy of the people in the front of the house. You must have a knowledge of all three areas." As demanding as the classes were, he did find time to pursue a small catering business with his fellow students. He also found time to pursue the "good life." In the early 1970s, McCarty was nineteen years old and had virtually no responsibilities. "It was pre-AIDS, pre–every crazy thing. We catered all the time. And we threw a lot of parties in this outrageous five-bedroom apartment we rented. It was a wonderful period."

Though McCarty believes absolutely in the essentials of French cooking, he did not entirely embrace the French system. It wasn't just that mistakes were paid for physically—McCarty even remembers being beaten on the head with a wooden spoon. It was also that students at hotel and restaurant schools are sent out on four- to six-month *stages,* during which they apprentice in the country's top restaurants. And they often apprentice for years. "You've got to peel potatoes for a year and then you're moved to the fish station for a year," before moving to another station. He found the process laborious and lengthy. There was something particularly anti-American about this, in McCarty's eyes. The Yankee way demands that smart, hardworking people get ahead by their initiative, merit, and ingenuity; they don't apprentice endlessly. It didn't help that, because he was a few years older than the other students, he was anxious to move through the system quickly. So, to expedite his education, McCarty used his earnings from catering to eat in the continent's best restaurants. "I could learn more from eating one meal out than from spending a year in a kitchen chopping onions." While some might see his attitude as arrogant, McCarty thought he was just being efficient. "I needed to move faster to the next level. It's not a lack of patience; it's just that the French system was archaic."

While McCarty found the French training outdated, there was a progressive culinary movement afoot, one which he was fortunate enough to witness up close. Nouvelle cuisine was a revolution—a method of cooking that emphasized lighter sauces, fresh ingredients, and simpler preparation techniques. "It wasn't what we learned about in America afterward, where it became a joke—a big, giant plate with one scallop on it. It was *pure* then. For the first time, we were seeing dishes such as grilled duck served medium-rare, not well done." McCarty paid particular attention to Michel Guérard, who was working at a great little restaurant, La Camélia à Bougival, on the outskirts of Paris. There Guérard worked with a classical yet innovative chef, and together they were making waves.

It was about this time that McCarty, who was still only nineteen years old, and a bunch of friends did something miraculous. Without any idea of what they were getting into, they opened up an informal twenty-two-seat restaurant, Xavier, on the Île Saint-Louis. It was there that he began to develop his own style, a blend of French techniques, ingredients borrowed from various ethnic cuisines, and the best of what he knew of American cooking—grilling and barbecuing. Though the press in France and in the United States would later describe McCarty as working in the nouvelle style, he insists that he never completely adopted all of its ideas. Nonetheless, he praises the movement for liberating French chefs. "It gave chefs the freedom to start experimenting, to start saying, 'I'm going to do a red wine sauce with the salmon. I'm going to serve that with a chilled Chinon. And on and on down to the composed salads. Prior to that, they didn't really eat salads in France." Greatest of all, perhaps, it *simplified* the food.

While he never completely bought into the nouvelle style, he did try to modernize the classics at his restaurant.

> *In the old days, for instance, scallops were cooked straight through. And they were usually cooked a little bit in advance. Our idea was to cook them* à la minute, *right between medium-rare and medium, and get them out to the tables as quickly as possible, so you'd have the freshness of the taste, not masked with tons of sauces. We also pulled the flour out of sauces, and the sugar out of pastries.*

This marked the beginning of McCarty's signature style, which he developed in Paris and used throughout his career.

After eighteen months, McCarty sold his share of Xavier and returned to the United States and **Cornell University's** summer program for hotel and restaurant management, which he found to be a perfect foil for his European training. From there McCarty went to visit his brother in Colorado, where he consulted for two different restaurants. It was an opportunity to learn about the *business* of running a restaurant from an American perspective, and he got to do it on someone else's dime. But it wasn't just the consulting that was beneficial. Colorado also presented him with a chance to extend his education in food and wine. When department heads at the University of Colorado at Boulder learned that he was fluent in French, McCarty was asked to teach French to students who could write and read it but had trouble speaking it. The idea was to get their minds off the language and onto food and wine. Speaking French, he and the students would seek out local farmers at the market and buy enough food for a five-course meal. "We'd buy whatever had been grown in Colorado right there. We'd look at the vegetables, we'd decide what was the best that day, and buy that," a departure for many students who were accustomed to cooking with frozen foods. Then they'd head off to an extraordinarily stocked wine store known as the Liquor Mart, where a man named Phillip Reich, a blues singer smitten with wine, helped McCarty select the appropriate wines to complement the meal. Though McCarty was a graduate of L'Académie du Vin, it was through Reich that he really began to learn the art of pairing the right wine with a specific food. These Liquor Mart lessons would influence his whole way of entertaining.

Colorado also offered McCarty the opportunity to get a formal, recognized American college degree. With the help of the teaching faculties and deans, he designed a program that consisted of six different business classes, from advertising to business and tax law. "It was perfect. It rounded everything out, and I got my degree in the 'Business of the Art of Gastronomy.' Once again, the business and entertainment worlds merged. McCarty later leveraged the degree to help Julia Child, Robert Mondavi, and Richard Graff establish the **American Institute of Wine and Food (AIWF),** an organization founded nearly twenty years ago to increase the appreciation of food and drink through its conferences and programs.

After graduating from the University of Colorado at Boulder, McCarty visited his parents, who had by this time relocated to Malibu, California. It was January 1975, and the thermometer never dipped below 70 degrees. He's been in California ever since. New to the West, McCarty sought out local people who were versed in food and wine. He called up Lois Dwan, the highly regarded food critic of the *Los Angeles Times.* "I explained my background, told her I was looking to find the best local minds on food and wine." Dwan told him to contact Jean Bertranou of L'Ermitage and Dennis Overstreet at the Wine Merchant. McCarty hooked up with Overstreet, and together they created a series of wine and food pairings at the Wine Merchant. Drawn from the store's mailing list, the customers came from the elite of Los Angeles and included, of course, a few of its celebrities. McCarty offered a five-course cooking demonstration, and Overstreet paired each course with a wine. "It wasn't a big dinner party but little tastes of many things." The pairing of the right food with the right wine was a relatively new and groundbreaking step. Their public was bowled over. McCarty and Overstreet even impressed the journalists, who began tracking them.

Meanwhile, Bertranou and McCarty got together frequently to cook, eat, and discuss the food-and-wine scene. Produce, meat, game, and some dairy products, they concluded, were the biggest culinary problem in America at that time. Rather than fuss interminably and reminisce nostalgically about the great products in France, they decided to raise their own game. "We bought some land and built a farm where we raised chicken, squab, pheasant, duck, and quail. We made (for commercial use) the first foie gras in America, and we made a lot of headway into the way birds were raised and fed." Their venture was a critical success. The *New York Times* ran an article, which not only raised McCarty's profile locally but also increased national demand for his and Bertranou's products. They shipped their products to La Tulipe, La Française, Lutèce, and Le Bec-Fin. It was one of the most labor-intensive enterprises McCarty had yet undertaken: "We'd take the damn duck, butcher it, package it in these little Styrofoam things, wrap it up, whip it down to the airport, and send it across the country. Of course, we wouldn't tell anyone, because it was illegal." Bertranou and McCarty also encouraged and supported farmers in Imperial Valley, California, and in Mexico, who were willing to try their hand at growing lettuces other than iceberg, such as Boston and Bibb, and even less familiar salad greens such as arugula, mâche, and radicchio. Their influence in this area went far beyond California.

The farm came to an abrupt end in 1978, when Bertranou died suddenly of cancer. Problems with the estate forced McCarty to liquidate the farm and all its assets. Rather than start another farm, he decided to open his own restaurant. He looked all over Los Angeles for a location, rejecting the college areas because most students wouldn't be able to afford his food and rejecting other areas because they were, at the time, too sleepy. Given the demands on a restaurateur's life, McCarty also wanted to be relatively close to his house. After a few deals fell through, he finally hit on a spot in Santa Monica. "In the deadest part of town, there was this little pub in an art deco building, called the Brigadoon. And there was this little red glow coming out of it." As with his first revelation at the French restaurant in Manhattan, McCarty knew he had found the spot. "I said, 'Voilà!' It *feels* great, and it's fifteen minutes away from my home in Malibu. There are very big houses all around, which meant it would be perfect for dinner, though I knew it certainly wasn't going to be a lunch spot, because it was so dead during the day. Then I see that in the back of the building, there's a huge empty lot, completely overgrown with weeds. And it just clicked right then." It was the outdoor dining that sealed the deal in McCarty's imagination, for it reminded him of his parents' style of entertaining—outdoor, candlelit dining in the middle of the Hudson Valley forest. He knew that customers would be unable to resist a California variation on the same theme. With all the pieces in the right place, McCarty negotiated a deal in 1978, immediately started building the restaurant and transforming the lot into a garden, and opened Michael's in April 1979.

Though the media knew about McCarty's farm, his tastings at the Wine Merchant, and his catering business in Los Angeles, McCarty had no way of predicting the deluge of publicity that Michael's received before it even opened. Suddenly, he was caught up in what he now calls a "troika"—a fortunate moment when the press, restaurateurs, and clients all are in alignment. One of the most influential articles was written by Ruth Reichl, later the editor in chief of *Gourmet* and former *New York Times* restaurant critic. In 1979, however, she was writing for *New West* (which became *California Magazine*). Reichl, who had worked at The Swallow, a communally owned restaurant in Berkeley, before she began writing about food, wrote a nine-page piece about McCarty and the restaurant. As she pointed out, McCarty was not your typical restaurateur. He wasn't out just to open a restaurant; he wanted to change the way Californians dined and to eliminate all clichés from the restaurant industry. He wanted to make a statement and, more particularly, he wanted it to be an *American* statement.

Not only did he create a sensational menu—for example, pasta with a Chardonnay cream sauce, roasted red and yellow sweet peppers, baby asparagus, and American golden caviar; grilled squab salad with curly endive; spinach with raspberry vinegar sauce—he also created an *atmosphere* by paying attention to every detail. In an almost comical contrast to French restaurants, he eliminated the formality of dining. He urged his Ralph Lauren–bedecked wait staff to be friendly to the public. And he traded in the "beveled glass" for works by contemporary artists—Frank Stella, Richard Diebenkorn, and Jasper Johns—which he procured in a very clever art-for-food barter. It's common now to see restaurants decorated with contemporary art, but when McCarty did it he was really breaking new ground, and everyone took notice. There were changes in the kitchen as well. The six young chefs, many of whom had approached McCarty before he opened because they heard such phenomenal things about him, functioned as his equals in the kitchen. "We didn't have a hierarchy like we had in Europe. It was a collaboration." The biggest draw of all was that he put half his customers outdoors in the garden. After Reichl's article appeared, it was impossible to get a reservation for months at a time. Michael's quickly became one of the most popular restaurants in the state. This was a joyous time, and McCarty, who was then only twenty-five, was "living large," wearing designer suits and driving fancy cars.

At this point, the press started using the sobriquet "California cuisine" to describe the food at Michael's. Though McCarty has never agreed with that description—he believes his food is broader than the term implies—he acknowledges that "the press labeled us California cuisine because we were the first of the regional cusines." Other regional cuisines that found a huge following included Louisiana (Cajun), Hawaii (Hawaii regional; see page 115), and New Mexico and Texas (southwestern cuisine), among others. What McCarty and his peers in California were doing prompted cooks and diners across the country to turn away from European food and European methods of preparation toward homegrown produce and techniques that were right outside their own back door.

As interest surged in the various branches of American regional cuisine and modern American cooking, McCarty, who by this time was known throughout the state, became involved with a very influential group of American food professionals—Julia Child and the vintners Robert Mondavi and Richard Graff (Chalone Vineyard in Monterey). They started "commiserating about why you can't get a degree in gastronomy" in the United States and why food studies had "always been relegated to home economics, when it's a discipline that combines history and art." Along with several other prominent food professionals, they started a movement to change that through educational conferences, tastings, and seminars.[9] And with the help of Bob Huttenback, then the chancellor of the University of California at Santa Barbara, the group approached the university for assistance. Eventually UCSB gave them land and support to launch the American Institute of Wine and Food (AIWF), but it was an uphill battle all the way. Among other issues, they were battling the perception that gourmet food and the idea of pairing food and wine were elitist concepts, and therefore not at all appropriate for a publicly funded university. Each professional also had his or her own priorities. "Mondavi wanted to prove that American wine was as good as wine all over the world. That was his mantra, still is today, and God love him for it, because that's why it is what it is today." McCarty wanted to emphasize food. And Child's emphasis was on motivating the "common person to get out there and be excited about food."

In an effort to clarify their mission and raise money for the AIWF, they held a massive fund-raising dinner at Jimmy Nassikas's Stanford Court in San Francisco on May 4, 1983. Three hundred seventy-two people paid $250 each to eat the food of chefs from around the country who were gathered together to talk about what was happening nationally on the food scene. James Beard was honored at this "American Celebration" dinner, making it, according to McCarty, the first of the annual James Beard Benefit Dinners. During the dinner, each chef's segment of the meal was paired with a video that featured art and music from his or her area as well as the chef's take on the food of the region.

It was an extraordinary gathering of food literati, groundbreakers in American regional cuisine. "No one had quite combined the French and the Latin the way Mark Miller did. No one had ever put chiles on quail and then put it on a bed of mesclun greens before." On top of that, people were stimulating each other and learning from each other; some of them were meeting, talking, and collaborating for the first time. Noël Riley Fitch writes in her biography of Julia Child, *Appetite for Life:*

> *When Jimmy Schmidt (Detroit) was preparing his stuffing of wild root vegetables, fiddlehead fern, and hazelnuts from Michigan, Larry Forgione (River Café in Brooklyn) and Bradley Ogden (Kansas City) rolled up their sleeves and helped him chop and slice. When Paul Prudhomme's blackened redfish was ready to be prepared, Jonathan Waxman (Michael's), Wolfgang Puck, and Mark Miller joined in the last-minute cooking. When Jeremiah Tower [Stars] was ready to put the chocolate and sabayon sauce on his pecan pastry, Alice Waters and Barbara Kafka (New York City) joined the assembly line.*[10]

It was a heady and exciting time, whose benefits we are still feeling—and not only in this country. McCarty asserts that the Europeans changed the way they cooked as well. They developed their own regional specialties. "I use the term *codifying*. Italy went through this; France went through it too. They've gone through the complete regional rebirth. And we were the leaders. We showed them that they had to get off their butts, straighten out their acts, and evolve. Because times change. You cannot hold on."

After the benefit, "having done his thing in the restaurant business," McCarty was now itching to take the California hotel scene to another level. He had his sights on and won the commission for a five-acre former private club on Santa Monica's coast. Yearning for an indoor-outdoor design similar to Michael's, he hired twenty-seven world-renowned architects and commissioned each one to do a bungalow. "It was going to be the new age of the hotel business." But an "elite" community group and its lobbyists fought him every step of the way. In a long and tiresome process, his detractors prepared to take the issue to the voters.

As the battle waged over the next several years, McCarty grew even more restless and needed more challenges. After all, by the time he was thirty-one he had already co-owned a restaurant in Paris, started a foie gras business, launched one of the most successful restaurants in Los Angeles, and made plans to open a second Michael's in New York City (which he did in 1989). Tired of waiting around, he decided to go back to what he knew best—restaurants. Between 1985 and 1989, McCarty and partner Jimmy Schmidt, who now heads META Restaurants and has been twice inducted into the Who's Who of Foods and Beverages, opened up three Rattlesnake Clubs—one in Denver, one in Detroit, and one in Washington, D.C. (Adirondacks). With no kids, McCarty was able to jet off from one location to the other to keep an eye on the restaurants. As he had done in France, he was living large. "All three of the Rattlesnakes were in big eighteen-thousand-square-foot historic buildings. The market was great. People were eating like mad. We were feeding four to five thousand people per night between the three restaurants. It was unbelievable. We thought it was never going to end." But it did, sooner than he had planned.

In 1990, McCarty lost the community referendum for his planned Santa Monica hotel. "It was the end of the eighties. Developers were bad, greedy, rich people. And through the buzzwords of pollution and traffic, the lobbyists were able to defeat me." But the vote wasn't all he lost. He was out $6 million. All that McCarty had worked so hard for had sunk into a black hole of political, legal, and design fees. His only recourse was to sell his interest in the Rattlesnake Clubs, leaving him with only the two Michael's and a still unsated desire to open a hotel.

With a manager, a chef, and a bookkeeper in both restaurants and bimonthly trips to New York, McCarty now focuses on "maintaining a level of service and a quality of food and product buying that is impeccable." While he has had to scale back, he doesn't consider the last few years a loss. Instead, he sees them as a time of regeneration. "Los Angeles had the riots in 1992, the fires in 1993, the earthquakes in 1994. I was going through my recovery while the whole town was going through its recovery. So we sort of survived it together." And he doesn't take lightly the fact that he's still standing. To celebrate the sixteenth anniversary of Michael's in Los Angeles and to benefit local museums in southern California, he invited back sixteen chefs who had worked for him over the years to cook for a benefit dinner (an annual event he throws to support the city's art institutions). Attendees included Gordon Naccarato (formerly of Gordon's in Aspen), Sally Clarke (from Clarke's in London), Mark Peel and Nancy Silverton (from La Brea Bakery and Campanile, both in Los Angeles), Zack Bruel (from Zack's in Cleveland), Jonathan Waxman (formerly of Bryant Park Grill), Ken Frank (of La Toque), and Roy Yamaguchi (from Roy's in Hawaii and New York City). These are important, active chefs in their own right, and their attendance speaks to the importance of McCarty's place in the annals of modern American cuisine.

Michael McCarty's

California Gazpacho

Chef's note: *When I was a kid, my mom used to make the gazpacho in the* New York Times Cookbook. *I always liked the way the cool tomato soup had all those fresh little goodies in it. I've adapted memories of that childhood gazpacho into the somewhat more fiery version here. The key to it, I feel, is to start with really impeccable ingredients: since you don't cook gazpacho, the soup has nothing to hide. Use a rich, high-quality tomato juice as your base; I like Sacramento brand. If Maui onions aren't available in your area, Walla Walla, Vidalia, or a good sweet red onion will do.*

(Serves 6)

6 cups of tomato juice

1 medium red and 1 yellow tomato (or 2 red tomatoes), peeled, seeded, and finely chopped

1 medium Maui onion, finely diced

½ each medium red and yellow bell pepper, stemmed, seeded and finely minced

½ jalapeño chile, stemmed, seeded, and finely minced

½ bunch of fresh cilantro, stemmed and finely chopped

1 medium garlic clove, finely chopped

Juice of 1 lime

¼ cup extra-virgin olive oil

¼ cup Cabernet vinegar or white wine vinegar

Salt and freshly ground pepper

3 tablespoons sour cream
6 small sprigs fresh cilantro

1. In a large mixing bowl, combine the tomato juice with the tomatoes, onion, bell peppers, chile, chopped cilantro, garlic, lime juice, olive oil, and vinegar. Cover and chill for several hours in the refrigerator. Season to taste with salt and pepper.
2. Ladle the soup into chilled serving bowls. Spoon a small dollop of sour cream into each bowl and top with a sprig of cilantro.

Michael McCarty's

Grilled Tenderloin of Pork with Apples and Calvados

Chef's note: *This is my California-style modern simplification of the classic Normandy sautéed or roast pork dish. If you like, you can add an additional garnish of a few strips of grilled bacon, cut into thin juliennne strips.*

(Serves 6)

6 pork tenderloin fillets, 6 ounces each

1 recipe Basic Marinade (see below)

4 tablespoons (½ stick) unsalted butter

2 medium-sized Red Delicious apples or other good, firm, sweet apples, peeled, cored, and cut into ¼-inch wedges

1 cup Calvados

2 medium-sized shallots, finely chopped

2 cups heavy cream

Salt and freshly ground white pepper

2 tablespoons chopped fresh chives

1. Put the pork fillets in a glass or ceramic bowl and add the marinade. Cover the bowl and leave the pork to marinate at room temperature for 1 to 2 hours, or overnight in the refrigerator.

2. Preheat the grill or broiler until very hot.

3. Melt the butter in a medium-size skillet over high heat. When the butter foams, add the apples and sauté them, stirring constantly, until they are golden, 5 to 7 minutes.

4. Remove the skillet from the heat and add the Calvados and shallots. Carefully return the skillet to the heat, taking care not to slosh the Calvados, and boil until the liquid reduces to ¼ cup, about 15 minutes. Add the cream and continue cooking until the sauce is reduced to coating consistency, 5 to 7 minutes more. Season to taste and keep the sauce warm.

5. While the sauce is reducing, wipe the marinade from the pork fillets and lightly season them with salt and pepper. Grill them 5 to 7 minutes per side for medium; halfway through the cooking on each side, rotate the meat 90 degrees to give it crosshatched grill marks.

6. Slice each fillet at a 45-degree angle into pieces about ½ inch thick and place them, overlapping, on a heated serving plate. Spoon the sauce and apples around the meat and sprinkle the sauce with chives.

Basic Marinade

Chef's note: *I use this marinade to give extra flavor and tenderness to duck, squab, or pork. If you're marinating quail or rabbit, add ¾ cup of Sauvignon blanc or Chardonnay to the ingredients listed below.*

(makes 2½ to 3 cups)
1 cup extra-virgin olive oil
6 medium-size cloves garlic, unpeeled, bashed
½ medium-size Maui, Walla Walla, Vidalia, or sweet red onion, sliced
1 medium-sized carrot, coarsely chopped
1 bunch parsley, leaves only, coarsely chopped
1 bunch fresh basil (about 12 leaves)
Cracked white pepper, to taste

1. Combine all the ingredients.
2. Pour over the poultry or meat to be marinated.

✳ DESIGN FUNDAMENTALS ✳

When Michael McCarty set out to design his restaurant in California, he decided to make the garden and artwork from contemporary artists—Frank Stella, Richard Diebenkorn, and Jasper Johns—the major visual focal points. When Steve Poses (page 256) first opened Frog, he adorned it with "tons of plants and . . . secondhand furniture and artwork given to him by aunts and uncles." By the time he had opened the last restaurant in his multimillion-dollar empire, he could afford to hire designers. According to **Larry Bogdanow,** of the design firm Bogdanow Partners, Architects, PC not everyone needs a designer. Some small restaurants, like Poses's first, can look and feel fine without one. "But just as there are certain things about cooking that a bartender can't take care of, or matters in the front of the house that a cook can't attend to, there are certain things about the design of a restaurant that go beyond the chef-owner."

Below, Bogdanow—who, with his partner Warren Ashworth, has designed dozens of restaurants, including Rubicon in San Francisco, and Union Square Café, Savoy, Follonico, Cub Room, and Union Pacific in New York—offers general tips on why you might want to hire a designer and how to find a good one.

Why a Designer?

"To give just two examples of concerns that most chefs and restaurant owners shouldn't be thinking about but designers routinely do, consider flow of service and seating.

"Just as chef-owners are very good at planning their own kitchens because they know how service flows in their kitchen, a good designer will program the flow of service in the front of the house so that there are no collisions with the public. But in a poorly designed restaurant, the kitchen and service areas are often located behind the bar. Consequently, you've got waiters with trays of food plowing their way through a crowded bar. Or you'll find the service and the bathroom-telephone areas sharing the same corridor, so you've got waiters and people en route to the bathroom sharing the space. Both of these mistakes are bad design choices; a good designer will know to avoid that.

"A designer also thinks about seating. And it's more than just, 'Is this table in the servers' path?' It's how we can make every table in the house a good one. Most restaurants have a few tables that are considered bad tables. But I try to work on a space so that even a table in the corner is appealing. It doesn't have to be considered Siberia. Instead, you can make it a romantic table for a couple who don't want to see and been seen, right in the center of the place. Good designers factor considerations such as these into their design."

Choosing a Designer—What to Look For

Once you've decided to hire a designer, you'll want to find the right one. Bogdanow suggests you judge designers not only by their style but also by their ability to listen to their clients.

"A good designer doesn't impose his style on the client but rather takes cues from his clients. For instance, Adam Tihany designed Le Cirque 2000 and Jean Georges, both in New York City, at the same time, yet they couldn't be more different, which means he didn't force his vision on his clients. He listened to what they had to say. So the first thing you want to do is find someone who listens.

"This brings me to the other key factor in choosing a designer. The contractor and designer you hire to build and design your restaurant had better be people you like, because it's a long process and you've got to talk on a regular basis. You had better understand each other. It's not quite like coupling, but you've got to have a good relationship and be able to talk honestly. This is almost as important as style compatibility.

"For example, as a designer, I like natural-fiber textiles, metals for accent, and wooden tables—wood is warm, it's earthy, it relates to food. But the client may not like these materials. I don't impose my will on the clients. I come up with suggestions based on the direction they're giving me. If they don't like it, they need to talk honestly with me about it: 'I really like what you did with the Union Square Café, but I'm not so fond of that other restaurant, which doesn't look as sophisticated to me.'"

Moving Toward a Design—Concept, Theme, Budget

Once you've hired a designer with whom you can communicate, you'll want to talk candidly about three things: (1) concept, (2) theme, and (3) budget and site selection.

Concept

"Before you get started it's important that you give the designer some sense of what the overall feel of the space should be. A good chef-restaurateur will be able to give a designer a concept: 'I want it warm and inviting, relaxed and homey.' Or, 'I want a more formal, white-tablecloth look.' Once a designer is given some direction, then he or she can come up with a menu of choices. If the client wants warm upholstered chairs as opposed to metal ones, then you can offer several different fabrics from which to choose.

"For instance, for Savoy, a restaurant in New York City that my firm designed, the husband-and-wife chef-owners told me to do something creative with simple materials because they like creative cooking with simple ingredients—heirloom tomatoes, pastas, poultry. That was good, clear direction, and I was able to show them things that I consider simple. The walls are made of blond Masonite with cherrywood trim, and the ceiling is covered with a vaulted-shape, bronze mesh window screen. When I proposed light fixtures made of onyx, which I thought were simple, they found it too fussy. In the end, we went with their preferences."

Theme

"The best clients—whether they're a chef or an owner who is working with a chef-consultant—give me a specific food theme, such as new American cuisine or pan-Asian. If they can describe their cooking to me, it helps tremendously with the design process."

Budget and Site Selection

Though every space is different, and the price of labor, materials, and the like varies regionally, Bogdanow offers the following general guidelines. "If you invest under $120 per square foot, it will be difficult for the designer to design a restaurant. Between $120 and $200, a designer can take a creative approach; and with $200 to $300 a square foot, a designer can make a really great-looking place. If you spend much more than that, it can feel a little overdone. In major urban areas, the required use of a union contractor can escalate the budget by 50 to 100 percent.

"While budget is really important, not every restaurant has to be a high-end one. The key thing to remember is that design has to coordinate with menu price point. A restaurant owner should not spend two million dollars to build a budget-minded restaurant. Site selection, therefore, is integral. You can't build a budget-oriented restaurant in a space with a high-priced lease.

"You also have to consider how much of the budget is just going into making the kitchen functional. If a space has an existing kitchen, air-conditioning, full amperage on the electricity, and a proper-size gas line, there's a lot more money left for the design— furniture, tabletop design, lighting fixtures, artwork, and so forth. But if the space is completely raw, and you need to install electric and air-conditioning systems and put in a flue to the roof, just to get the kitchen to be operational, then you have less money to design the front of the house. The earlier a designer gets involved in site selection, the more efficient the design and planning process will be."

To find a designer in your area, talk with other restaurateurs, contact local industry organizations, and consult *Interior Design* magazine's annual roundup of hospitality giants, as well as *Hospitality Design* magazine.

✳

Cowboy Cook Tom Perini

TURNING YOUR PASSION
INTO YOUR LIVELIHOOD

He's a cowboy cook who, with self-depreciating wit, makes light of his own accomplishments. Fortunately, others in the food establishment take Tom Perini quite seriously. Though his Texan restaurant is located far from America's food capitals, he has managed to catch the attention of the movers and shakers in the food world. The James Beard Foundation has twice invited him to cook at Beard House in New York, and Neiman Marcus features his mesquite-smoked, peppered beef tenderloin in its Christmas catalogue. Tom Perini's life is a perfect example of what happens when you follow your passion, if your passion happens to be food.

If you're looking for Tom Perini, your best bet is to first try Buffalo Gap, Texas, a little bitsy place fifteen miles south of Abilene. With a population of 499 people, Buffalo Gap is a town where the animals far outnumber the people. It's also the home of the Perini Ranch Steakhouse. The town got its name from an opening in the Edward Plateau mountains through which big buffalo herds used to migrate as Comanche Indians and buffalo hunters fought for control of the route. When Perini is at the Ranch, he is hard at work—supervising the kitchen staff, greeting the steakhouse regulars, picking vegetables in the garden, or playing plumber to a clogged drain. But he's not always there, and that's when finding him gets tricky. He's often invited to cater a shindig in some other part of the Southwest. He might even be in another country, promoting Texas beef and the Texas way of smoking meat in places as far-flung as Mexico and Japan.

Promoting Texas beef is not exactly what this former cattle rancher envisioned himself doing back in the 1960s, when he began raising and selling cattle to feedlots and restaurants. But increasingly he found himself hanging around the chuck wagon, more content to cook steak and potatoes—or, when the weather turned cold, chiles and other stews—for the scores of men who worked his ranch than he was to work beside them mending fences and running after fugitive cattle. At first the food wasn't very fancy:

> *When you're cooking on a chuck wagon out in the middle of a 4,000-acre pasture with cowboys, you forget all this fancy stuff. We were feeding men who had hard jobs, so we were fixing really heavy things—steak and potatoes in the winter and hearty stews when the weather turned cold. And we learned to cook things that tasted good, because if you cook bad food out in the wagon, you're in trouble. Your critics will tell you. For example, when you fix beans, you'll use some salt pork or you'll use bacon because that's the flavor—might not be the healthiest, but it damn sure tastes good.*

His peers protested neither the food nor the loss of an able body; they knew they were getting the good end of the stick. "I would be invited to go on deer hunts or different things with the guys, and it took me a little while to realize that I was being invited because they wanted me to do the cooking." Pretty soon word of mouth spread from one ranch to another, and before long, people on neighboring ranches started asking Perini to cater special events. "I'd get a bunch of cowboys together and we'd go over and cook for a party. And one day I thought: You know, we ought to get paid for this." And that's how in 1974, Perini Ranch Catering, a sideline to his ranching responsibilities, was born.

Though Perini started out catering primarily in Abilene, word got around throughout Texas. Eventually, people and organizations in most of the western states were bidding for his services as well. He catered at the Sleeping Indian Ranch in Colorado, the Coyote Ranch in Sabinal, Texas, the Western Chuckwagon Association in Oklahoma, and the Cowboy Artists of America. Like most caterers, Perini soon learned that he couldn't always rely on the host to have adequate kitchen supplies. He got around that by getting into the habit of taking his own barbecue pit and *Stella*, his hundred-year-old chuck wagon, with him wherever he went. Named after the *Playboy* playmate—and his former acquaintance—Stella Stevens, the wagon holds Perini's gear. This includes the spices and herbs he cooks with—onion powder and garlic powder along with thyme and rosemary—and his pricelessly seasoned equipment: lots of cast-iron pots, cooking utensils, and lanterns for illuminating the dark when the sun dips under the western skyline. And because cooking with mesquite is a Texas tradition, he and his crew also started taking with them, wherever they went, hundreds of pounds of mesquite wood from trees that grow on his ranch.

Perini can't imagine cooking without mesquite. "In our part of Texas, there are two different theories of cooking. There's the smoking theory, and then there is a roasting theory." With the smoking method, you pull smoke across the meat. "That's good, but it can be a little smoky. I prefer a roasting method, where you actually shovel mesquite coals under the meat and the smoke goes up so your heat goes up. You get more of the flavor and not quite as much of the smoke."

By 1983, his barbecue techniques had found such wide acceptance he could no longer split himself between cattle and catering. Instead of leaving ranching altogether, he decided to simultaneously run a catering company and turn his ranch into a restaurant, only he'd never call it that. "It's a joint—you don't wear a coat and tie." The Perini Ranch Steakhouse is a place you go to have fun, drink a few beers or margaritas, listen to some country-and-western music, and enjoy some mesquite-grilled steaks, slow-cooked pork ribs, or Cajun catfish. But his patrons don't just go for the food. They drive for miles for the complete sensual assault, or what Perini calls the *sizzle*—the music, the winter fire in the redbrick hearth, and the waiters in their cowboy boots and hats. In the trade, his is what is known as a *destination* restaurant, a place people specifically go to, not somewhere they just happen to walk or drive by on their way to someplace else. "We have people who drive from within a hundred-fifty-mile radius for dinner, and then they go back home. But in that part of Texas, where the land is big and flat, we grow up doing that kind of thing." And it's not just locals and everyday Texans who make Perini's their destination; a few celebrities—Robert Duvall and Clint Eastwood, for instance—have been known to frequent the joint as well.

Even politicians turn to Perini's for authentic Texas food. One of the most memorable catering events for Perini has to be the Totally Texas Tailgate Party, hosted by Governor and Mrs. George W. Bush for the football game between the University of Texas and the University of Virginia. A staffer from the governor's mansion inquired about Perini's food and reputation. Rather than boast over the phone, Perini replied, "Next week, I'm going to be in Austin to cook for the **Texas Restaurant Association (TRA)** at their office. So why don't you just send over your decision-maker for a taste?" Perini was a bit surprised when Laura Bush herself showed up at the TRA. When Perini asked why the taster hadn't come, he was told something to the effect of, "You asked for the chief decision-maker at the governor's house, and that's what you got."[11]

Despite the enthusiasm and caliber of his patrons, Perini does not consider himself a chef. "I'm a cowboy cook, not a chef." There are a few key differences between someone like himself—a cook who turned a hobby into a career—and someone who was professionally trained to cook, Perini would argue. "Chefs are taught about seasoning" and "how to gauge the temperature of a fire, and so forth, in school. Whereas I learned through trial-and-error, through, 'Well, next time, I won't put as much salt into it.'" Another way he's trained himself to be a better cook is by walking through his restaurant—a homey place where chile riastras dangle from the ceiling, railroad ties adorn the walls, and mesquite trees grow between tables on the adjoining terrace—to see what's being left on the plates. If a steak, or one of the sides—say the roasted acorn squash or a "cowboy potato" (a potato that's cubed with its own skin on it and cooked in a little butter and garlic)—is repeatedly left behind, he knows the item is a problem, menu-wise. For Perini, "plating," or elaborate plate design, is something else that separates the chuck wagon cooks from the real McCoys, the professionally trained chefs. In fact, you definitely won't see any fancy designs on dishes coming out of Perini's kitchen. "If you find a leaf on my plate, you send it back to the kitchen."

Though he doesn't consider himself a chef, the world thinks otherwise. The James Beard House even invited him to be a guest chef in 1995, an invitation that indeed signals acceptance by the food establishment. "The first time they called me, I was kind of embarrassed." With a name like Perini, he thought they were mistaking him for a fancy Italian chef. Once the Beard House staff assured him that he was their man, Perini agreed to do it. As Hal Smith reports in an article on Perini in *Texas Highways,* while prepping in the kitchen, Perini "half-heard someone on the intercom. 'Chef, line one.' I paid no attention. 'Chef, pick up line one.' It went over my head. 'Chef, please answer.' Finally, someone came in and said, 'Mr. Perini, you've got a phone call.' Well, you know, I'm a chuck wagon cook. I assumed the call had to be for someone else."[12]

As is clear from the Beard dinner (for more on these dinners, see page 113), his reluctance to embrace his success is matched only by the enthusiasm with which the food cognoscenti have courted him. In 1995, just before he went to New York City for the Beard event, someone in Abilene talked him into submitting his mesquite-smoked-peppered beef tenderloin to the *New York Times* and *Parade* magazine for their Christmas mail-order issues. When the *New York Times* called him back and asked for another tenderloin, he figured he was the butt of a bad joke. "Well, I thought, you know, I'm a country boy and these guys are out in the park having sandwiches with the tenderloin." He sent another one anyway. Months passed before he heard from the *Times,* but finally, "This guy calls me and says he's a fact checker from the *New York Times.* He asked, 'How do you spell Perini?'" When Perini asked why he wanted to know, he got a vague answer. But the fact checker did give Perini a tip. He told him to get a toll-free number immediately. The very next day Perini's "superlative and spectacular" peppered tenderloin was listed as the first choice by the *Times*'s holiday roundup of the country's top mail-order food items. *Parade* and the Neiman Marcus catalogue followed suit. Since that article appeared, Perini's toll-free number hasn't stopped ringing; calls come in to his full-service mail-order business from around the world.

He's so popular now that when the James Beard House called again in 1997, he knew they had found the right Perini. But fame had not gone to his head. He still went as a cowboy cook, not a chef. In an environment where it's often wine and Champagne, he and his right-hand person, Dale Crock, served cold Lone Star and Shiner bock beers. The drinks were accompanied by an array of appetizers. Mesquite baby back pork ribs and chilled pickled okra were on hand, as were calf fries—aka mountain oysters, a euphemism for bull testicles—and spicy pork tamales. Perini wrapped up the appetizer section with a Bacon-Wrapped Quail Breast stuffed with jalapeño and onion. (Bacon is a meat he does like to smoke, as opposed to roast. "I love bacon with a lot of different dishes. It's a neat seasoning.") For the main course, he served his now world-famous mesquite-seared peppered beef tenderloin with chilled baked apples, and fried Cajun catfish with a tartar sauce, a red sauce, and lemon. He accompanied those with green chile hominy and a green salad with roasted pecans. Even the bread, grilled sourdough bread with Texas onion butter, was distinctly southwestern. When that was all polished off, he served his trademark sourdough bread pudding with pecans, to which he added a wild plum sauce, sealed to perfection with a splash of a second sauce made with Jack Daniel's. Everything was prepared in the same manner as it usually is back at the Ranch. With cowboy music coming from the speakers, Perini wanted the guests to experience more than just good food. He wanted them to have the *sizzle*.

For Perini, determining how to create that sizzle and finding out what will differentiate one restaurant from another is something restaurateurs and aspiring restaurateurs must constantly strive for. "Every restaurant that's successful is successful for a reason—say, the type of food they cook or their location. Whatever it is, it's a niche. You have to be different to make it work. So I don't want to do everything that the steakhouse across the street does. There's no reason to." And even though he's found his specialty, it has still not been easy:

> *I didn't have any idea what I was getting into when I started. From cleaning the buildings in the morning to locking up in the evenings, a restaurant is an ongoing business with a payroll that starts first thing every morning. Now, I've enjoyed it and I've had a good time with everybody raising Cain. But it's been tough. You don't get into the restaurant business to make a whole bunch of money and go, "Boy, this is a good deal." You have to really love it.*

Take the Beard event in 1997. After dinner, as Perini walked around and everybody slapped him on the back and congratulated him, he was deeply satisfied. He even smoked a cigar, later that night. But he'll never forget that for those five minutes of glory, he and his crew had put in ten hours of sweating and chopping: "It's not all glittery lights." Still, all the sweat-inducing work that goes on behind the scenes is worth it, because he enjoys it.

Fifteen years after Perini first opened his own restaurant doors, he was elected to serve as president of the **Texas Restaurant Association,** the country's largest state restaurant association. It has over 5,500 members who do approximately $21.6 billion per year in business. This brings him into contact with all kinds of cooks—some fancy, some not; some who smoke their meat; some who, like Perini, prefer to roast it over mesquite charcoal; some who draw on Texas's southern traditions, its use of hominy and black-eyed peas; and others who borrow from its Mexican traditions, its tamales and quesadillas. Running the Texas Restaurant Association for one year is quite an honor. But, like his fame, it hasn't gone to his head. As with the Neiman Marcus catalogue or the *New York Times*'s recognition, he hasn't forgotten his roots. He's a cowboy cook through and through, not a chef. "If I had to put on one of those fancy chef hats, hell, I wouldn't know what to do. I'd be scared to death."

Bacon-Wrapped Dove Breast or Quail Breast

Chef's note: *This is a favorite hors d'oeuvre especially during hunting season, and it works with both quail and dove. Chicken can also be substituted. This is an incredibly easy recipe to double or triple.*

(Serves 6 as an appetizer)

6 dove breasts, 6 quail breasts, or 1 chicken breast (see Note),
   split and deboned

1 fresh jalapeño pepper, deseeded and sliced into 6 thin strips

3 strips of bacon, ½ strip per breast

Equipment: toothpicks

1. Fold breast around pepper, and then wrap with bacon and secure with a toothpick.
2. Roast over mesquite until bacon is done.

Note: If chicken breast is being used, cut the breast into 6 pieces.

Tom Perini's

Perini Ranch Steakhouse Rub

Chef's note: *This Perini Ranch Steakhouse dry rub is excellent on beef.*

(Makes enough for 3 to 4 large steaks)

2 teaspoons cornstarch or flour

2 teaspoons salt

2 tablespoons coarsely ground black pepper

½ teaspoon lemon pepper

¼ teaspoon ground oregano or rosemary

4 teaspoons garlic powder

4 teaspoons onion powder

1 teaspoon paprika

1 teaspoon beef bouillon granules

1. Combine all ingredients, mixing well. Store tightly covered in glass or plastic. Shake before each use to remix.

2. Rub generously on both sides of meat.

3. Let meat sit in the refrigerator for 1 to 2 hours to absorb flavors before grilling.

✳ THE AMERICAN CULINARY FEDERATION, INC.; ✳
THE JAMES BEARD FOUNDATION;
AND THE INTERNATIONAL ASSOCIATION
OF CULINARY PROFESSIONALS

The largest and oldest professional organization of chefs in the United States, the **American Culinary Federation, Inc. (ACF),** is a professional, nonprofit organization for chefs that was founded in 1929 in New York City by three chefs' organizations. Its principal goal is to promote a professional image of the American chef worldwide through education among culinarians at all levels, from apprentices to the most accomplished certified master chefs. The ACF was the pioneer organization responsible for elevating the status of the executive chef from the *service* category to the *professional* category in the U.S. Department of Labor's Dictionary of Official Titles, in 1976. Registered with the Department of Labor, the ACF runs the only comprehensive certification program for chefs in the United States. A national organization, with chapters everywhere, it also awards a scholarship to junior members enrolled in postsecondary culinary arts programs and ACF apprenticeship programs.

Founded in 1986 by friends and colleagues of James Beard, the legendary "father of American gastronomy," the **James Beard Foundation** promotes the culinary arts through its award programs, dinners, scholarships, and library. A number of the chefs who appear in *If You Can Stand the Heat* have ties to the James Beard Foundation. Rick Bayless, Frank Brigtsen, Bobby Flay, Thomas Keller, and Alan Wong, among others, have been recognized as outstanding chefs at the foundation's annual award ceremony. Every May, at the James Beard Awards Dinner, which is often referred to as the "Oscars of the food world," chefs and restaurateurs are recognized alongside cookbook authors, print and electronic journalists, winemakers, and restaurant designers.

In addition to the annual awards gala, chefs work with the foundation by helping to raise money for its scholarship fund. Across the nation, chefs are asked to cook at "Friends of James Beard" benefit dinners, which the public is invited to attend. Others, in a program pioneered by Wolfgang Puck in 1986, come to New York City to prepare, in their signature style, a four- to eight-course meal at the James Beard House. (See Tom Perini, page 104, for one chef's experience of cooking at Beard House.)

These prestigious dinners help raise scholarship money, which is then redistributed to aspiring culinary professionals who might not otherwise be able to afford cooking school. Since its inception in 1990, the Beard Foundation has given away over $400,000 worth of scholarships.

The **International Association of Culinary Professionals (IACP)** is a nonprofit organization that promotes the culinary arts throughout the world. Its members are primarily "food and drink" journalists, educators, or practitioners (chefs, food stylists, marketers, scientists, etc.). A research and networking organization, the IACP also hosts an annual educational conference, which culminates in the prestigious Julia Child Awards. The awards recognize excellence in cookbook writing and food journalism. Other activities of the organization include fund-raisers for culinary scholarships and hunger relief programs and the establishment of professional and ethical standards through the Certified Culinary Professional program.

Information about contacting all three organizations can be found in Appendix D.

Alan Wong

HAWAII'S REGIONAL CUISINE

Many would find it astonishing that less than twenty years ago, the culinary highlight for most tourists to Hawaii was either a luau (pig roast) or dinner at a continental European restaurant. It was only with the ascension of American regional cuisine (see Michael McCarty) that people began to realize they were doing themselves a disservice by not trying Hawaii's incredibly varied and flavorful cooking, which blends local ingredients, Asian spices, and Asian-influenced methods of preparation. Alan Wong, one of the top restaurateurs in Hawaii—along with a few other talented Hawaiian chefs—was a key player in this change. He and his peers have done for Hawaiian food what Mark Miller and Alice Waters, for example, have done for southwestern and California food respectively—by spreading the news that the fiftieth state to join the Union has its own enviable foodways. Despite his repertoire and knowledge of Pacific-influenced cuisine, however, Wong is adamant in maintaining that any chef worth his or her salt must be familiar with the essentials of French cooking.

To know anything at all about Hawaii's food, we need to know something of the waves of immigrant labor sent to work in the backbreaking and spirit-numbing sugarcane fields. The Chinese were brought over first, in 1852; then the Portuguese. Next to arrive were 180,000 Japanese. Some immigrant groups tended to intermarry with each other or with the Polynesians, Hawaii's first settlers; others sent for "picture brides" from home. As if the cultural gumbo weren't thick enough, within fifty years of the arrival of the Chinese, Koreans were encouraged to emigrate to Hawaii; and soon thereafter, in 1910, Filipinos were brought over to work in the pineapple fields—pineapples having replaced sugar as it began to decline. Each group carried its own religion, familial structures, and ceremonies. And of course the many languages collided and fused in the labor camps to form a lingua franca known as pidgin English.

Language wasn't the only area where cultures would mix. As the historian Ronald Takaki notes in *Strangers from a Different Shore*,[13] the immigrants also began to share and exchange their food:

> *In the camps could be found an interesting and unique variety of Asian ethnic foods—Chinese* char siu *(barbecued pork) and* manapua, *or* bao *(bun with pork stuffing), Korean* kimchi *(pickled cabbage laced with garlic and hot red pepper), Filipino* adobo *(stewed garlic pork and chicken), Japanese* sashimi *(raw fish) and* sushi *(rice with seafood). . . . As the laborers and their families mingled together in camps, they began to exchange their different ethnic foods, including not only various Asian dishes but also Hawaiian* kalua *pig (baked in the ground) and* lau lau *(fish and pork wrapped in* ti *leaves) and Portuguese hot sausage and sweet bread. . . . Crossing ethnic lines, workers would taste each other's food and exclaim in Hawaiian:* "Ono, ono!" "Tasty, tasty!"

Alan Wong, who grew up in Oahu's pineapple fields, witnessed firsthand this crossing of ethnic and culinary lines. If it's evident at all, it's palpable in the food that Wong—who in 1996 was named best chef of the Pacific Northwest by the James Beard Foundation—has been cooking in the latest phase of his career as chef and co-owner of AlanWong's. He had a Japanese mother and a Chinese grandfather, both of whom cooked at home, so he grew up in an environment where he was "blessed with good food" at almost every meal. The meals were neither *authentic* Japanese nor *authentic* Chinese, but rather a fusion of this and that. Indeed, long before it became chic to call such food "Asian fusion" or "Pacific rim," Wong and most other Hawaiians were eating an ethnically diverse cuisine, which is now known to many as Hawaii regional cuisine. Wong is one of its most accomplished devotees.

Despite being years ahead of the culinary curve, he did not always intend to be an expert on Hawaiian food. In fact, he originally set his sights on playing professional baseball. But to pay his bills, he found work at a local hotel restaurant; and as he worked his way up from dishwasher to busboy to waiter to cashier, and ultimately to restaurant manager, he found that he had no time for baseball practice sessions or weekend games. When it became clear that professional baseball wasn't an option, he began thinking seriously about his future career. To be a more effective manager, to really know how to manage people in the front and back of the house, Wong decided to go to cooking school. "If you're a restaurant manager and you don't know food, the chef is going to run circles around you." He applied to the culinary program at **Kapiolani Community College** in Honolulu in 1978.

Wong planned to study management, but to his surprise he excelled more in the cooking classes than in any other sector of the program. Cooking came naturally to him, and he credits his instincts in the kitchen to his family. Between the Japanese- and Hawaiian-based comfort food his mother prepared and the elaborate Chinese meals his grandfather cooked, he developed his palate and an innate sense of what tastes good as he was growing up. His instincts landed him at the top of his class, and upon graduating, he was recognized as the most outstanding student in the program.

Honors in hand, Wong soon jettisoned the idea of managing a restaurant, and he applied for the prestigious apprenticeship program at the **Greenbrier** in West Virginia (see page 127). "There were many applications from across the United States, and I was fortunate to be chosen as one of ten." He didn't always feel so lucky, however. Physically, psychologically, and culturally, the Greenbrier was far from home. It was so alien that he remembers crying on the first day. He quickly adjusted, though, and after graduating two years later, he headed to New York City.

Though New York was even farther from home, its appeal was irresistible. It was the city that seemed to most enchant instructors at Greenbrier. Returning from trips to Manhattan, they would sing the praises of the '21' Club, La Côte Basque, the dining room at the Ritz-Carlton, and of course Lutèce. Wong had interviews with a number of leading chefs from all these restaurants. But he had read about Lutèce, and his heart was immovable. It was a "four-star *New York Times* restaurant and it always appeared in the top-ten lists of most people's best restaurants in the United States." He had also been reading a lot about André Soltner, "one of the leading culinary figures in the city"— a chef about whom much had been written. Soltner, who had agreed to interview Wong, promised him a job as soon as there was an opening. In the interim, Wong had to hang out in the city because the position, when it became available, would be filled quickly.

Wong, who had virtually no experience living in a big city, learned the ins and outs of Manhattan the hard way. He accepted an interim job at the Ritz-Carlton and moved to New York the day after New Year's in 1982. The very little cash he had was supposed to pay for his first and last month's rent on an apartment, his transportation, and a wardrobe full of warm clothes. After one night in a costly hotel, he knew he was in trouble. He called a friend of his mother's—one of the only two people he knew in the city—and was quickly escorted to a church, where he spent his first three weeks until he had saved enough money to rent an apartment in Queens. In the meantime, he was still anxiously awaiting the call from Soltner, which had not come. With his patience fraying, he urged his boss at the Ritz to remind Soltner of his promise. Wong's hand-wringing came to an end when he was told to report to Lutèce the following Monday.

Though he had spent the last several years of his life surrounded by food professionals, first at hotels in Hawaii and later at the Greenbrier and the Ritz, nothing matched the esteem and enthusiasm with which the staff of Lutèce regarded food. "This was the first time I was with people who truly loved what they did, the first time I had seen such appreciation, such respect for food." Wong recalls seeing unique delight in their faces when products such as wild mushrooms, seafood, or fish came into the restaurant. He also remembers his new peers as having a genuine "passion for hospitality, for making people happy, for treating people as if they're coming into your house." Though he spent three years in an intimidating and demanding situation, he learned an invaluable lesson about life as a cook: "You work hard, and you go home, and the next day you start all over again. You've got to love what you do in order to survive."

Under the direction of Chef André Soltner, Wong stayed at Lutèce from 1982 to 1985, working his way up to chef de partie, or line cook. Beyond developing Wong's ardor for food, Soltner trained him in the fundamentals of French cuisine, which now informs everything Wong makes at his own restaurant, Alan Wong's, even though he has chosen to cook food that is vastly different from French food.

I think there are two great cuisines in the world, the French and the Chinese. Chef André Soltner says you have to learn the base, which is the foundation of French cooking. When you learn the base, you're cooking with two feet on the ground. A lot of guys today are creative, but they're cooking with one leg in the air. There's no concept of what actually works or what makes sense.

After five years away from home, Wong decided to return to Hawaii. In 1985, he was asked to open the Canoe House at the exclusive Mauna Lani Bay Hotel and Bungalows. Wong was given total freedom, which doesn't come easy in the world of union-dominated hotels, but the Canoe House had good reason to give in to Wong. Word of his talent spread, and reviews started pouring in. Eventually, he was asked to take over the hotel's Le Soleil restaurant as well. In 1984, his efforts were acknowledged by the Robert Mondavi Winery, which named him one of the Thirteen Rising Star Chefs in America, and by the James Beard Foundation, which named him Best Chef in the Northwest.

Apart from recognition, the Canoe House also gave Wong the opportunity to improvise with fusion cuisine. While he was there, he participated in "Cuisines of the Sun," an annual event, sponsored by the hotel, that brought chefs who specialized in cuisines "from sunny climates" to Hawaii. Wong's role was to make "East-West" dishes that went with each year's theme. If, for example, the theme was Mediterranean, he would come up with dishes like seared ahi summer roll with tapenade and chiso. It was out of necessity, then, that he began to think broadly about fusing Eastern and Western ingredients. But because of his French training, he was not with "one leg in the air" but with both feet planted solidly on the ground. Though his dishes were unusual, he never abandoned the basics of French cooking.

After five and a half years at the hotel, he was presented with a new opportunity when a friend approached him to ask if he had ever thought of opening a restaurant. Though the idea had crossed Wong's mind—when André Soltner had told him that "nothing would make me more happy for you than to see you have your own restaurant one day"—he had put it on the back burner, where it quietly simmered while he was working at the Canoe House. Now, when his friend proposed the idea, he jumped at it. "I went and cooked a nine-course dinner for the investors, three prominent business people in Honolulu." Wong got an enthusiastic phone call the next day; he and his friend were in business.

With the same naiveté that allowed him to go to New York with $2,000 and seek out a job at the Ritz and Lutèce, Wong set about the task of being an entrepreneur. He had absolutely no idea of what lay ahead. "I didn't worry about the little things; all I knew was that I wanted a restaurant." He knew a lot of things about the food side of the business, but next to nothing about the "business" side. He didn't think about whether or not it was an appropriate time, economically, to open a restaurant or even about location—an approach that would make a consultant blanch. Nonetheless, in 1995 Alan Wong's opened its doors to the public. "We broke all the rules. The restaurant is on the fifth floor of an office building complex. For the first year, we had no signage. It was sort of like a secret for a while. I called it the 'Hole in the Wall on King Street,' but people found us and we were busy. For the first two weeks of business, I had only forecast sixty to eighty customers a night. On the very first Saturday we opened, we had one hundred fifty people." He was so overwhelmed that he had to call his chef friends for fish and then send his dishwashers to pick up five pounds of mahi mahi or six pounds of onaga in the middle of the night. They've been going full steam ever since. In the first three years, the accolades have been endless: *Honolulu Magazine* has bestowed three awards—Best New Restaurant and Restaurant of the Year, followed by Restaurant of the Year again in 1997. The James Beard Foundation has also saluted Alan Wong's with a nomination for Best New Restaurant, and the *Honolulu Advertiser* has recognized the restaurant as well.

Wong does not consider the food at Alan Wong's to be fusion food, which is what he prepared while hosting "Cuisines of the Sun." Rather, it's very much rooted in the flavors of Hawaii—known as Hawaii regional cuisine (HRC), a term preferred by a number of leading Hawaiian chefs.[14] "It's the contemporary style of cooking found in Hawaii today." Though his menu changes daily, examples of HRC include standbys like nori-wrapped tempura ahi and lamb chops with coconut-macadamia crust and star anise sauce. According to Wong, HRC has four components. First, it's multi-ethnic in that it draws from the cultural melting pot found in Hawaii; any dish served at Wong's, for example, could have four or five different ethnic influences. Second, HRC also uses as many locally grown ingredients as possible. This has been a boon for Hawaiian farmers, and it contrasts with the time when 80 percent of Hawaiian agricultural products were from abroad—California and farther—and only 20 percent were grown in Hawaii. Third, it tends to be healthier than butter- and cream-enriched foods. Fourth—and according to Wong this is its most important characteristic—HRC emphasizes flavor. "First and foremost, food has to *taste* good. No matter what you do, how you get there, it doesn't matter. It has to taste good." All of the above come together in dishes such as ginger-crusted onaga with miso sesame vinaigrette and terrine of grilled eggplant and maui onions, items he couldn't take off the menu even if he wanted to, such is the public demand. With tables hard to come by and recognition from both the press and the public for food, service, and atmosphere, Wong seems to have hit on a formula that gives the public what it wants. He's cautiously jubilant about this success. He figures that you're only as good as your last plate, a sentiment echoed by many a chef-restaurateur.

The cost of the ticket to success has, of course, been a toll on his life outside work. When he's not traveling—and he travels regularly to cook for special groups, to speak with the media, or to expand his knowledge of other Asian cuisines—he's always on site. His staff even jokes about his single focus: "I'm married to the restaurant, and I've got fifty-five kids." The "kids" give him their time and their sweat (start-ups are even more demanding than those of the usual restaurant), and in return he puts a special emphasis on retaining and training them.

Not everyone he works with comes in with the same base of knowledge. Though he'd prefer to work with cooks who know exactly how to handle knives and product, it's even more essential that they have the right spirit and demeanor.

> *I hire an attitude. I don't want to hire people who are going to tell me how they want to do something. I want to hire people who are going to listen to me when I tell them this is the way we're going to do it. Culinary degree or no degree, I look for foodies who are enthusiastic and want to learn, to be on the edge, because you can teach anybody anything, if a person has the right attitude.*

Once he finds people with those qualities, Wong spends a lot of time training them, both in one-on-one sessions and in the weekly seminars that he holds at the restaurant on issues germane to excellent food. One week, for example, it will be on the "five classical mother sauces taught in the French kitchen" (even though Alan Wong's doesn't use any of them), and the next week he'll teach the staff how to fillet a whole fish, explaining not only how it's done but how it breaks down in terms of cost—why one fish is $25 on the menu instead of $30, and so forth.

Between cooking, managing, and nurturing his staff, he's at Alan Wong's an average of fourteen hours a day. He doesn't seem to mind it. "There's just so much more satisfaction" in owning and operating your own restaurant, compared with working for somebody else. "I don't mind working up to twenty hours a day, because I know why I'm doing it and who I'm doing it for." His passion notwithstanding, he doesn't advise everyone to follow his path. When aspiring cooks come to him for advice, he cautions them to think long and hard before taking the leap. "It's hard work, it's greasy, it's hot. Your legs get sore, your feet get sore, your back gets sore. It's not glamorous. When everyone is out partying, you're *providing* the party."

While the lifestyle of a chef may not appeal to everyone, Wong is glad he made the transition into the kitchen. Not only is he energized by the rewards of working for himself, but he also revels in the nature of the work, the endless possibilities. "One of the reasons I enjoy this business so much is that it keeps me constantly stimulated. As you travel, as you come across people and their cultures, their food and ingredients, you learn something. I could go on for the rest of my life and not learn all there is to know about food." The endless possibilities of it all make cooking an alchemist's dream, and with his knack for fusing flavors, Wong is nothing if not an alchemist.

Alan Wong's

Grilled Lamb Chops
with Macadamia-Coconut Crust, Cabernet Sauvignon Jus, and Coconut-Ginger Cream

Chef's note: *These lamb chops are a marvel of tenderness edged with the intensity of the Cabernet Sauvignon sauce. The macadamia-coconut crust doesn't come across as too sweet, as it's balanced by this pungent sauce perfumed with star anise and fennel seeds.*

(Serves 4)
Macadamia-Coconut Crust

¾ cup honey
¾ cup grated coconut meat
¾ cup chopped macadamia nuts
3 tablespoons chopped fresh parsley
3 tablespoons chopped fresh thyme leaves
1 tablespoon minced garlic

Coconut-Ginger Cream

1 cup canned unsweetened coconut milk
1 piece fresh ginger (2 inches long), smashed
2 tablespoons sugar

Cabernet Sauvignon Jus

1 cup Cabernet Sauvignon
¼ cup mirin (sweet rice wine)
¼ cup mushroom soy sauce
1 cup Lamb Stock (see recipe, page 126)
8 star anise
2 teaspoons fennel seeds
2 cinnamon sticks
2 teaspoons coriander seeds
Salt and pepper to taste

Lamb

¼ cup olive oil
2 racks of lamb (¼ pound each), cut into double chops
Salt and pepper to taste

1. *For the crust:* Mix all the ingredients in a small bowl. (Can be prepared 1 day ahead. Cover and refrigerate.)

2. *For the cream:* Bring all of the ingredients to a boil in a heavy medium saucepan. Boil until reduced by half, about 5 minutes. Transfer to a bowl, remove the ginger. (Can be prepared 1 day ahead. Cover and refrigerate.)

3. *For the jus:* Boil the Cabernet Sauvignon in a heavy medium saucepan until reduced to ¼ cup, about 10 minutes. Add the mirin and soy sauce and boil until reduced by half, about 3 minutes. Add the remaining ingredients, reduce the heat to low, cover, and simmer 15 minutes. Season with salt and pepper. Strain into another heavy medium saucepan. (Can be prepared 1 day ahead. Cover and refrigerate.)

4. *For the lamb:* Prepare the barbecue grill (medium heat). Rub oil over the lamb chops. Let stand 30 minutes. Season the lamb with salt and pepper. Grill the lamb to the desired doneness, about 5 minutes per side for medium-rare. Preheat the broiler. Place the lamb on a baking sheet. Press the crust mixture over the chops. Broil until golden brown, about 3 minutes.

5. Meanwhile, bring the jus and coconut cream to a simmer in separate saucepans. Ladle the jus onto plates. Spoon the cream decoratively in 4 to 5 nickel-size dots atop the sauce. Top with lamb and serve.

Wine Note: Cabernet Sauvignon seems to be the definitive partner, and one with generous, ripe fruit and medium to medium-high tannin is the way to go. Many fine examples are produced in California. You could also pair this dish well with moderately aged, well-made Italian Barolo or Barbaresco. These wines are hard and unyielding in their youth, yet perfumy and elegant with age. A well-stored 1978 would be right in between and still possess enough fruit and tannins for the lamb.

Lamb Stock

(Makes 6 cups)

6 pounds lamb bones
4 carrots, chopped
3 celery stalks with leafy tops, chopped
1 large onion, chopped
1 large leek, chopped
1 large tomato, chopped
1½ cups dry white wine
12 cups water
12 whole black peppercorns
4 fresh parsley sprigs
3 fresh thyme sprigs
1 large bay leaf

1. Preheat the oven to 400°F. Arrange the bones and the vegetables in a roasting pan. Roast until brown, stirring frequently, about 40 minutes. Transfer the bones and vegetables to a large, heavy pot.

2. Add the wine to the roasting pan. Set the roasting pan over medium-high heat and bring to a boil, scraping up the browned bits.

3. Pour the wine mixture into the pot containing the bones and vegetables. Add the water, peppercorns, parsley, thyme, and bay leaf and bring to a boil. Reduce the heat and simmer until the liquid is reduced to 6 cups, about 4 hours.

4. Strain the stock. Cool, then degrease.

Advance preparation: Can be prepared ahead and refrigerated up to 2 days or frozen up to 6 months.

✳ THE GREENBRIER APPRENTICESHIP ✳

The **Greenbrier Apprenticeship Program** is for chefs with at least five years of practical experience who have graduated from high school and achieved at least an associate degree from a higher-education culinary curriculum. It runs for three years and includes at least twenty-two months of hands-on cooking at the Greenbrier Hotel, a luxury 6,500-acre resort in West Virginia. The remaining months can be spent at the hotel, business permitting, or, during the off season, at another property run by the group that manages the Greenbrier. Robert Wong (no relation to Alan), the executive chef in charge of the apprenticeship at Greenbrier, sees the program as an opportunity for cooks to work throughout all stations. This gives the apprentice "a well-rounded, in-depth foundation for all aspects of the culinary arts. Our apprentices also learn about professionalism, and respect for food and one another."

In addition to attending lectures and demonstrations, apprentices do rotations in various stations. Demonstrations and lectures may include ice carving, menu planning, fish, consommés and soups, sauces, wines, smoking and curing, nutrition, quality control, chocolate, buffet platters, hors d'oeuvres, and desserts. Stations range from breakfast to buffet, from pastry to cold meats, and more.

While these apprenticeships are paid, participants are responsible for their own housing.

Information about contacting the Greenbrier is available in Appendix D.

✳

PART 3

Border Crossing

From Cambodia to Boston:

THE ELEPHANT WALK'S FAMILY-STYLE APPROACH TO MANAGEMENT

Nadsa, Bob, Longteine,
and Longteine's sister Sourath.

Though Cambodian food uses spices and ingredients similar to those in Thai and Vietnamese food—coconut milk and cilantro, lime and lemongrass—it differs from both. Bolder than Vietnamese and more subtle than Thai, Cambodian food falls comfortably somewhere in between the two. The De Monteiros were one of the first groups to introduce Cambodian food to America. But that's not the only thing that distinguishes this restaurant group. While family-run restaurants are fairly common, The Elephant Walk is run by an international, multigenerational family of six. Those who have willing business partners in their extended family might take inspiration from the De Monteiro family. Theirs is a tale of determination and grit, of creating something out of nothing, and in the process creating new cuisine.

The **Elephant Walk—the name** itself evokes another era. It conjures up visions of colonial mansions set alongside dense jungle and indigo waters. But the colonial legacy informs only half of The Elephant Walk's story. The most immediate impulse behind the restaurant is the Khmer Rouge's reign of terror.

Before 1975, Longteine De Monteiro, the original head chef and chief inspiration behind The Elephant Walk, had never worked a day in her life. She belonged to the Cambodian aristocracy, and as was customary for those in her social circles, she never expected to have a job. She was a housewife, and her husband Kenthao De Monteiro, the man whom she had married at the age of eighteen, was the breadwinner. With degrees in literature, political science, and law (the last from the Sorbonne), Kenthao was not only well educated but also politically astute. Over time, he worked his way up through Cambodia's foreign corps to become an ambassador, with postings in the Philippines, Yugoslavia, and Taiwan.

In Taiwan, far away from what would come to be known as the "killing fields," theirs was an idyllic life. They had two beautiful and talented daughters, Launa and her younger sister Nadsa. While the ambassador conducted foreign affairs, Longteine, in her capacity as his wife, presided over numerous diplomatic luncheons and dinners. Though she often received help from the Cambodian cooks who traveled with the family wherever they went, she wasn't without her own formidable cooking skills. Longteine had learned how to cook Cambodian food when she was just a girl, and by the time she was a teenager, she had taught herself how to cook French food. She began with simple soups and appetizers; by the time she worked her way through several French cookbooks, she had come to divine the secret of making the perfect soufflé au chocolat. "When I was seventeen, I started to cook French food for my father every day, twice a day, first lunch, then dinner." But her enthusiasm wasn't limited to French food. Once Longteine—or Nyep, as she is called—moved to Taipei, she enrolled in the local Chinese culinary school, where she continued to pursue her hobby.

But Eden as the De Monteiro family knew it ended when the Khmer Rouge marched into Phnom Penh on April 17, 1975, toppling the Cambodian national government. Suddenly, they were citizens without a country. They couldn't return to Cambodia, as the Khmer Rouge brutally tortured or executed all known politicians allied with the former government, as well as most known intellectuals and professionals, including several of their relatives. With few options, they stayed in Taiwan until 1978, when they moved to France, where they were granted safe haven. Though they were fortunate to have survived one of the worst atrocities in the history of modern civil war—an estimated 2 million people were killed—they would still know their share of unhappiness.

Once in France, the De Monteiros applied for political asylum in the United States, where Kenthao could teach diplomacy at an American university. But the U.S. government refused their request because they had already resettled in France and were no longer considered refugees. Because it's virtually impossible for foreigners to find "gainful employment" in France, Kenthao couldn't find a teaching position. Unexpectedly, the breadwinner had no access to a realistic means of support.

Desperate but practical, Nyep knew there was one thing she could do to support the family: she could cook. Risking it all, and with no experience whatsoever, the De Monteiros literally pawned what family jewels they had with them when they fled Southeast Asia to raise the cash necessary to open their first restaurant, Amrita, a Cambodian restaurant in Béziers, west of Montpellier. Unlike many people the world over who fantasize about opening a restaurant or a café, the De Monteiro family had never even considered it. In the beginning, Nyep recalls, "I didn't have a clue about the business. I tried very hard to put everything together, to work hard, to organize myself. It was really hard. I had never cooked for fifty people five nights in a row."

A fifty-seat neighborhood restaurant, it required all of the family's muscle. But it was Nyep who worked the hardest. Suddenly, at forty-two, a woman who had never worked a day in her life found herself working round the clock, slow-roasting and caramelizing chicken for *mouan tum,* to be served with bean thread noodles and whole cloves of garlic, lotus seeds, and shiitake mushrooms, or making Cambodian curry with giant freshwater prawns. For the entire ten years they ran the restaurant, she was the only line cook—a position believed by many in the business to be the most demanding in any restaurant. She worked from sunup until late in the evening, five days a week. She had no choice; the De Monteiros had invested their life savings. If the restaurant didn't survive, neither would they.

As they persevered, assistance came in the form of Gérard Lopez, a charming and highly energetic Frenchman, who in 1985 married the De Monteiros' daughter Launa. Just as the De Monteiro family had never imagined owning and working in a restaurant, neither had Gérard, his appreciation of food notwithstanding. Gérard had grown up in a household run by a Spanish father and a French–North African mother, and his early meals ran the gamut from couscous to paella, from sopa de ajo to coq au vin. But this wasn't enough to entice him to work with food professionally. Instead, he worked as a salesman, a job that took him all over France. It was on these trips that he sampled poularde de Bresse truffée, sauté de veau Marengo, and bouillabaisse—and even lunches and dinners at Michelin-starred restaurants such as Troisgros or Paul Bocuse didn't lure him into the business. The pull had more to do with his heart than with his palate.

Five years after the De Monteiros opened Amrita, Gérard started casually helping them out in the restaurant, whenever his work schedule permitted. He didn't go into the business naively. In his two years of courting Launa, he was exposed to the unglamorous side of the business. But still he loved helping out. What inspired him to make the switch? Apart from an emotional attachment to Launa and her family, Gérard credits it to an impulse common to many: "For me it was the opportunity for something different, something new." The need for exposure to new ideas and activities was quickly met. Gérard started out as a general handyman, helping with whatever was necessary, from plating desserts and putting up drinks to helping out in the dining room and general maintenance. "It was a small restaurant, about fifty seats, so I could wait tables and *watch* what was going on in the kitchen at the same time." During the many years he helped out at Amrita, he absorbed so many things about running a restaurant that he eventually proved to be indispensable.

Gérard wasn't the only one who would be drawn into the De Monteiro family circle—first emotionally and then professionally. Like Launa, the younger daughter—Nadsa—would also find a mate who would become closely involved in the family business. But for Nadsa, it was not so easy. Before her Prince Charming appeared, she would know her share of love lost and loves found, of separation and reunion.

Though born in Massachusetts, Robert Perry grew up in Asia, where his father worked in the electronics business. His family did stints in Hong Kong, Okinawa, and Korea, and Taiwan, where he met Nadsa in the spring of 1977. Bob and Nadsa were both students at the American School in Taipei. She was seventeen and he was fifteen. When he describes his romance with Nadsa, he uses language straight out of a Doris Day movie. They fell madly in love, but within three months after they started dating they were subject to the vagaries of corporate planning. The company Bob's father worked for unexpectedly relocated the Perry family back to America, truncating the budding romance.

Back in the United States, Bob finished high school in Connecticut and enrolled in Tufts University. Although college is supposed to be an exciting time in a young person's life, Bob found it hard to focus. His heart was definitely elsewhere, and so was his mind. To earn money, he started working with Steve Herrell, the Steve of Steve's Ice Cream. Located throughout the Northeast, Steve's ice cream parlors were among the first to encourage people to add cookie bits and candy to their ice cream. Bob quickly worked his way up from a scooper to a manager, all the time losing interest in his classes, and eventually in Nadsa, with whom he was carrying on a long-distance relationship. Finally, they broke up.

After college, Bob met another young woman, and in October of 1985 they decided to take their first European vacation together. They visited West Germany first and then went to Paris, where Nadsa was living. In Paris, their trip took an unexpected turn. While Bob had probably buried his feelings for Nadsa so deep that he could manage to ignore them, his girlfriend needed reassurance. She convinced Bob that he needed to look Nadsa in the eye and admit to himself that he wasn't still in love with her. It was a test he would fail. With deep apologies to his new girlfriend, Bob was reunited with Nadsa, and he married her six months later.

Since Bob's French was limited and Nadsa was fluent in English, they decided to move to America, leaving Launa, Gérard, Kenthao, and Nyep behind at least until they could bring Kenthao and Nyep over. Back in America, Bob started his own business—a small company manufacturing and distributing gourmet ice cream and frozen yogurt. He sold wholesale primarily to small mom-and-pop ice cream places in Boston and to a couple of bakeries, like the revered Rosie's. Though business was fair, Bob blames the recession of 1989 for depressing his profits.

It was about this time, in 1990, that his in-laws were finally able to emigrate to America. If Bob had planned a surprise homecoming party for them, they had a bigger shock for him. Once they had settled comfortably in their new home, a home they would share with the newlywed couple, they turned to Bob for counsel. "They put the proceeds of the sale of Amrita, sixty to seventy thousand dollars, on a table in front of me, pushed it toward me, and said, 'Whatever you decide is okay with us. We'll do whatever you think is right.' It totally freaked me out," he admits.

He was only twenty-nine years old, and his own business had yet to take off. By any objective standard he wasn't the best investment adviser, and he knew it. "I started thinking, 'My God, the risk that they are taking, moving to this country, giving up every-thing to come here and take one more shot. Hell, if they're willing to risk it all, I have to be too.'" So he did what any good son-in-law would do. He upped the ante by selling all his own assets—both his personal assets and those of his business—and contributed them to the family. With a pot of cash in front of them, the next question was what to do with the money. After much deliberation and with some hesitation, they decided to risk it all on another restaurant.

But what type? A straight Cambodian restaurant, along the lines of Amrita? There was not one precedent in Boston, and no reason to believe such a restaurant could be a success. And there was the problem of perception. It's no longer unusual to meet a group of friends for Thai food, but in 1990 many "ethnic" restaurants, with the exception of a few cuisines such as Italian or Japanese, still occupied a marginal position. They were only for the adventurous of heart, places where you went when you wanted to go "slum-ming." "I was afraid that a Cambodian restaurant would be relegated to the status of a curiosity, another 'cute little ethnic hole in the wall.'" So they decided to include Nyep's other strength, traditional French food:

> Generally, because Asian food is unfairly perceived by Westerners as perhaps not requiring as much skill or creativity as continental cuisine, there's a cultural bias that says, "If you're preparing continental cuisine you're a chef, but if you're preparing Asian cuisine, you're just a cook." So I suggested we offer both French and Cambodian, hoping that the public would conclude that if my mother-in-law was cooking French food, she must be a chef, which means that her Cambo-dian food must be really good.

In the business, this is part of developing a concept. First the De Monteiros planned a menu (classical French and traditional Cambodian), then they picked a memorable name (The Elephant Walk). Their next step was to scout for a location (Somerville). The space, the basement of a police station in a working-class district of Boston, was raw and needed about $120,000 worth of renovation. They invested $60,000, and their ex-tremely generous and helpful landlord put in $60,000. But money wasn't their only con-cern. "Initially, we worried that a blue-collar neighborhood would not support our restaurant, that the residents simply wouldn't be curious or interested in our food." But they decided to go for it, and within eight months, in August 1991, they were ready to open their forty-seat restaurant.

Despite what they thought were smart strategic decisions, and despite the financial breaks that their landlord provided in helping them build out the raw space, they still came close to losing everything. Completely unknown at first, located in a space that had not hitherto been a restaurant, and classically undercapitalized, the business got off to a very bad start. But when they were within $2,000 of going bankrupt, they got their first review. Robert Levey of the *Boston Globe* gave The Elephant Walk three stars, and business exploded almost immediately. With Bob manning the front of the house and Nyep and Nadsa running the kitchen, people poured in with the review in hand, ordering the exact dishes that Levey had suggested.

From the day of that first review—and dozens have followed in newspapers in and outside of Boston, as well as national publications such as the *New York Times* and *Travel and Leisure*—the restaurant has stayed packed. Some people come craving French food, others Cambodian. Some enter desiring steak au poivre and leave having had sweet and sour lemongrass fondue. The more adventurous mix and match. For appetizers they may try both the salade aux crevettes chaudes (a salad of shrimp flambéed with anisette and served on a bed of greens) and the calamar Napoléon, a tower of alternating layers of crisp fried wonton skins and calamari cooked with basil and extra-virgin olive oil, topped off with a mussel-and-saffron sauce.

The first Elephant Walk formula was so successful that after nearly three years, the De Monteiros and Bob Perry decided to open up a second restaurant in Brookline, a much more affluent quarter of the Boston metropolitan area. This time they were more ambitious. Their new restaurant would seat 140, more than three times as many as their first. As their ambition grew, so too did the amount of capital they needed. They had invested $60,000 to start the Somerville restaurant, but they needed ten times that for the second. What accounted for the increase? According to Bob, who now acts as the general manager of both restaurants, "We opened in a better economy the second time around," and people assume that "if you have a successful restaurant running you must have deeper pockets." Consequently, at the Brookline location, they "got no help from the landlord, no discounts from anyone." Still, they knew that they had a good thing going, so they took the risk.

When they faced the challenge of running two restaurants, the family realized that they could use more hands. At a minimum, they would need another chef. They didn't want to open up the second restaurant without the help of Gérard and Launa, who were still in France. After one phone call, Gérard and Launa sold their house, quit their jobs, and moved to America. Nyep put the relatively inexperienced Gérard in charge of the Somerville kitchen, while Nadsa set up shop at the new location. Nyep would be the chef de cuisine.

Having once again sunk all their assets in the new business, the family must have felt some trepidation about letting Gérard run the Somerville restaurant. If the ratings of The Elephant Walk in Somerville declined, all would be lost. Save for one pastry class, Gérard had never been trained formally. Most of his culinary education had been informal. As a child, he would watch as his parents adjusted their paella, cassoulet, and tagines by adding a dash more saffron, a bit more thyme, or a touch more cumin. And at Amrita he had spent some time in the kitchen, but he had never been in charge before. Fortunately, there was no need to worry. Between what he had learned from his parents and what he had learned while working with Nyep at Amrita, he had picked up so much that the rave reviews continued to pour in. In eleven months, he was responsible for planning the menu, serving 420 people per night, and adding his creative touch to the food. One might say that he was suited for the job by virtue of his nationality: "In France, men cook; it's normal."

With Gérard holding the fort at Somerville under Nyep's watchful eye, Nadsa ran the new Brookline restaurant. Both restaurants drew fine reviews and big crowds. In a recent Zagat survey, The Elephant Walk was ranked as one of the five most popular restaurants in Boston. Nyep credits both restaurants' success to the boldness of the American palate. Compared with the French, she finds Americans "more daring." They go for things that the French aren't as enthusiastic about—bold displays of fried garlic and lemongrass; the distinctive Khmer marinade, tuk trey, which combines Asian fish sauce with vinegar, sugar, and garlic; and exotic entrées like amok, small pieces of catfish mixed with spices and coconut and then steamed in a curl of banana leaf.

But it's not just good food that makes a restaurant successful. It's good service and smart management as well. On management, the family has some very strong views. For Bob, the first step is to remember that "restaurants are theater. It's a performance. The waiters are the players, the chefs are the directors, and the owners are the stage managers.

You have a performance every single night. No one will pay you tomorrow for what you did today. They will only pay you if you do it well again tomorrow." To this, Gérard would add that the most important priority of any restaurateur, even more than hiring a chef, is to "get a good manager, and be prepared to pay him or her well." A competent manager will then hire the host and wait staff or, in Bob's lexicon, the stage players. The manager will want skilled people in the front of the house because "they come under more fire than almost anyone else in the restaurant."

For the host, the psychological pressure can be excruciating. According to Bob, after the line cook "the second toughest job is at the reception desk on a busy night." Bob finds this especially true for the Brookline restaurant, which caters to a more professional and wealthier clientele. It's not at all unusual for a Brookline diner to offer the host money. "They say, 'Listen, if I give you a fifty, will you seat us right away?'" That doesn't happen in Somerville, the more working-class neighborhood; there according to Bob, the clientele is much more relaxed and understanding.

In terms of pressure, the wait staff rank next, because they have to balance the needs of a demanding clientele *and* a demanding kitchen. Waiters get it coming and going. While the public can make nasty demands on their waiters—"Where's my dinner? Where's my warm bread?" and so forth—waiters must answer back politely and humbly. Then, when they go into the kitchen to pick up an order, they're often greeted with language as foul as anyone could find on a trading floor. Chefs don't have to edit their language for the public, so if a waitress or waiter has screwed up, it's not unusual to hear a remark spiced with expletives: "Hey, come on, make sure you're timing your food right. Your food has been up five minutes, you *!?!*." In compensation for this pressure, Bob adamantly refuses to have the wait staff pool tips, as they are required to at some restaurants. Consequently, at The Elephant Walk, waiters make twice or even three times the amount the kitchen staff does. It gets political, but this arrangement encourages loyalty among the staff.

Bob is also adamant in his insistence that it makes business sense for a restaurant to be open to the public all seven days of the week:

We went the seven-day route because if you open seven days it means you can't do it yourself, and that forces you to hire people and delegate. Once you do that, you're empowered; you're free. You can take a vacation, you can take a day off. You get the job done by coordinating the efforts of other people. There are days when we've had two restaurants running with no owners anywhere near them. That's good management. I feel sorry for these control-freak owners who can't leave their restaurants. That's bad management because they can't figure out a way to train people to do the job as well as they do.

Apart from easing some of the psychological pressure, opening those two extra days also has the obvious benefit of bringing in more money. Bob insists, "If you're open only five days, you can have forty percent more sales by opening the other two. You've already decided that you're paying all your bills in those five days, and this means that any profit, any margin that you make in the next two days all goes to you. *Open those two days!*"

In December 1997, with great management and enough public enthusiasm to support their ambitions, the family opened their third restaurant, in Waltham, Massachusetts. Unlike the other restaurants, Carambola serves only Cambodian food. Less than a year later, in October 1998, the family moved the Somerville restaurant to Cambridge, where Gérard—who eventually enrolled in **Cambridge Culinary Academy** and graduated as the top-ranked student in his class—is now in charge, particularly of the French menu. His wife Launa is the manager of the Cambridge restaurant's retail shop, which sells hard-to-find Cambodian ingredients and handicrafts. As for the two who started it all— Bob is president and CEO of the group, and Nadsa is the executive chef of all three restaurants, with special responsibility for the Cambodian menus. Kenthao is the chief taster and helps monitor the finances; Nyep, who was the spark behind the entire enterprise, is the consulting chef emeritus. With her entire family to rely on, Nyep is finally in a position where she doesn't have to work the line every day. Instead, she gets to promote Cambodian food through her new line of Cambodian spices as well as her long-awaited book, *The Elephant Walk Cookbook*. She also gets the word out by leading cooking demonstrations around the country, whether it's at the **James Beard House** or the **Greystone Campus of the CIA.**

On the assumption that things will continue to go well, Bob—who, with a surplus of energy and ideas, can't envision "running exactly three restaurants for the next umpteen years"—is looking for new locations, some outside of Boston. If they really want to promote Cambodian food nationally, perhaps the best gift the family could give to the country would be to introduce The Elephant Walk to the West Coast, somewhere nearer to the Pacific and the China Sea, the body of water that surrounds Cambodia. Maybe then it will be easier for Nadsa and Launa to reimagine and return to the country they left more than twenty years ago—a place Nyep and Kenthao are hesitant to return to for fear that memories of all they lost will crowd out all that they have built for themselves; a place Gérard has been to only aromatically; a place Bob knew as a young man, a boy so inexperienced that it would have been impossible for him to envision the long journey that would lead to The Elephant Walk.

Trey Trung Kroeung
Royal Catfish Enrobed with
Coconut Milk and Lemongrass

Chef's note: *As the name indicates, this dish is considered very fancy, and in Cambodia when I was growing up, it was served only in aristocratic homes for festive occasions. But for all its elegant appearance and rich sauce, Royal Catfish is actually quite simple to make when you have a blender. The spice paste can be prepared quickly; the fish is fried; and all that remains is to cover the fish with its succulent "robe." This dish pairs nicely with jasmine rice. Royalty has rarely been achieved so easily.*

(Serves 4)

Paste

3 dried New Mexican chiles, soaked, seeded, and deveined
1 tablespoon sliced lemongrass
3 garlic cloves
2 medium shallots, coarsely chopped
5 kaffir lime leaves, deveined
2 teaspoons peeled, coarsely chopped galangal
¼ teaspoon turmeric
1½ tablespoons shrimp paste
½ cup water

6 tablespoons vegetable oil

4 catfish fillets (about 2 pounds)

1½ cups unsweetened coconut milk

1 tablespoon fish sauce

2 teaspoons sugar

4 kaffir lime leaves, finely julienned, for garnish

1. *To make the paste:* Put all the paste ingredients in a blender and blend until smooth, 2 to 3 minutes. Set aside.

2. Heat ¼ cup of the oil in a large skillet over medium-high heat. Fry the fish until firm and golden-brown, turning once, about 6 minutes per side. Set aside, covered, to keep warm.

3. *To make the sauce:* In a second large skillet, heat the remaining 2 tablespoons oil. Add ½ cup of the coconut milk and cook over medium-high heat until the oil separates from the coconut milk. Add the paste and cook for about 2 minutes, stirring constantly, until the aroma is released. Add the remaining 1 cup coconut milk, the fish sauce, and the sugar and cook for 5 minutes more, stirring all the while.

4. Remove from the heat and add the fish. Spoon the sauce over the fillets to cover fully and allow to sit for 1 to 2 minutes. Carefully transfer the fish and sauce to a platter. Sprinkle the kaffir lime leaves over the top of the fish.

Note: Kaffir lime leaves and galangal are available in Asian food markets.

✳ LOCATION: PICKING THE RIGHT SPOT— ✳
WHAT TO CONSIDER

When Michael McCarty was looking for the right location for Michael's in Los Angeles, he rejected one neighborhood because it was full of college kids (who probably wouldn't be able to afford it) and walked away from another because it was "too sleepy." The owners of The Elephant Walk were just about to sign the lease for their second restaurant when a hunch told them they should wait until they found a spot with more parking and better access to the T, or subway. When Bobby Flay and his partners opened Mesa Grill, they looked for an up-and-coming neighborhood in New York City, though they didn't go so far as to "trailblaze." And Rick Bayless had all but negotiated a deal for a spot in Los Angeles when it occurred to him that he had not only the wrong location but the wrong city altogether. In effect, McCarty, The Elephant Walk's family, Flay, and Bayless conducted their own "feasibility studies" to make sure the neighborhood they had their eye on could support the kind of establishment they were hoping to open.

According to Brendan Keenan of the **New York Restaurant School,** location feasibility studies essentially look at the daily traffic and the competition at the site that is being considered as well as the demographics of the population in that neighborhood: "Does the area cater to lunchtime diners and empty out at 7 P.M. as most financial districts do? Is it an area full of takeout places where people grab their food and run, or is it an area that can support another formal dining room?"

There are two ways of conducting feasibility studies, according to Keenan. "You can get a group of friends together, stand on a corner, and literally count the people and check out the competition. Or you can bring in some professionals—which you'll probably want to do because there are a lot of nuances in the information and they can help you interpret the data, especially if you don't have experience or formal training."

Karen Karp, a business development consultant who has taught management and entrepreneurial skills at NYU and Northeastern University and lectured at Cornell University's School of Hotel Administration, is one such professional. When working with her clients, many of whom are aspiring restaurateurs or food specialty entrepreneurs, she helps them assess a location by inquiring about the following.

Economic Climate

The general economic climate in a particular city or town will help define possible radii of location. If the economy is growing, and funky neighborhoods are starting to go more upscale, then it may be a good idea to look on the fringe, to be a bit of a pioneer. If there is no sign that the neighborhood is turning around, it is important to consider what that will mean for your customer base.

You can find out a lot about the direction a neighborhood is headed in by talking to real estate brokers to find out who is renting and building there. Economic development agencies, chambers of commerce, and tourism offices are also good resources, as are other shopkeepers.

Clientele

When looking at locations, you want to consider mostly what kind of people an area will attract—residents, workers, tourists, students? In addition to looking at their economic bracket, you also want to ask yourself the following questions:

- What alternatives does this market have for eating—lots of upscale places, no upscale places? What about casual cafés and bistros, bars, coffeeshops, and so on?
- Do the alternatives indicate that there is a need your concept can fill?
- Would an upscale concept fit into a neighborhood with primarily casual cafés? (Probably not.)
- Would a casual café fit into a neighborhood with a lot of expensive eateries? (This is more likely, but can you pay the rent with a lower-priced menu?)

Neighbors

In addition to exploring what kind of customers the neighborhood attracts, you'll want to know as much as you possibly can about your neighbors. Here are some factors to consider:

- What is the neighborhood like?
- Who are and who *will be* your neighbors?

- Do the existing businesses complement your concept, at least stylistically?
- Are people (businesses and individuals) moving out of or into this neighborhood? Chambers of commerce and local trade associations are often good sources of information.
- Is it a destination area for people who don't live or work there?

Access

You also want to check out access.

- Is there parking, particularly in the suburbs or in a city that doesn't have a heavily used subway system?

Here are some other questions to ask:

- If the location is in a city, can you get there easily by subway or bus? Do taxi drivers know how to get there?
- Is the street well lit at night?
- During the day, is the place on the sunny or busy side of the street? (This helps more than you can imagine.)

Lease

Probably the most important concern is the lease. Before you fall in love with a space, you should ask the following questions:

- What is the price per square foot? What is the length of the lease?
- Are you going to get free rent while you're renovating the place?
- How much will the rent increase annually?
- What is the percentage of real estate taxes you may have to pay?
- Will you have to pay a percentage of gross sales to the building owner as part of your rent? If so, would this be to your advantage?

Before you sign the lease, you need to balance the answers to the questions against projected sales, and keep in mind the percentage of gross sales that is the industry standard for rent: 8 to 12 percent (see page 254).

*

Rick Bayless

SOUTH OF THE BORDER:
THE ART OF CHOOSING
THE RIGHT LOCATION

When you consider that parts of California, Texas, and the Southwest were once part of Mexico, it makes sense that Mexican ingredients heavily influence our national diet. Whether it's the use of chiles, the preference for salsas, or the arrival of "wraps"—the newly popular burrito derivatives—Mexican traditions have an impact on the way Americans eat. One of the most important people working in the Mexican tradition in the United States is Rick Bayless, a self-described gringo from Oklahoma. A consulting editor to Saveur, national chairman of the Chefs Collaborative 2000 (see page 157), and a guest instructor at the Culinary Institute of America's Napa Valley campus, Bayless has acquired so much knowledge about Mexican food he has, as Alice Waters eloquently described it, "mastered the line in order to walk outside of it."[15]

If **Gary Goldberg—the restaurant** consultant and director of the **New School's Culinary Arts** program—had to prioritize what aspiring restaurateurs should focus on, menu planning would rate extremely high. (For more on menu planning, see pages 216 and 219.) According to Goldberg, until you've planned the menu your hands are tied with regard to just about everything else. Will your kitchen be large or small? Will the dining room be formal or informal? What about the wait staff's uniforms and the tabletop design? As a consultant who is called in to fix problems, Goldberg sees his share of restaurant owners who leave menu planning to the last moment. But while this is a problem many new restaurateurs fall prey to, Rick Bayless never did. Long seduced by its bold flavors—its use of chiles, spices, and nuts to enrich its moles; its infusion of wild greens and tomatillos; its extensive use of corn masa—Bayless knew that at his future restaurant he'd serve Mexican food, a cuisine that revels in what Octavio Paz has called the "shock of tastes: cool and piquant, salt and sweet, hot and tart, pungent and delicate."[16] His biggest question was what American city would he serve it in.

Bayless's almost atavistic love of Mexican cuisine started when he was a kid in Oklahoma. With two sets of teachers—his parents, who ran the family barbecue restaurant, and the inimitable Julia Child, whose television show he watched religiously—Bayless was cooking before he had even reached adolescence. He was so enchanted by Child that nothing short of her written masterpiece would do. He hesitated before asking his parents for her book; it seemed like such an expensive indulgence. But with his older brother being showered with presents at the dawn of each new sports season—a baseball here, a football there—he figured he deserved a gift of his own. "It was the beginning of the baseball season, and my brother, once again, got all this new gear. I told my parents, I want something that's important for me. I asked for *Mastering the Art of French Cooking.*"

Bayless was only ten years old, and yet by that time, not only had he figured out that he was a good cook but also he had worked out that it would be financially impossible for his family to take many trips, particularly abroad. "Growing up in a very middle-class family in the restaurant business, there is not a lot of time or money to do much traveling." This presented a problem for Bayless, a peregrine by nature, who would never be content to stay in Oklahoma his entire life. But Mexico was only a bus ride away, and though that might be as far as he'd ever get, he was determined to get there. In preparation for his trip, he enrolled in Spanish classes. Finally, at fourteen, he took the first of what would eventually be dozens of trips across the border. That first trip, and later ones, ignited a passion that inspired him to pursue a college degree in Spanish language and literature and Latin American studies and, eventually, a doctorate in linguistics. It was in Ann Arbor, Michigan, while he was working on his doctoral dissertation, that he first started teaching cooking classes and catering. That was when he met Deann Groen, a fellow graduate student. After a courtship that revolved around their shared love of cooking, Deann eventually became his wife, though not before cooking a multicourse meal that indelibly impressed him. Together, they traveled throughout Mexico. And it was on one of these trips that Bayless realized he'd much rather teach people about Mexico's culinary history than teach them about its language. Distracted by his love of cooking, he stopped short of the Ph.D.

Having been covered in the *New York Times* and its Sunday magazine, and in *Wine Spectator* and the *Chicago Tribune*, the story of how the Baylesses diligently collected recipes during their trips thoughout Mexico may be familiar. No matter what the town or region, Bayless made it his business to stop at every roadside and market stall he could find. On one trip during the Día de la Independencia (Independence Day) holiday in September, Bayless stumbled on a recipe for an absolutely classic holiday meal—chiles nogada, roasted poblano chiles stuffed with a mixture of shredded pork, dried and fresh fruit, and various spices. The chiles are then covered with "a classic and unctuous white cream sauce made from barely ripe walnuts whose skins have been individually hand-peeled." Given the complexity and seasonality of the dish, Bayless thought it would take forever to find someone who still made the recipe, let alone someone willing to share it with him. But the first time he inquired in a market stall, he found not one but five women who were willing to confide in him. One woman even sent her daughter out to buy all the ingredients—the nuts, the cream and the cheese—and then sat down with Bayless and wrote down every detail of the recipe. "Because it's so complex and time-consuming, I couldn't believe that such a luxurious meal was being made at a market—you have to hand-roast the chiles, hand-peel the walnuts, and shred the pork. But in Mexico, preparing dishes for special occasions is so much a part of life that even market stall vendors make the effort."

He complemented such trips to markets with visits to cheesemakers, farmers, and the homes of friends he met along the way. Throughout his culinary journeys, which totaled more than 35,000 miles, he took copious notes on the technique with which each dish was made and the origin of the ingredients. Having once considered teaching, Bayless was heartened when he had an opportunity to transform these notes into the basis of an educational multi-episode PBS television series, *Cooking Mexican*. He also used them as the basis of *Authentic Mexican: Regional Cooking from the Heart of Mexico*—his first book, which he wrote with Deann and published in 1987.

So with hundreds of recipes for both television and the book in his pocket, Bayless began to design a menu for his future restaurant with relative ease. He didn't want to open a restaurant with Tex-Mex or Cal-Mex food; he wasn't interested in serving rice-bean and enchilada combination plates. He wanted to serve authentic food, food he himself had enjoyed during his trips to Mexico—things like mole poblano de Guajolote, a dark and spicy mole with turkey; or Tomatillo-Braised Pork Country Ribs with Mexican Greens and Potatoes. By authentic, Bayless didn't mean according to some Platonic ideal. Nor did he mean that it had to taste exactly as it would in a Mexican home. For Bayless, a dish is authentic as long as it respects Mexican techniques and ingredients, even if the chef puts his or her own imprint on it. Take beef with a chile oaxaqueño sauce. In Mexico, the beef would probably be a shoulder cut that's been browned and simmered in the sauce till it resembles a stew. In a variation of that, Bayless will "take a shoulder of lamb, cut it up, and simmer that in a sauce so we get some of the flavor in the sauce. And then I'll roast the rack of lamb separately, and I'll serve that with the sauce." Though different, his variation isn't an ounce less authentic.

> *I don't think every dish should be made and presented the same way for eternity. Mexican culture is full of whimsy, spontaneity, and vitality, and it's so much in line with what nature is like. You plant a seed, you never know exactly what you're going to get out of it. Sometimes it will grow up to be a gorgeous bush that flowers and flowers, and sometimes it won't produce very much of anything. And that I think is a perfect description of Mexican cuisine. Mexican is a folk cuisine, and everybody does things slightly differently.*

Bayless was confident that there were diners who would want to eat his interpretation of authentic Mexican cuisine. It was the question of where to find them that perplexed him.

In 1986, Bayless turned first to southern California. With its large Mexican-American population, its proximity to Mexico, and the plethora of chains offering fairly predictable food, he thought Los Angeles was the perfect city. That it was enjoying a restaurant boom only encouraged him. Yet just as Bayless was about to sign the lease for a hip spot on Melrose, he got cold feet. A hunch told him that the people in Los Angeles were not going to like his food. "I could see the glass ceiling and I knew I'd end up either going way down the scale," serving a taquería kind of food, because such places were so popular in these areas, or closing down altogether. He had similar reservations about northern California and the Southwest, where he sensed that people were resistant to the notion that Mexican cuisine could be anything other than inexpensive poor people's food. (For a discussion of prejudice in attitudes toward southern food, see "Southern Revival.")

Prejudice against Mexican food has deep roots in western history. As the noted journalist and poet Victor Valle points out in *Recipe of Memory,* the tendency of Americans to denigrate Mexican food dates all the way back to the late 1800s, when early settlers thought they could make Mexican food sound more palatable by calling it Spanish. Not only did masking its roots—according to Victor Valle, Mexican food is primarily a hybrid of mestizo, native, and to a lesser extent African—help to perpetuate the myth of a romantic mission-era California, where "gentle padres presided over vast pastoral domains"; it also allayed people's fears that the food was somehow tainted and unhealthy.

This perception of "unhealthy" food is another obstacle Bayless factored in when choosing a location. Though Mexican food is no longer thought of as tainted, it still suffers from a reputation for being heavy and rich. This does not accurately describe the way Mexican food is served in Mexico, though it does apply to a lot of Tex-Mex or Cal-Mex food. According to Bayless, "Traditionally in Mexico, they eat really small amounts of meat during the week, and then on Sundays they want to eat nothing but meat." For many Mexicans, when they are not feasting, their primary foods are "beans and corn tortillas. The tortillas have no fat added to them, just ground corn and water. No salt is even added to that. Together, corn tortillas and the beans provide all the amino acids that you need for synthesizing proteins. And then there's the chile sauces [high in vitamin C], which they eat with a lot of greens and vegetables and small amounts of meat." While Bayless knew about the nutritional benefits of Mexican food from his travels and research, he had still to convey it to the dining public and the food critics. He thought he'd have a harder time doing that in regions of the United States where there was emotional and historical baggage attached to Mexican culture or where people thought that the standard American interpretation of Mexican food was all the cuisine had to offer. So when it came time for Bayless to choose his location, he didn't have the luxury of just focusing on one particular neighborhood or the rental cost per square foot (see page 144); he had these larger cultural issues to consider.

With northern and southern California ruled out along with the Southwest, the Baylesses had yet to find the ideal city. It was only after several trips to Chicago, where Deann's parents lived, that they realized how apropos a city Chicago was for what they hoped to accomplish. Not only were there hundreds of thousands of Mexican Americans living in Chicago, but also Mexicans were considered "hardworking, good people." Added to that, "There were no chain restaurants right in Chicago, no Chi Chis. All that people knew about Mexican food in Chicago is what they had eaten in the ma-and-pa kinds of places" near the city's South Side and West Side. There were also good markets, where Bayless found he could get better ingredients than he could in Los Angeles. The final draw was that Mexican food hadn't been "Chicanoized" in the minds of Latin and non-Latin Chicagoans—a situation unlike that in Los Angeles.

> There is such a strong Chicano personality in Los Angeles that even recent immigrants throw off what they have from home and adopt this Chicano spirit. And that says to them, Look, we can get everything that we need to eat here. And really, what we want to eat is hot dogs and hamburgers with a little Mexican food thrown in. And the Mexican food is sort of that Los Angeles–style Mexican food. It has a relationship to the food in Mexico, but it is not very strong.

Finally Bayless realized that in Chicago, he was free to be innovative with the food, to represent its integrity accurately, and to convey that respect to his diners.

With the question of where to open the restaurant finally resolved, Bayless presented his version of Mexican food to the public in 1987. He opened not one but two adjoining restaurants: Frontera Grill, a casual seventy-seat restaurant; and Topolobampo, a more elegant seventy-five-seat dining room. They have been a critical and popular success since they opened, regularly appearing at the top of most "best of Chicago" lists. Bayless has also been recognized by his peers. Perhaps most significant of all, in 1995, the unprecedented happened. Both the James Beard Foundation *and* the International Association of Culinary Professionals (better known as the Julia Child Awards) named Bayless as Chef of the Year.

Despite all the acclaim, including nods from chefs throughout Mexico, Bayless still feels he has a lot to learn. Toward that end, he makes four to five pilgrimages to Mexico a year, ever on the lookout for new techniques and ingredients; but more than that, he goes just to stay grounded. It's such a valuable experience that he and Deann, who works as the operating manager, close down the restaurants for four days each July to take the staff to a different region of Mexico. Though the restaurants lose money while they are closed, Bayless is convinced that he is paid back many times over in intangibles. "If you don't know this food firsthand, it's very hard to know how to make it, how to serve it, how to describe it. I think food always tastes better if you know somebody made it just for you. So, if we get that *connection* with another person and then that person makes you something to eat, it can be a very transcendent experience." It's not only a treat for the staff, who work very hard at this labor-intensive cuisine—the chiles alone have to be peeled, seeded, soaked, and ground before they are ready to be added to dishes; and tamales take a herculean effort to make by hand—but it's also a way to keep the staff renewed.

A fresh staff, in turn, helps Bayless accomplish better what he set out to do as an evangelist for Mexican food, turning as many people as he possibly can on to its depth and complexity. This is a message he conveys through his restaurants, culinary tours of Mexico (see page 301), classes, and books. (*Authentic Mexican* was followed by *Mexican Kitchen: Recipes and Techniques of a World-Class Cuisine,* both of which were called masterly; and by the latest, *Salsas That Cook.*) And though he's a writer and a scholar, deeply committed to the written word, Bayless also uses and recognizes the value of television. Just as Julia Child inspired him to cook, he knows that some of the chefs on the Television Food Network will inspire an entire new generation of up-and-coming cooks. "Up until the mid-sixties, the doors to all kitchens were closed, and it was rare that you would ever see a menu with the name of the chef on it. That showed our total lack of respect for the craftsmanship of cooking." Television has helped broaden the country's interest in and respect for this craft by making it exciting and accessible, according to Bayless. And that's a good thing. "I don't think that a culture can really progress unless it has a respect for all the arts, including cooking."

Rick Bayless's

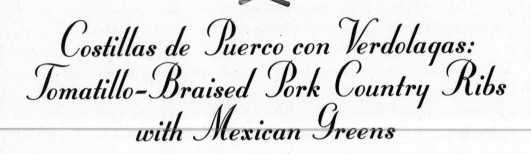

Costillas de Puerco con Verdolagas: Tomatillo-Braised Pork Country Ribs with Mexican Greens

Chef's note: *This is a typical Mexican one-pot meal that could not be more authentic or more widely embraced by just about everyone. If you like lemony flavors, you will be taken with the combination of purslane and tomatillos. The browned pork, of course, brings richness to the pot, and the potatoes are a wonderfully gentle foil to all this boldness.*

Purslane, sadly, is not in many grocery stores yet, so you probably will be making this when purslane is in the farmer's market; or you will use chard, which makes a great dish, though one that is not as lemony and soft-textured. For wine, I would recommend a full but dry Gewürztraminer.

(Serves 4 to 6)
For 2¼ Cups of Essential Simmered Tomatillo-Serrano Sauce Base

1½ pounds (15 to 18) tomatillos, husked and rinsed
Fresh hot green chiles to taste (roughly, 5 serranos), stemmed
½ cup chopped fresh cilantro, plus a few sprigs for garnish
Salt, about 1½ teaspoons, plus some for sprinkling on the meat

2 tablespoons vegetable or olive oil

3 pounds (about 6 good-size pieces) pork country ribs
   (or 1-inch-thick blade pork chops)

2 small white onions, finely chopped, plus a couple of slices separated
   into rings, for garnish

3 garlic cloves, peeled and finely chopped

8 medium boiling potatoes (like the red-skin ones), quartered

3 cups (about 12 ounces) fresh purslane (verdolagas), rinsed and thick
   bottom stems removed; or 6 cups loosely packed, sliced (½-inch
   pieces) chard leaves (you'll need a 12-ounce bunch)

1. *Making 2¼ cups Essential Simmered Tomatillo-Serrano Sauce Base:* Lay the tomatillos and chiles on a baking sheet and place about 4 inches below a very hot broiler. When they darken and soften, about 5 minutes, turn them over and broil the other side.

2. Roughly chop the chiles, then transfer them and the tomatillos (along with any liquid) to a food processor or blender. Puree, then add the chopped cilantro, ¾ cup water, and the salt.

3. *Meat and potatoes:* Over a medium-high burner, heat the oil in a Dutch oven or Mexican *cazuela* large enough to hold the meat in a single layer. Sprinkle the meat with salt, then brown on all sides, 10 to 15 minutes. Transfer to a plate.

4. Preheat the oven to 325° F. Pour off all but a thin coating of oil from the pan. Add the onions and cook until translucent, about 4 minutes; add the garlic and cook 2 minutes. Stir in the tomatillo sauce base, let come to a rolling boil, then return the meat to the pan. Cover and bake in the oven until the meat is just tender, about 45 minutes. Remove from the oven and skim off any fat that has risen to the top of the sauce.

5. Add the potatoes to the hot pot, push them down into the sauce, cover, and continue baking until potatoes are tender, about 20 minutes.

6. *Finishing the dish:* Stir the greens into the meat and potatoes, set the cover in place again, and bake 10 more minutes. Taste and season with a little more salt if necessary.

7. Transfer the ribs to a warm, deep serving platter. Arrange the potatoes around them, then spoon the sauce and greens over and around the meat. Strew the onion rings over the top, garnish with the cilantro sprigs, and carry the impressive platter to the table.

Advance preparation: The dish can be prepared very successfully through step 3; then cover and refrigerate. Bring to a simmer on top of the stove before continuing.

Shortcuts: Two 10-ounce packages frozen leaf spinach—thawed, squeezed dry, and roughly chopped—can replace the fresh greens; add it just before serving.

Pictured with Rick Bayless (right) at the
Halcyon/*Gourmet* Magazine–sponsored
"Great American Chefs" series is John Halligan,
the executive chef at the RIHGA Royal Hotel.

✳ OLDWAYS AND ✳
CHEFS COLLABORATIVE 2000

Increasingly, chefs and industry professionals are concerned with the strain that we consumers are putting on the earth's natural resources. Below, are two groups that chefs in this book belong to, including Rick Bayless, who chairs the Chefs Collaborative 2000.

Oldways

Established in 1988, Oldways is a nonprofit educational organization whose goal is to promote healthy eating based on the traditional cuisines of cultures around the world that are grown in environmentally sustainable ways. Oldways organizes international conferences and seminars on the relationship between food and culture and invites scientists, food writers, nutritionists, and chefs to participate. It also has a range of publications, including newsletters, monographs, and brochures.

Chefs Collaborative 2000

A nonprofit organization, founded in 1993 by Oldways Preservation Exchange Trust, Chefs Collaborative 2000 (CC2000) is dedicated to promoting sustainable cuisine, educating children about food, supporting local farmers, and inspiring customers to choose clean, healthy foods. Members are committed to maintaining the integrity of the environment and supporting every human being's right to safe, wholesomely grown, minimally processed, seasonally available food. Included in its charter is a recognition that "cultural and biological diversity is essential for the health of the planet and its inhabitants," and that "preserving and revitalizing sustainable food and agricultural traditions strengthen that diversity." Programs range from farm-to-restaurant projects to in-school education. Chefs Collaborative 2000 has developed an adopt-a-school program for teaching elementary school children about sustainable agriculture, foods from many cultures, and simple cooking techniques. Rick Bayless is chairman of the Board of Overseers of CC2000, and Frank Brigtsen is a member.

Information about contacting both organizations can be found in Appendix D.

Linda Rodriguez

JAPANESE FUSION

Even though she had a culinary degree and over four years of professional experience behind her, Linda Rodriguez was so determined to be a chef at Nobu that she would have started as a dishwasher just to get her foot in the door. Instead, Nobu offered her the only position available at the time of her interview—assistant pastry chef. She took it, though she had no aspiration to become a pastry chef. Indeed, whenever there was a no-show on the line, Rodriguez pleaded for an opportunity to substitute. Her tenacity paid off, both at Nobu and then at BondSt, a popular and acclaimed Japanese fusion-sushi restaurant where she is the executive chef. Here, she talks about why Japanese foods inspire her creativity and how she simply ignored any obstacles that may have come her way as a result of being a woman from a non-Japanese background in a traditionally male-dominated field.

Growing up in tourist-saturated Florida, Linda Rodriguez could always find a restaurant job. By the time she headed off to Baton Rouge, Louisiana, after high school, there was nary a front-of-the-house job she couldn't do—from waiting tables to tending bars to busing dishes. Eager for pocket change, she immediately set out to find a job, and within hours of arriving she was gainfully employed as a waitress at Maison Lacour. After all the years she had spent working at restaurants, she never once thought of working in the kitchen. So she surprised no one more than herself when she asked the chef-owner, Jacqueline Gréaud—a Chinese woman born and raised in France, who was knowledgeable about both French and Chinese cuisine—if she could move from the dining room to the kitchen.

After a quick assessment of Rodriguez's potential, Gréaud agreed to train her; and from that point on, the two worked side by side making classical French for the dining room and everything from Thai to Indian for the family meals (the food the staff eats before service). During their two years together, Rodriguez grew quite attached to Gréaud. So she was heartbroken when, unexpectedly, Gréaud suggested that she leave Maison Lacour for cooking school. Having taught her the *hows* of the kitchen, Gréaud wanted Rodriguez "to find out the reasons *why* cooks do certain things, and why certain ingredients react chemically to others." Those reasons were nearly compelling enough to persuade Rodriguez to leave a place she had grown fond of, but it was something else Gréaud said that ultimately convinced her. A formal culinary education would provide Rodriguez with a skill that "nobody can take away from you," Gréaud advised. With a culinary degree, she'd always have a way of providing for herself, a sense of security that she would learn to appreciate later in life, especially as a woman.

In 1992, Gréaud helped Rodriguez with her application to the **Culinary Institute of America (CIA),** particularly the financial aid forms and the letter on why she wanted to become a chef. Six months later, Rodriguez moved to Hyde Park to become a culinary student. If she had any anxiety about leaving the South, it was short-lived. For her externship, she went to Louisiana, this time New Orleans, where she had long yearned to live. She would have returned to the South again after graduation, had she not been granted a six-month fellowship to work as an assistant to a chef-instructor at the CIA. The only thing she enjoyed more than teaching—"I love watching the students evolve within just seven days of instruction"—was visiting Manhattan, which was only a quick train ride away. "During my fellowship, I'd come to New York every chance I could get. It seemed to me like the center of the food world, because you could go to any kind of restaurant—Chinese, Thai, Korean. I'd just walk into the kitchens and volunteer to work for free at all these really cool restaurants, including Le Bernardin." By the time Rodriguez completed her fellowship at the CIA, she had decided to move to New York City, putting Louisiana, though certainly not Gréaud, behind her.

Within no time, she found a job at the River Café, Brooklyn's world-famous romantic restaurant, revered for its modern American food, its spectacular view of Manhattan, and its alumni, who include Larry Forgione (An American Place), Charlie Palmer (Aureole), and David Burke (Park Avenue Café). She started out in the fish station, earning approximately $350 for a sixty- to seventy-hour week, though she can't say for sure what her hours were because she didn't count them. "If you did, it wasn't for you." Like Anthony Bourdain (who describes his initiation on page 28), she was nearly worked to death and "dearly" abused. "It's like the military—no matter what the head of the kitchen tells you, even if it is very annoying, you do it." And just like Andrew Pforzheimer when he first started out (page 13), she quickly learned the value of time in the kitchen. "If you didn't have speed, you wouldn't make it." But beyond anything Bourdain or Pforzheimer experienced, Rodriguez was also harassed for no other reason than her gender. "When it got really rough and busy, most people thought I couldn't take it because I was a girl. I didn't let it bother me. I never showed any signs; I never complained. I cooked like the men did. I just loved it." (For more on women and the business, see Patricia Williams, page 3; and Anne Kearney, page 189.)

Rodriguez stayed at River Café for two years—a relatively long time for someone just out of culinary school—rotating every few months to a new station in the kitchen, from fish to garde manger (cold appetizers and salads) to hot appetizers to the grill. Just as she was starting to get restless, rumors began to fly about a new Japanese restaurant that was generating quite a bit of publicity and buzz before its opening. Having spent a couple of years as a young girl in Japan, she was eager to work in a nontraditional Japanese restaurant; and in 1995, a friend put her in contact with the general manager of Nobu. After waiting five hours for her interview, she got her chance to tell the manager that she "wanted to work at Nobu, no matter what the position was." When he told her that his only opening was in pastry, she accepted without hesitation:

I took it even though I was a line cook, not a pastry girl. But in this industry, you take what you can get; it doesn't matter. I'd probably have taken a dishwashing job just to get my foot in the door. Sometimes, you have to be prepared to take anything, just to see what is going on around you—because if you work hard for what you're hired for, you'll move up. People will notice you.

While she had no idea what went into Japanese pastry, she did have some experience with pastry, from both the CIA and Maison Lacour. She figured that she could learn what she didn't know on the job.

With her hands embedded in flour—which was used to make chocolate cakes that resembled maki rolls—Rodriguez kept her eyes open for any new positions that might become available outside the pastry kitchen. Though Nobu Matsuhisa (partner with Drew Nieporent) wasn't against her moving up, the kitchen manager, a traditional Japanese man, wasn't comfortable with the idea of having a woman work in the kitchen. Whenever she asked for a chance, "he'd say things like, 'It's really hot over there. Do you think you can deal with that?' I never responded." Even though the pastry chef supported her ambition to go work the line and endorsed her work, she got nowhere with the kitchen manager. She was stuck. Indeed, she might never have moved out of Nobu's pastry kitchen had it not been for a no-show. Short one person at the garde manger station, the kitchen manager had no choice but to let her work. She started out working as garde manger cook, making soups and salads. Soups were particularly important, and within no time she had her first lesson in making dashi. Made from kelp and bonito, dashi is to Japanese cuisine what the "mother sauces" are to French haute cuisine; it's used in everything from soups and broths to noodle dishes. From there she moved throughout the kitchen, working every other station except the sushi bar.

When the head chef was fired, Rodriguez got her next break. She and two other cooks were asked to split the responsibilities. Rodriguez was assigned the non–sushi and sashimi portion of the *omakase* menu (which means "Let the chef decide"). "Nobody thought it was a big deal at the time because Nobu had just started doing these tastings, but they got to be very popular"—which is a bit of an understatement, considering that people from all the world would visit Nobu for the *omakase*. Once she got the hang of the fundamentals, she found that her biggest challenge lay in constantly creating new specials.

It was while coming up with different specials every week that Rodriguez experimented with and learned from three stylistic elements critical to traditional Japanese cooking that have been adapted for a Western audience. First, since what's not eaten with chopsticks will be eaten by hand, and Westerners prefer not to touch bones, she couldn't serve meat on the bone. If Rodriguez wanted to serve a rack of lamb, for instance, she would have to come up with a way to make it palatable. "It was either cut the meat up in small pieces for them" or come up with something creative. She went for creativity: "I wrapped the bone in raffia so that they could pick it up with their fingers and not feel like they have to touch the greasy part of the bone." She'd pair the rack of lamb with a sauce she made by reducing a lamb stock and infusing it with Asian pear and shiso, an herb unique to Japanese cuisine that is related to mint and basil, though its fragrance resembles neither. With its dramatic raffia costume and its herb-spiced sauce, Rodriguez's rack of lamb was so widely accepted that it became a mainstay.

Second, early on, Rodriguez was also introduced to the traditional Japanese notion that "if you're going to cook a fish, you should try to use every part of the fish, even the bone." Knowing that some Westerners are uncomfortable with looking at a whole fish, Rodriguez once again solved the problem creatively, if a bit whimsically. "For my fried flounder with sweet-and-sour yamamomo sauce, I'd deep-fry the flounder *and* the bone. Then I'd shape the bone into a boat, put the meat on top of the 'boat,' and serve it with a sauce made from yamamomo, which is like a Japanese mountain peach; it's really sweet, like a cherry."

Third, she applied the all-important concept of visual harmony in the food she prepared. "They say that Japanese people eat eighty percent with their eyes. The other twenty percent is what they smell and what they taste in their mouth." Visual refinement not only affects how Rodriguez plates dishes but also influences how she cooks. "I've gotten to the point where I can't mix too many ingredients in one dish," she says; and she prefers no more than two to three things on a plate. This aesthetic purity is reflected in the clean taste that the food leaves on the palate. Or, as a restaurateur in Tokyo, Michiko Yamamoto, expressed it, traditional Japanese cuisine is so clean it's like "a very clear lake where you can see everything beneath the water—the different-shaped pebbles, the plants, and the fish."

After working for Nobu for two and a half years, Rodriguez started getting restless. As a solution, Nobu Matsuhisa proposed that she go to London to open a Nobu there.

"It was a whole new experience for me. Even though I was still doing the same food, I was doing it in Europe, so I was learning about European produce and fish." Working with chefs from different backgrounds also kept her experience fresh. Because she was teaching Japanese concepts and ingredients to French and Italian chefs who didn't speak English very well, one would suppose that it would have been difficult to communicate. But since American kitchens are frequently multilingual, with Spanish often being used, she had no problems. She ended up loving London so much she made plans to move there permanently. Unfortunately, the British immigration service saw things differently. Without a visa, she had to return to the United States.

In the midst of moving out of her London home and saying a very emotional good-bye to her staff—as well as the friends she had grown attached to in her seven months at Nobu—she got a call from a group of New York restaurateurs who wanted to talk to her about their next venture. Among other businesses, the group owned and operated Indochine, one of the oldest—and perennially chic—Asian fusion restaurants in the city; and Republic, a funky modern incarnation of a noodle shop. Indochine and Republic had together established a very solid niche. For their next venue, the group wanted to open up a Japanese fusion-sushi restaurant. Their reputation and track record spoke volumes, and Rodriguez knew that a liaison with them could be an exciting development in her professional life. There was still her loyalty to Nobu Matsuhisa to consider, however: he was a mentor to whom she had grown close over the years. But after talking with Nobu, who was one hundred percent behind her, she decided to plunge into this new chapter of her life.

As the workmen built the front of the house at BondSt in the winter of 1998, Rodriguez experimented with specials, which she tried out on her new bosses and the investors in the kitchen, as the contractors were finishing the space. Though she had grown accustomed to hard work and long hours, working in a start-up was so demanding that she spent many nights sleeping on the floor, not even bothering to go home. For her menu, she brought with her variations of the dishes she had created at Nobu, such as rack of lamb and fried flounder, and she added entrées like potato-crusted chicken in sansho pepper sauce (sansho pepper is a spice and herb used in Japanese and Chinese food) and broiled Chilean sea bass, marinated in saiko miso. While her food is inspired by the Japanese principles she learned at Nobu, and by French techniques she learned with

Gréaud and at the CIA, it's neither French nor purely Japanese. Instead, "it's a very New York kind of thing," a hybrid cuisine, and a homage to the city she grew to love once she left the South. A typical example is her vegetarian Matsutake Hari Hari Nabe, a Japanese noodle dish that is traditional except for the fact that the broth, or dashi, is made out of vegetables rather than fish.

In her own small way, Rodriguez has added to the diversity of New York City's cuisine. But as executive chef, she has more on her mind than simply coming up with new dishes. She worries about quality and control; she monitors the inventory to check costs; she searches out the best purveyors of different foods, such as fish and produce; and she orders and receives food. But more than anything, perhaps, she focuses her energy on managing a staff:

> *Being an executive chef, a manager, is a hell of a responsibility. It's not about the food anymore. It's not about the establishment. It's about the people, having everybody come together to form a good working relationship. There's a lot of hand-holding. You have to keep your eyes and ears open all the time and be able to come up with results very quickly should something go wrong. On top of that, you must be able to do a thousand things at one time.*

From experience she has learned that "you can't be afraid to have people help you. You have to have good people around you, because they will take some of the weight off." At BondSt, she's helped by the owners and by Hiroshi Nakahara, the sushi chef with whom she developed the menu.

Though it's too early to say for sure, given the odds against success for restaurants in New York, the first indications that BondSt will have some longevity are strong: tables are booked several weeks in advance, and the first reviewers were enamored of both the food and the clientele. One local restaurant critic, Moira Hodgson, writing in the *New York Observer,* called the food extraordinary: "Dinner reminded me of Nobu."[17] The critic of New York's Sidewalk.Com, a guide for computer-savvy diners, wrote, "If the Fashion Week parties were any indication—Donatella Versace schmoozed here with the likes of Elizabeth Hurley and Minnie Driver—BondSt should prove to be the next big thing." Encouraged by press like this, BondSt has added a second dining room, and plans are in the works to add a lunch menu. But while Rodriguez is optimistic that BondSt will have the staying power of some of the other restaurants in the group, she knows that customers are fickle. The Versace-clad crowd could move to the new best thing, and then where would she be?

She's not sweating it too much. At barely thirty, she is a rising star with a solid educational background and, now, years of cooking experience under her belt. She also possesses a fondness for teaching. She has all that Jacqueline Gréaud once hoped she would have: marketable skills that no one can take away from her.

Linda Rodriguez's

Vegetarian Matsutake Hari Hari Nabe

Chef's note: *This traditional dish is usually made with dried bonito flakes, but here I've incorporated vegetables and dried mushrooms to keep the broth totally vegetarian. This soup is an ideal winter treat, when matsutake mushrooms are in season. Although they are quite expensive, the flavors they release in the broth are irreplaceable.*

(Serves 8)
Vegetable Dashi

12-inch strip of konbu
1 pound onions, roughly chopped
½ pound celery, roughly chopped
½ pound carrots, roughly chopped
1 whole head fresh unpeeled garlic, cut in half
2½-inch piece fresh ginger, roughly sliced
2 tablespoons fennel seeds
2 tablespoons coriander seeds
8 whole dried shiitake mushrooms, reconstituted in cold water for 3 hours
   until soft
1 tablespoon black peppercorns
3 tomatoes, halved

1½ cups soy sauce

2 cups mirin (Japanese rice wine)

1 pound dried udon noodles ¼- to ½-inch wide

1 pound matsutake mushrooms, sliced thin (chanterelles may
be substituted)

4 ounces fried tofu, cut crosswise into ½-inch strips, or 4 ounces
thinly sliced, firm tofu, lightly coated with flour and pan-fried in
2 tablespoons of vegetable oil

1 pound mizuna (Japanese leaf lettuce)

Pinch yuzu-skin powder (optional)

Pinch toragashi (cayenne pepper can be substituted)

1. Place all ingredients for the vegetable dashi in a stockpot with 4 quarts of water, bring to a boil, and simmer for 30 minutes; strain.

2. Put 2½ quarts vegetable dashi into a stockpot with the soy sauce and mirin, bring to a boil, and simmer for 10 minutes. Cook the udon noodles separately according to package instructions; drain and set aside.

3. Add the sliced matsutake mushrooms and tofu to the broth and bring to a boil. Just before serving, add the udon noodles, mizuna, yuzu-skin powder, and toragashi. Serve immediately in large bowls.

Note: Konbu, rice wine, and matsutake mushrooms are available at Japanese food markets.

✳ RESOURCES FOR WOMEN ✳

"A Woman's Place Is in the Kitchen": The Evolution of Women Chefs, by Ann Cooper, lists a number of resources for women in the culinary field, and is itself a wonderful source of information, both historical and contemporary. There are also a number of professional, educational, and networking organizations that support women working in the industry, including these.

Arizona Women in Food and Wine (AWFW)

This professional support organization for women working in Arizona's food, beverage, and hospitality industries promotes educational programs, higher standards, and networking opportunities. AWFW also offers scholarships to young women who choose to pursue a culinary education in Arizona.

Les Dames d'Escoffier International (LDEI)

LDEI is a unique worldwide society of professional women of high achievement in the fields of food, fine beverages, and hospitality. With a highly diversified membership, reflecting the multifaceted field of contemporary gastronomy, Les Dames d'Escoffier is dedicated to supporting and promoting the achievement of women in the culinary professions and to fostering excellence through educational and charitable activities. Each member has at least five years' professional experience; all have distinguished themselves in their fields. Membership is by invitation only.

Network of Executive Women in Hospitality, Inc. (NEWH)

Members of this national nonprofit group come from all segments of the hospitality industry and related fields: management, design, architecture, production, education, sales, marketing, and communications. NEWH serves its members and the industry through scholarships, fund-raising, education, and information exchange.

New York Women's Culinary Alliance (NYWCA)

NYWCA promotes cooperation and education among women in the food industry. The membership of the Alliance, which includes a cross section of food professionals, share information through member-generated programs and seminars. Ongoing food and wine tastings, lectures, and field trips provide organization members with continuing education. The Alliance also participates in community affairs through volunteer work and fund-raising.

Roundtable for Women in Foodservice (RWF)

The RWF is a national nonprofit organization with local chapters that support the development of industry leaders. The mission of RWF is to provide its members with educational, mentoring, scholarship, and networking opportunities. Its "point of differentiation among food-service industry organizations is that it is the only association focused on the development and enhancement of women's careers throughout all corporate and entrepreneurial operator, supplier, and service segments of the industry."

Wider Opportunities for Women (WOW)

WOW is a women's employment organization that strives to place women in areas of the workforce, such as the culinary and hospitality industries, where they have a better chance of gaining economic self-sufficiency. Since 1964, WOW has trained more than 10,000 women for well-paid work. In addition, through programs like the National Workforce Network—a group of more than 500 independent women's employment programs and advocates in every state and the District of Columbia—WOW has improved access to good jobs for tens of thousands more women and girls.

Women Chefs and Restaurateurs (WCR)

WCR was organized in 1993 by eight industry leaders to advance the role of women in the restaurant industry and to promote their culinary education. The founders are Lidia

Bastianich (of Felidia, Becco, and Frico Bar in New York City), Elka Gilmore (of Kokachin, New York), Joyce Goldstein (a former restaurateur and the author of many cookbooks, including *Back to Square One,* San Francisco), Johanne Killeen (of Al Forno, Providence), Barbara Lazaroff (a restaurateur with her husband, Wolfgang Puck), Mary Sue Milliken (of Border Grill in Santa Monica, California), and Barbara Tropp (author of *China Moon Cookbook).* In addition to advancing the education and role of women in the industry, WCR works to promote the betterment of the industry as a whole. It has a job bank, for members only.

Information on contacting organizations is available in Appendix D.

Sonia Urban

PASTRY CHEFS AT WORK

Though she was trained in classical French culinary techniques, Sonia Urban looks to her own Caribbean background for inspiration in her work as a pastry chef. In addition to working at various restaurants and pastry shops in New York City, this working mother continues a self-improvement course that has taken her from the kitchen of the artisan breadmaker Amy Scherber of Amy's Bread to the pâtisserie of François Payard. Together with Patrick Terrail—the former owner of the fabled Ma Maison in Los Angeles and executive director of the United States Pastry Alliance—Urban reveals how the world of a pastry chef differs from that of a chef, and explains why—whether they're working at a café, a bakery, a hotel, or a restaurant—pastry chefs work in a world apart.

Sonia Urban is a former hairstylist. That may sound like an unusual background for an acclaimed pastry chef, but according to Patrick Terrail, the former director of the **United States Pastry Alliance,** Urban is not such an anomaly. "There's a direct correlation between the pastry world and other visual arts. In fact, if you go into the background of most pastry chefs, you'll find a lot of former and aspiring architects, carpenters, or other artists—which is not surprising, since so much of what we enjoy about desserts is visual." To illustrate his statement, he points out that David Brown, the executive pastry chef at the Hilton on Hawaii's Big Island, is an aspiring sculptor and a former carpenter; and Donald Wressel of the Four Seasons in Beverly Hills loves to restore old furniture.

Locks, not furniture, was Urban's medium. She started styling hair just about the time that Bo Derek put cornrows on the map of popular culture. So along with perms, cuts, and color rinses, Urban added braids to her repertoire as a hairdresser. And she would have happily continued teasing, braiding, and curling her clients' locks had she not developed severe allergies to the chemicals, which forced her to embark on a new career. Encouraged by friends and neighbors, who had long taken pleasure in her wedding and birthday cakes, Urban decided to go to culinary school. With two young girls and a husband to care for, she chose a school close to her Bronx home, the **French Culinary Institute (FCI).**

The FCI has an ace faculty, which now includes the esteemed dean chef Alain Sailhac and visiting dean Alice Waters, as well as Chefs Jacques Pépin, André Soltner, and Jacques Torres, and is run, in Urban's view, like a military academy. "They were and still are strict about everything, but the training is worth it because most of the graduates are highly organized and disciplined in French techniques when they leave." In fact, Urban is convinced that her training—which included both pastry and culinary arts, as most certificate and degree programs do—is one of the reasons she can confidently navigate her way around any kitchen. "French techniques teach you how to make stocks and sauces correctly, how to cut vegetables and butcher meats properly, and, on the pastry side, how to make proper pâte sucrée, ice cream, sorbets, and the like."

After graduating second in her class in 1989, Urban got a chance to put her training to immediate use when she went to work for an American chef who had contacted the FCI placement office looking for an assistant to help with culinary and pastry prep. When that restaurant folded some five months later, Urban was surprised to find herself, suddenly, without a job. But given the number of restaurants that close each year, people who work in the industry have to expect sudden unemployment at some time in their career. Urban quickly turned the situation around, however, through contacts she had made at the **James Beard House,** where she was volunteering as a prep cook. (For more on the Beard House and Beard Foundation, see page 113.) Of the many people Urban assisted in prepping multicourse meals, two influential cooks—and cookbook authors—proved to have an enduring influence on her career: Madeleine Kamman, author of *Making of a Cook* and founder of the Modern Gourmet Cooking School, which together influenced a whole generation of cooks; and Christopher Idone, author of a number of cookbooks, including *Glorious Food.* Noting Urban's intensity as the two worked together, Kamman reminded Urban that "great culinary artists treat food with utmost respect. They never rush, but allow the natural process to evolve as it is meant to be."

Urban took that to heart and has applied it as a working philosophy in almost every kitchen she's ever set foot in, including that of Christopher Idone, who, after working with Urban at the Beard House, offered her the joint position of pastry assistant and line lunch cook at his new contemporary American restaurant, 1022. Once again, Urban worked both services, barely stopping from five in the morning to six at night, rolling out pastry dough before dawn and prepping soup for lunch. "I worked so hard, but I had so much of a fever for cooking that I didn't care. I would've done anything I was asked."

Working in both pastry and lunch service gave Urban a good perspective on the similarities and differences between the two kitchens, though at that stage in her emerging career, she was most impressed by the similarities. Prep work for both pastry chefs and prep cooks is grueling. Where someone on prep might be asked to peel 100 onions, a pastry prep cook might be ordered to peel 100 apples for apple crisps or glaze 200 fruit Danish. At a hotel or a restaurant where complimentary sweets are brought to the table at the end of each meal, a prep pastry cook might be responsible for mixing and scooping out, by hand, a ten-gallon batch of chocolate chip cookies, or cutting and arranging petit fours throughout the dinner service.

Both kitchens also exact an extraordinary physical toll. Whereas a *poissonier* gets nicks from fishbones, a pastry chef gets calluses from holding a knife too firmly while cutting through an entire box of peaches, to say nothing of routine bruises and burns, and the back strain that comes from lifting heavy pots and pans. Some pastry chefs, including Urban, develop "baker's lung," allergies to starches and flours. (For Urban, this is ironic, since it was because of allergies that she left professional hairstyling to become a baker.)

But there are differences between being a pastry chef and being a chef, and because there aren't enough hours in the day to do both, most chefs eventually have to choose between the two careers. For Urban, it wasn't a hard decision; there was something more scientific and precise about pastry, to say nothing of the artistry involved in the final product. "I found that there was more creativity in a pastry kitchen. A chef's raw ingredients are meat, fish, or vegetables. In a pastry kitchen, the possibilities are almost limitless." She also felt that her sweet tooth would make her more "open-minded about experimenting with different products," and therefore a better pastry chef.

Having made up her mind to become a pastry chef, Urban started taking supplementary classes in chocolate, candy, and sugar-flower work—the process used for designing wedding and birthday cakes. Sugar work was her favorite of all, both because it tested her knowledge of the science behind it—the ratio of sugar to water, the degree at which the cooking process is stopped, and the speed with which it is cooled—and because flower-making classes put her in touch with nature. "You have to know what flowers look like in order to excel at the work, which means you're constantly observing what a particular type of flower looks like in the spring versus the summer, or noticing things like there are more orange flowers in June than May."

With a growing portfolio of skills, Urban wasn't too worried nine months later when it looked as if 1022 was going out of business. She decided to look for work in a hotel rather than in another small restaurant. Apart from having better personnel benefits, she knew that hotel chefs gain experience in volume, wedding and birthday cake design, and centerpiece work. In addition, whereas most restaurants serve primarily plated desserts with sugar or chocolate embellishments, hotels also offer a variety of pastries, including Viennese pastry, Danish, croissants, and brioches. Though she could have turned, once again, to the helpful placement office at the FCI—a service most culinary schools offer their graduates—Urban turned instead to the men who delivered milk to 1022. "I said to the guys, 'You take milk all over the city. You see all the hotel and restaurant bulletin boards. Next time, look and see what's around.'" Ten days after hatching her clever plan, Urban was working at the Mark, a luxury hotel in Midtown Manhattan.

Urban started out at the Mark as a pastry prep cook but was rapidly promoted to pastry sous chef under the direction of Susan Bolout. With Bolout, Urban "went over the production of what was needed each day and oversaw what the rest of the pastry staff did." She was also responsible for overseeing production for big parties and special events, for ordering products for day-to-day operations, and for overall general operations when her boss was on vacations. Customers' requests ranged from the standard salted peanut-butter cookies for room service to plated desserts for sit-down banquets. One of Urban's most unusual events occurred when a woman hosting a sit-down dinner wanted pans of apple tart, hot out of the oven, ushered into the dining room so that the smell of baking apples would penetrate the air, reminding her guests of home.

As she worked her way up from pastry sous chef at the Mark to pastry chef, over the course of three and a half years, the differences between pastry and culinary chefs and kitchens became more apparent. First, pastry chefs work different hours. According to Patrick Terrail, the chef who first brought us Wolfgang Puck, "Because the preparation time is so complex for a pastry chef, he generally arrives in the morning and prepares everything so that it's ready for dinner that evening. During service, the only thing that has to be done is the plating of the dessert." Not only do pastry chefs work different hours from chefs; but also, as Urban points out, in a proper restaurant pastry shops are segregated from the main kitchen, so that the pastry staff works in relative isolation. And even if there isn't a separate kitchen, pastry staffs usually have special equipment, which they keep off limits to everybody except themselves:

> Pastry has to be stored properly. Otherwise either it becomes spoiled or it takes on the flavor of everything else. If, for example, you put a strawberry sauce in a container that had onions in it, you're going to have an onion taste in your strawberry sauce. So, we need separate containers that no one else can use.

This segregation can sometimes cause tension between pastry and culinary, but according to Urban, there's little way to avoid it.

Pastry cooks also feel that they need more precision than cooks do: "We have to weigh all our ingredients, and the temperature of everything has to be exact. Not only that, we need really good, working ovens, whereas cooks can use any ovens, because they don't really need precise temperatures." Terrail agrees, and he further points out that in a proper pastry shop, there should be no humidity because pastry chefs work with products such as butter, pie dough, and chocolate that are very sensitive to temperature. Ideally, different sections of the kitchen will even have different temperatures. It's because pastry chefs *can't* stand the heat that they go in early, before the kitchen heats up; work in a separate area, space permitting; and, when necessary, work in walk-in refrigerators. Fortunately, the Mark, like most hotels, had a proper pastry shop. But since most restaurants lack the extra space, Urban had to improvise a bit more at Patria, the restaurant she moved to when her mentor, Susan Bolout, moved to Portland, one of the emerging food meccas of the Northwest.

Urban was born in the Dominican Republic, and she has long been interested in using Latin ingredients and flavors in her professional baking. So when Douglas Rodriguez, a nominee for the prestigious James Beard Rising Star Award and owner of Patria—a restaurant at the forefront in revolutionizing the way Latino food is prepared and served in New York City—offered her a position as executive pastry chef, she couldn't resist the opportunity to work with him. Whereas Bolout had trained Urban to emphasize freshness and simplicity; Rodriguez inspired her to seamlessly blend a number of different flavors on a plate. One example is Patria's signature "Cuban cigar," an almond cake accompanied by a "cigar" made of chocolate mousse and a "box of matches" made with edible sugar and *tuile* cookies. It's a playful, pretty dessert that not only blends many flavors but also requires the chef to have scientific knowledge of chocolate and sugar work, as well as the ability to create and present a beautiful finished product.

Adapting Rodriguez's emphasis on multiple flavors to her own style, Urban developed a few house favorites of her own. For example, she improvised with a fruit soup she had learned from Bolout at the Mark. Whereas Bolout used vanilla bean and lemongrass to flavor her fruit soup, Urban infused hers with accents of jalapeño and black peppers. A similar burst of flavor characterized her piña colada flan, which was made with pineapple and coconut milk, and her unusually flavored sorbets. Drawing upon a Latin palette of flavors, Urban added tamarind- and sangria-flavored sorbets to the menu, eliciting approval from Ruth Reichl, the former restaurant critic for the *New York Times* and author of *Tender at the Bone: Growing Up at the Table,* who wrote: "Don't let the [visually restrained] desserts fool you: each has a surprising intensity of flavor. Try the flan, with its deep milky taste, or the raspberry sorbet, with its hint of cinnamon. Or for sheer flavor shock, the powerful tamarind sorbet. And then, for the fun of it, have the smokeless Cuban cigar, a trompe l'oeil chocolate cigar with a book of sugar matches. It will leave you laughing."[18]

In addition to making multiflavored desserts that complemented Chef Rodriguez's boldly flavored food, Urban was also interested in playing with texture. To a milk chocolate flan, for instance, she added shavings of dark chocolate. "With each bite, you'd taste the two different chocolate flavors. Sometimes I'd add a crust of cashews and chocolate on the bottom as well," which would be yet another layer of flavor and texture. Indeed, these desserts helped Patria scale new heights. In 1996, while Urban was heading the pastry kitchen, the *New York Times* awarded Patria three stars.

But having worked for others for over eight years, Urban and her husband, also a culinary professional, were ready to start working on a business plan of their own. Since it would be impossible to scout locations, develop menus and business plans, and get financing while holding a full-time job, Urban left Patria to start developing her own ideas. In the meantime, she works as a freelance consultant specializing in Latino menus, advising chefs and restaurateurs about pastry to complement their lunch and dinner menus. She also trains the staff in her techniques and recipes.

Urban's counseling is not limited to restaurant owners. She has advice for the next generation of pastry chefs as well:

> Give, give, give, give. If you're going to work in a place and a chef says "I need you to stay tonight," you have to say yes—because he'll like you that much better, and will consider you part of the "brigade" that much faster. He will then give you more chances, and keep promoting you. And volunteer whenever your schedule permits. If you are great at chocolate but you want to be more skilled with pastry, go trail one of the best pâtisseries in town.

In addition to working with other bakers, pastry chefs, and artisans, she advises new pastry chefs to take supplementary classes to develop a portfolio of skills.

An aspiring pastry cook may not necessarily be a good baker, but this doesn't mean that he or she won't excel at cake decoration, chocolate, pastillage, pulled sugar, or confectionery work. As Patrick Terrail emphasizes, "There are a lot of pastry chefs who are wonderful decorators, wonderful artists, yet they have no palate. Likewise, there are a number of pastry chefs who are not the world's best dessert makers, but they excel at sugar work or at making roses on a wedding cake." As Terrail sees it, the field is so diverse and is growing so rapidly that there's room enough for artists of every stripe.

Exotic Fruits in Consommé

Chef's note: *This recipe reminds me of wonderful sunny days in Santo Domingo, where as kids my brothers and I would head to the open fields in search of an afternoon snack. There we would pick wild tropical fruits as other children might buy candy at a candy store. This luscious way of serving fruit is a modern interpretation of those memories. I learned from my Mexican friends to spike fruit with hot pepper sauces. So do use additional jalapeño (if you dare) as a garnish. A fruit sorbet and a fancy cookie will also add texture, contrast, and elegance.*

(Serves 4)
Zest of 1 orange
Zest of 1 lime
3 cups filtered (or spring) water
¾ cup sugar
1 inch ginger, peeled
4 sticks lemongrass (if market has already trimmed stalks, use 6)
½ cup packed mint leaves
1 teaspoon whole black peppercorns
One 1½-ounce (1 medium-sized) jalapeño, seeded and chopped

Fruits

Pineapple, mango, papaya, passion fruit, or any combination of fruits
enough for 4 servings; uncommon fruits such as mamey or star fruit
are also good

Special Equipment: 2-quart heavy-bottom stainless steel or ceramic pot;
cheesecloth; medium-size, fine-mesh strainer; zester (if not available, a
vegetable peeler will do)

1. Thoroughly rinse the orange and lime; then zest both, making sure there is no pith (the white part) on the skins. Set zest aside.
2. Put water and sugar into the pot.
3. Chop peeled ginger; add to the pot.
4. Remove any discolored or brown tips, roots, and leaves from the lemongrass and rinse well. Crush the lemongrass by hitting it with a large knife from top to bottom. Chop into small pieces and add to the pot.
5. Remove mint leaves from stems. Rinse well and add leaves only to the pot.
6. Add the black pepper to the pot.
7. Place the pot on medium heat. Bring to a low boil, uncovered. Skim liquid to remove foam that settles on top. Lower heat to just a simmer, add the chopped jalapeño and citrus zest, and simmer for an additional 5 minutes, still on low.
8. Remove from heat. Allow infusion to cool before straining through cheesecloth. If using immediately, chill over ice. Or, at this point, you can refrigerate overnight, but use within 24 hours.
9. Peel and slice fruit. Use ripened, seasonal, good-quality fruit for the most flavorful results. Arrange artistically in soup bowls (for example, use a rose-petal design). Spoon about ½ cup of consommé over the fruit and serve.

Note: Use organic produce to avoid pesticide residues.

✳ THE UNITED STATES PASTRY ALLIANCE ✳

Founded in 1994 by Gilles Renusson, in response to a tremendous growth in the pastry industry, the United States Pastry Alliance (USPA) is a nonprofit organization that supports pastry chefs across the country. Its mission statement includes (1) promoting continuing education for pastry chefs, (2) facilitating communication among its members, (3) disseminating information about new products and available tools to facilitate the art of making pastry, and (4) assistance at pastry competitions recognized by the Alliance. (Competitions are usually judged according to a combination of visual presentation, utilization of product, and taste.) The USPA also supports the **Careers Through Culinary Arts Program (C-CAP),** a culinary scholarship program for minorities.

Like many professional organizations, the USPA maintains a job bank for its members (see page 185). Judging from the number of jobs that come through his office, as well as from discussions with pastry chefs across the country, Patrick Terrail, the Alliance's former executive director, believes that the future is bright for pastry chefs. "Because the American palate has grown, and more and more Americans recognize what a good dessert is, restaurants are raising the bar. It's now a commonly held notion that the end of the meal is just as important as the center."

But this doesn't stop with restaurants, as Terrail points out: "We're seeing better desserts everywhere, from coffee and pastry shops to takeout gourmet stores such as Eatzi's and the frozen-food section of neighborhood grocery stores. Even the companies who sell premanufactured pastry to restaurants are growing by leaps and bounds." To meet this demand for pastry chefs at cafés, bakeries, hotels, restaurants, and home replacement stores, the number of schools with two- and four-year programs, as well as the number of confectionery schools, is "on the rise."

As Terrail points out in "Pastry Chefs at Work," (page 178), there's something for *almost* everyone in the world of pastry.

For information on contacting the United States Pastry Alliance, see Appendix D.

✳ RESOURCES ON THE INTERNET ✳
FOR FINDING JOBS

The chefs in *If You Can Stand the Heat* have found jobs in both traditional and unusual ways. When Sonia Urban was ready to work in a pastry kitchen doing big volume, she asked the men who delivered milk to the restaurant in which she worked to keep their eyes out for openings at luxury hotels. More typically, as Anthony Bourdain explains, cooks will follow their sous chef or executive chef from one restaurant to another.

The alumni job placement office is another wonderful resource for those who have gone to cooking schools. And if you're new to a city and have absolutely no contacts, there is always the want ads, which is exactly how Brigtsen found a job with Paul Prud-homme (see page 221).

The Internet is the latest source of information on job openings in the restaurant and hospitality field. A few popular sites are listed below. In addition to these, if you are affiliated with a culinary school, be sure to consult their Web site. And if you're interested in working in a hotel, it's helpful to know that most hotels have their own Web sites, many of which list job openings.

- http://www.acfchefs.org/jobbank.html—the **American Culinary Federation** is a nonprofit organization for culinarians: cooks, chefs, educators, and food purveyors. Résumés are posted for one year and can be viewed by the general public. Job openings are posted for sixty days and may be accessed by members or nonmembers who have paid a fee.

- http://www.culinary.net/cgi-bin/iccentry.cgi—Though anyone may access the Women Chefs and Restaurateurs Web site, its job listings are for members only.
- http://escoffier.com/nonscape/employ.shtml—Escoffier on Line is a Web resource with a special emphasis on employment and food service education for chefs, pastry chefs, cooks, culinary educators, food and beverage managers, and food professionals.
- http://www.iacp-online.org—The International Association of Culinary Professionals has a members-only, password-protected job site.
- http://www.kitchenette.com/jobs/index.html—A source for restaurant jobs (chefs and managers) in the San Francisco Bay area. Catering opportunities are listed as well.
- http://www.pastrywiz.com/talk/job_toc.htm—In addition to chat rooms and other resources, this online discussion group offers people an opportunity to post and look for jobs. This site is not limited to pastry jobs.
- http://www.restaurantreport.com/Jobs/index.html—The industry magazine *Restaurant Report* has an online edition, which encourages hotels and restaurants to post job openings.
- http://www.starchefs.com/CCC_helpwanted.html—A guide to openings submitted by potential employers as well as a site where people looking for work can post their résumés. The site, just one segment of this very popular food site, is updated daily.
- http://www.uspastry.org—Sponsored by the United States Pastry Alliance, this job site posts positions for pastry chefs only. For members of the USPA, the service is free. For nonmembers, there is a $50 fee.

Chef-Owners on the Business of the Business

Anne Kearney

WHAT NINE YEARS OF BEING A COOK CAN'T TEACH YOU ABOUT BEING A PROPRIETOR

Anne Kearney can't remember a time when preparing and consuming food weren't a central part of her day. During summers at her grandfather's lodge in Michigan, it was mandatory that Kearney and her siblings participate in all phases of the meal, from fishing for the main course to sitting through lengthy dinners with the paying guests. Once school rolled around—with her brothers away at soccer practice and her sister learning drill team routines—it fell to Kearney to help her mother prepare meals and set the table. Though she had cooked professionally for several years before she bought her own restaurant, Kearney knew very little about the "business" of the business. At the risk of losing it all, however, she learned quickly. Here she shares how she transformed her near pitfalls into learning experiences and her learning experiences into entrepreneurial successes.

On the surface of things, life has gone pretty much as Anne Kearney hoped it might when she wrote in her high school yearbook that she wanted to be a chef within five years of graduating and a restaurateur within ten. But if you scratch a little deeper, it's clear that she was nearly derailed a couple of times.

First, before she even graduated from high school, Kearney was talked out of becoming a chef altogether. According to one of her high school guidance counselors in Dayton, Ohio, "there was no future in cooking." She was also advised that professional kitchens were too "blue-collar," too "male-dominated," and not at all in line with the goals that her college prep school set for its class of 1985. While cooking may have been considered blue-collar at the time, the counselor couldn't have been more mistaken about there being no future in the industry. According to recent projections by the Bureau of Labor, the fastest-growing occupations through the year 2006 will be in the food preparation and food service sectors, with over 1.25 million new jobs to be created *each* year.[19]

The counselor had foreseen neither this growth in the numbers of people who would be employed in this industry nor the prestige that a lucky few would confer on the entire profession. Thus discouraged, Kearney went to college instead of cooking school. Her mother calls it her social year: She spent all the money and got really bad grades. After one year, she left to pursue her original dream of going to cooking school, but because she had done so poorly in college, her parents offered her little financial support. To save money for culinary school, she started working in a local kitchen, making club sandwiches for lunch, baked potatoes and prime rib for dinner. In between, she waited tables.

By the fall of 1987, she had saved up enough money to enroll in the **Culinary Arts Academy** in Cincinnati.

During my first week there, they totally wiped out and retaught everything I had learned in my previous job. It was hard, but I enjoyed it so much and got the best grades I had ever gotten in my life. Reflecting on school now, I realize that the most important thing I learned was technique. School teaches you how to do things properly. It doesn't make you a chef. It doesn't make you a genius at writing menus or combining flavors. What it does do is say, Sauté: Grab a proper-size pan; heat until hot; add a small amount of butter.

Right out of school, with a working knowledge of various techniques—sautéing, roasting, braising, etc.—Kearney was asked to work with one of her instructors from the Culinary Arts Academy in his restoration of Grammer's, one of the oldest restaurants in Cincinnati. The restaurant, which had been closed for five years, was in such a disastrous state that Kearney and four other students had to clean and scrub everything from the kitchen equipment to the floors and walls. Then they had to set up brand-new systems, including developing and costing out a menu. In hindsight, this opportunity to put into practice all that she had learned in school was the perfect complement to her technical training:

> So many people get out of school with the idea that they know everything. And then they go into a restaurant, where either they are in charge too early or they're being told to do things in compromising ways. As a result, they quickly lose sight of proper technique and the proper ways to handle food.

Though she couldn't know it then, this opportunity to build a restaurant from the ground up would serve her well in the future. Still, there was a price to pay for all this valuable knowledge. The experience was critical, but at a wage of $5 per hour, it was also financially destabilizing. "I had nothing, literally. Not even a car. My father asked, 'What in the world are you doing? You're working sixty hours a week, yet you're making less than three hundred dollars a week.' I told him, 'Dad, I'm paying my dues. Because that is what you do in business: You pay your dues.'"

After twelve months, however, even Kearney grew weary of this lifestyle. So when a restaurant in her native Dayton began tempting her with promises of working with a young, reputable French chef, she was only too happy to move back home. In an unexpected turn of fate, two weeks after she got there, "the French chef was deported because he didn't have a green card." Unfortunately, the replacement chef ran an unorganized, dirty kitchen, made Kearney serve rotten food, and insisted that all his cooks work a double shift, the first from 9 A.M. to 2 P.M. and then another from 4 P.M. to 11 P.M. What had started out as an opportunity quickly turned into a bitter disappointment. "I would get home just after two P.M., sit down on the couch, stare at the television, and then Oprah would start. And I'd say to myself, I don't want to go back. I don't want to go back. I hate it." Kearney came as close to losing her way as she ever would.

Four months later, salvation came when the owner of Grammer's back in Cincinnati called to tell her that their executive chef was leaving. They wanted Kearney and two of her classmates, both also women, to run the entire kitchen. At the incredibly young age of twenty-two, Kearney and her friends were in charge. As night chef, Kearney got to use the creative half of her brain in the kitchen for the very first time in her professional life. Rather than execute orders of the executive chef, she got to design the menu. "When I look back on those menus now, I see they were very remedial—hollandaise on fish with a garnish of fresh herbs and an accompaniment of a green vegetable or a starch; or the southwestern thing, black bean sauce with fried tortillas and salsa cruda. Not very original," she reflects years later. At the time, though, she was having fun experimenting with different food combinations.

If the job entailed nothing more, it might have worked. But as one of the executive chefs, she also had to *manage people,* and that was the hardest part of it all, particularly when it came to managing people for whom Grammer's was a job, not a career. "I was twenty-two. The dishwasher was coming in on crack. I was hiring and firing people who were older than me, and I was thinking, 'This is not fun anymore; this is when people burn out; this is why people in the industry do drugs, and I don't want to burn out!'"

Added to that stress was the sexual tension she encountered in the kitchen. Although Kearney never made a big deal out of it, she admits that harassment has been a factor at every place she has ever worked:

People always ask if it's been hard being a woman in this business. Well, it's hard being in this business period. Whether it's been harder for me than a man, I don't know. I do know that every job I've ever had, I've been harassed in some capacity—whether it was being patted on the butt, or having someone gaze at me or tell me nasty jokes all day. I've encountered all sorts of stuff from coworkers to owners to chefs. I don't think that men have to put up with that, but I don't know if that's harder or easier. At some point, you take a stand for yourself and you say to people, "You can talk about whatever you want, just don't talk to me about it."

For many women, constant harassment might have been the final straw. But Kearney didn't let it get to her. Instead, she hung tough until a friend who had spent her externship in New Orleans suggested that the two of them head south to look for work. (An ex-

ternship is a paid or unpaid training position in a restaurant or hotel or on a food magazine or television show, which most culinary schools either mandate or encourage as a
way to bolster their students' work experience.) Kearney jumped at the chance to live in
a sunny city, especially one that took its food seriously. Also, a move would allow her to
refocus her energy on food rather than on managing people.

Kearney had been one of three people in charge at Grammer's, but in New Orleans she
had to start all over again because she had no contacts. Through the want ads she managed to find a local job; and after a couple of months she landed an even better one—as
sous chef to John Neal, the chef of the Bistro at the Maison de Ville. Finally, it appeared
that she was on a steady course. Neal, a French-trained southerner, took an interest in
Kearney's development and became her mentor. First he unveiled for Kearney the se-
crets of her own palate; then he taught her depth and meticulousness, and how to look
for texture and color on a plate. In Neal she found a patient, thorough teacher: "We were
very much into the history of cuisine and flavor combinations." When Neal and two
other owners left the Bistro at Maison de Ville to open a new restaurant, Peristyle, he
took Kearney with him. (As Anthony Bourdain points out, this is customary.) But after
two years, he had taught her as much as he could, and in October of 1992 she decided
to leave. "We came to a place in our relationship where it was time for me to learn again.
He needed to be refueled and to teach somebody else. And I needed to be taught by
someone who had something different to teach me." The split was completely amicable;
she left with their friendship and mutual respect intact.

   With a lot more to learn about the business, Kearney decided to accept a job working for Emeril Lagasse, the owner and impresario behind the restaurants Emeril's
and NOLA, and the host of *Essence of Emeril* on television. Soon after she started at
Emeril's, Lagasse moved her to the food bar, a cooking station in the middle of Emeril's
dining room. It was simultaneously the best and worst of worlds. With Lagasse screaming at her as he was expediting orders, it was a very high-pressure job, where she got her
"butt kicked" every night. "People are watching you cook for four hundred people and
Emeril is screaming at you, expediting, *'If you don't give me that food in five minutes, I'm
going to come over there and work your station. Do you want me to work your station?'* And
you're saying back to him, *'Yes, sir, right away, sir!'*" There was an upside to all this: Kearney learned how to communicate with the public. If people asked how something was

prepared, instead of replying, "We take the scraps from the fish and make a court bouillon, or fumet." She learned to say, *"We take the trimmings and we make a fumet."* Instead of embarrassing somebody by asking, "Do you know what this is?" she learned to ask, *"Are you familiar with radicchio?"*

Though she now recognizes how much she benefited from working at the food bar for eighteen months, at the time she couldn't wait to get out of the line of fire. Finally, she asked Lagasse to transfer her to another job within his operation. First he moved her to his test kitchen, where she developed recipes for his second cookbook, *Louisiana: Real and Rustic;* then she began writing for his television show, *Essence of Emeril.*

Just as she was starting to want even more new challenges, Kearney got a devastating phone call. Her mentor John Neal had passed away. Knowing that Neal and Kearney had been extremely close and that she would preserve the integrity of Peristyle, on the first of August, 1995, the family offered her the first option to buy it. She had only five days to decide. With no savings to speak of and no entrepreneurial experience at all, Kearney might well have been deterred. Instead, she decided to find a way to come up with the money. She wanted a restaurant of her own.

She immediately marched into Lagasse's office and announced her resignation. When he was reassured that this was no passing whim, and after a serious meeting with the bank executives in which Kearney presented a formal business plan, Lagasse pledged his full support. "He got on the phone and called his bank and said something like, 'If you don't give her the money, I will. She is a good investment. If you lose the money that you loan her, she has the potential to make it back in less than five years on the market because she is a very good cook and she will make it.' He went to bat for me." With someone of Lagasse's stature behind her, Kearney was able to get the financial backing to buy Peristyle, even though she herself had less than $300 in the bank.

As at Grammer's, before she reopened Peristyle—which is housed in a canary-yellow converted masonry building in the French quarter—Kearney, the preexisting staff, and her supportive parents cleaned and refurbished the kitchen and dining room. Then Kearney developed a new menu and several specials. She decided to draw on the abundant local produce. But she also wanted to feature foods native to her own cultural background—German, Scandinavian, and Irish—as well as those of Italy. She prepares most of her food using classic French techniques. She describes it as Louisiana–French bistro fare, and her specials might include Hand-Rolled Ravioli with Roasted Tomatoes, Mushrooms, and Goat Cheese with Artichoke Brown Butter or a crabmeat salad, which she teams up with horseradish, beets, and pickled onions—a colorfully seductive dish where the stark white of the crab serves as a perfect foil for the red beets and the green herbs.

Once the building was spruced up and the menu planned, she thought the customers would come, as if by magic, the very day she reopened for business in October 1995. Yet for months she had trouble filling more than fourteen tables on a good night, six on a bad one. Finances were tight and business looked grim. When she could no longer afford to pay a pastry chef, and had to let that person go, Kearney would get to work at four in the morning, make bread, and start the pastries herself before making the soups and dashing home at one-thirty for a quick nap. She was willing to do whatever it took to stay afloat, but how long could she sustain this pace?

While most experienced entrepreneurs and restaurant consultants know that it takes six months for any new restaurant to get established enough to break even, Kearney was surprised. "I used to sit there and beg. I mean I used to cry every night. Every time the phone rang, I would think, Please be a reservation." Soon enough, she realized that if she wanted to survive, she'd have to hustle. With no budget to hire a public relations firm, she hit the pavement herself. First she put together packets containing menus, details of the venue, and business hours. Then she went around introducing herself to the hundreds of concierges in the hotels of New Orleans. "Some of them threw the packets in the garbage after I left, I'm certain of it. And others thought, 'Oh, what a nice girl. We'll throw her some business.'" To further promote her restaurant, Kearney also did cooking demonstrations and benefits on Saturday mornings at different farmers' markets, at gourmet shops, and at Williams Sonoma. "I just got my face out there. I had no clue what I was doing. I was so naive. But the less I knew what I was up against, the better off I was. I just kept saying, 'I can do this. People think I'm going to fail. But I can do it.'" Kearney did succeed, but not without some near misses.

As the owner of a new business Kearney had to contend with at least three categories of problems. First, she had to ferret out real assets from unexpected liabilities, a problem faced by anyone who buys a preexisting restaurant. She was told, for example, that all the accounts payable were paid in full when she bought the restaurant. But several weeks after opening, she was presented with an invoice for $5,000 worth of china that she couldn't even confirm still existed. "I spent the first couple of years trying to figure out, Is everything really paid for? Am I really legitimate?"

The second category of problems Kearney faced is also universal among owners of new businesses—getting a realistic hold on monthly expenses versus what she had budgeted for. Kearney knew she had to buy flowers, linen, food, and wine, for example, but she hadn't anticipated the need to pad her budget with extra money to replace the case of wineglasses that break every month through sheer carelessness and accidents.

More than any budget item, she admits, she was most naive about payroll expenses. She found out, for instance, that the previous owner wasn't paying workers' compensation. Consequently, when she added that to her payroll, expenses were suddenly much more than she had anticipated. There were also federal and state insurance taxes. While a more seasoned owner may have known that employers have to match their employees' FICA taxes, this was news to Kearney. "I didn't understand that for my whole life, my employers had been matching my FICA taxes on my check." When she got her first payroll statement as owner of Peristyle, she was shocked. She had budgeted $7,000 per month, but she actually owed nearly 60 percent more. In that same vein, she suddenly looked at waiters' tips in a new light. "By law, your waiters have to claim all their tips, and if they don't and they get caught, you have to match their back taxes. So it's in your best interest for them to be legitimate. But if they're legitimate, then you're paying their matched taxes. Either way, they're going to get you!"

Kearney's rude awakening regarding hidden payroll costs is not surprising. As Carol A. King, a consultant to the hospitality industry, wrote in *Professional Dining Room Management*, "Payroll is by far the largest cost in the operation of a dining room. It includes not only the direct hourly wages of service staff but also a number of related costs, sometimes referred to as fringes."[20] By law, employers have to pay social security taxes, workers' compensation, FICA, and state insurance. In some cases, they also pay union fees, health and life insurance, a payroll service or a bookkeeper, and sick leave and vacation time. (See also "Getting Started: Projecting an Accurate Budget," page 201.)

In addition to budgeting properly, Kearney had to learn how to plan around the seasonal tourist and convention cycle. This is a third category of problems common to almost all restaurants in a heavily visited area such as beach, desert, and mountain resorts. And Kearney hadn't anticipated that although New Orleans is flush with tourists from January through May, business drops off significantly in the summer and to some extent even in the fall. Consequently, just as Kearney's hard public relations work had begun to pay off, with Peristyle routinely serving more than fourteen tables a night, the tourist season ended and she was back asking the bank for more money. "I hadn't wasted money; it just took more to get it going than I had anticipated. I borrowed enough money to cover cash flow, payroll, and inventory for New Year's Eve because that is your biggest night of the year." From that moment on, she knew that as a chef-proprietor, she had to do more than make delicious food. She had to make sure that the front of the house provided excellent service; she had to manage her staff; and she had to manage the restaurant's cash flow.

Three years into Kearney's stewardship, with excellent local reviews—the *Times-Picayune* critic called her a "genius"—and referrals from hotels in the area, Peristyle has moved up in the rankings. It went from being a restaurant with a few walk-ins to one that tourists and conventiongoers might rank as seventh or eighth on their list. According to *Gourmet* magazine's 1998 restaurant survey, it's now the second most popular restaurant in New Orleans, and ardent diners book months in advance.

Beyond the local press, Kearney is also reaping the kind of national media attention that she couldn't buy even if she wanted to, a far cry from the days she had to walk around hot and humid New Orleans begging for business. For *Wine Spectator*'s story on "The Rising Stars of American Cuisine" in 1998, a beaming Kearney graced the cover. Just a few months later, in *Food & Wine*'s cover story and its photo of the country's top young chefs, Kearney was nestled comfortably and confidently among her peers. In 1999, she was nominated for a James Beard award. How does she prevent success from going to her head? By reminding herself that success in this business often has no correlation with how hard one works. "I'm just really lucky, because you don't always get rewarded for hard work." And it's precisely because of this that she cautions against going into this business just for fame or a chance at being a celebrity. "Fame can't be your motivating factor, because you can work hard your whole life and fall through the cracks without anyone ever taking notice."

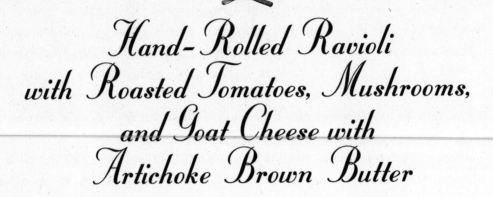

Hand-Rolled Ravioli with Roasted Tomatoes, Mushrooms, and Goat Cheese with Artichoke Brown Butter

Chef's note: *I was on an endless search for the perfect meatless starter when I came up with this ravioli, a dish that has the textures and visual appeal I was looking for. It is now so popular that I cannot remove it from the menu. The flavors are complex—raisins for sweetness, goat cheese for tanginess—without being overbearing. And the simple sauce doesn't mask the delicate vegetables it is meant to highlight.*

Pasta

(Serves 6 as a starter)
Four 12-inch fresh pasta sheets, 3 inches wide (At the restaurant we
    make our own, but there are some awesome fresh products at
    specialty markets.)
1 egg, beaten (to make an egg wash)
Salt

Filling

½ cup Roma tomatoes, cut into bite-size pieces and dry-roasted
1 tablespoon roasted garlic paste
½ cup rough-chopped spinach, squeezed free of any excess liquid
1½ teaspoons pomace or light olive oil
1½ cups sliced fresh shiitake mushrooms
Salt and white pepper to taste
¼ cup grated aged goat cheese
½ cup ricotta, preferably goat's-milk ricotta
1 tablespoon chopped golden raisins
1 tablespoon chopped fresh basil

1. While you dry-roast the tomatoes and roast the garlic, blanch, shock, and chop the spinach, then squeeze it free of any excess liquid.
2. Heat pomace. Sauté mushrooms until tender. Season with salt and white pepper.
3. Combine tomatoes, garlic, cheeses, raisins, basil, and mushrooms in a medium bowl, season, and chill for 30 minutes.

Assembly

4. On a dry surface lay out 1 sheet of fresh pasta. Using a pastry brush, lightly cover the entire surface with a thin layer of egg wash. Using roughly 2 tablespoons of filling, place 6 oblong (tightly packed) mounds of filling evenly spaced over the surface of the pasta. Make sure you allow at least 1½ inches of space between mounds.
5. Carefully lay another sheet of pasta over the mounds. Gently press the pasta sheets together, making a secure, air-free seal over each mound. Using a chef's knife, cut each ravioli free from the others. Repeat with the remaining 2 pasta sheets to make 6 more ravioli.
6. Store on a lightly floured surface in the refrigerator until you are ready to cook.
7. Bring 3½ quarts of salted water to a boil. Carefully add the 12 pieces of ravioli. Cook for 3 to 4 minutes at a gentle simmer. Remove. Place 2 ravioli in each bowl and top with Artichoke Brown Butter.

Artichoke Brown Butter

2 artichoke bottoms (After all the leaves have been removed, use a paring
    knife to cut all the dark green from the base and stem of the choke.)
½ cup dry white wine
3 cloves garlic, cut into thin slivers
30 picked fresh sage leaves
4 ounces (½ cup) unsalted butter
Salt and white pepper to taste

For garnish

2 tablespoons freshly grated Parmesan cheese
1 tablespoon chopped parsley

1. Place the artichoke bottoms in a medium-sized pot. Cover with wine and ½ cup water. Simmer until tender.

2. Place the artichoke bottoms, garlic, sage leaves, and butter in a small sauté pan and cook slowly, stirring until the butter begins to gently brown. Season with salt and white pepper.

3. Divide the ravioli evenly among the plates. Top each portion of ravioli with a little of each garnish and a drizzle of butter.

✳ GETTING STARTED: ✳
PROJECTING AN ACCURATE BUDGET

When it comes to opening a restaurant, most people underbudget. Perhaps they don't allocate enough for construction, or they fail to anticipate that restaurants can take at least six months to find an audience, or both. Here, **Karen Karp**—coauthor of *Gourmet-to-Go: A Guide to Owning and Operating a Specialty Food Store* and founder of Karp Resources, a consulting company that counts several restaurants and food specialty companies among its clients—addresses eight areas in which underbudgeting frequently occurs, and offers suggestions on how you might avoid some common pitfalls.

Business Plan

Very few people actually write their own business plan, because they're too close to the information to be effective. So when you're projecting start-up expenses, you'll want to factor in the money it costs to pay someone to write your business plan. Business plans can run anywhere between $10,000 and $20,000 depending on the extent of the project (concept, total capital investment, and legal or partnership structure), the knowledge base of the client, and how much the client himself or herself can contribute to the plan (research, writing, etc.).

Legal and Accounting

Legal expenses will include negotiation and preparation of the lease, incorporation, and partnership papers—all of which (except, perhaps, incorporation) can happen several times before an agreement for the location and deal you ultimately get is final. For example, I have a client who has in excess of $75,000 in legal expenses for a project that, after three years, did not happen due to an unresolvable issue in the partnership agreement.

Construction

This line item always goes over budget. After you have picked a bid, have the contractor *guarantee* the bid. And even with this precaution, you still must plan a contingency in your budget for overages (15 to 20 percent is recommended).

Design and Architecture

Some concepts don't need a "big" design—they're well suited to a coat of paint and mix-and-match furniture. But anytime you are executing a "concept" restaurant, design is a key element, and it costs money. Plan accordingly. (For more on design, see page 100.)

Graphic Design

Often, people underbudget for design and architecture, either because they have a "friend" who wants to design the place or because they figure that they themselves can assist the architect so much that it won't cost a lot. When it comes to graphic design (cards, matches, press kits, menus, and postcards) the pitfalls are pretty much the same as for architecture and design, except there is much less money at stake when you hire someone to do a professional job. Printing costs are also frequently left out of the plan.

Preopening Rent

If you have to pay rent while you are renovating, it is very costly. See if you can negotiate for free rent while you renovate, or have the landlord contribute to the renovation. (See Bobby Flay's Story, page 205; and Elephant Walk, page 131.)

Staff Training

You will need your staff working prior to opening, so be sure to factor their wages and salaries into your budget. Depending on the size of the venture, chefs and managers can be on board up to six months before opening; kitchen staff, one to two weeks; floor staff, one week. And there are payroll taxes on top of that! Many new restaurateurs forget to add payroll taxes onto their payroll budget, for pre-opening as well as operating budgets.

Working Capital

Increasingly, new owners seem to know that they have to prepare sales and expense projections. Nonetheless, many still experience cash flow problems and underestimate expenses, particularly those related to food and staff.

- Working capital cash flow: The best restaurants take about six months to build up business and work out the operating kinks before they approach breakeven (unless you are an instant hit—and then, after the dust settles, you may have the problem in reverse). You need to budget for losses during this period. To estimate the amount of money you will need to make it through the first year, project and add up the net losses for each of the first twelve months and add to that a contingency amount of 5 to 15 percent.

- Food cost: If the new owner is a chef, he or she will possibly have a handle on the food cost from a previous venture, but many don't factor in what it takes to maintain appropriate cost of goods sold—from storing food to pricing the menu and figuring out portion sizes. To maintain food costs: (1) Determine what percentage of sales you want your food costs to be. The acceptable standard is 25 to 33 percent. (2) Create a recipe for each dish, cost out each of the ingredients in the dish, and then add up what it will cost to put that recipe on a plate. It is crucial to purchase wisely. Ask yourself which vendors will sell you the products you want at prices that will help you stick to your projected food costs. (3) Factor in a percentage for food that will get eaten by staff, trimmings of food that is being prepared, mistakes, spoilage, food that falls to the floor, and other waste. (4) Factor in the all-important (and often neglected) menu mix: How many of each dish is going to sell? Remember, it is important to monitor what's selling to be sure that a good number of lower-cost dishes are being sold along with those great but costly dishes that raise your food costs.

- Staff: As a consultant, I make all my clients do at least one full staff schedule: I ask them to imagine a complete week and then get them to itemize the number of people per staff position they will need to make the restaurant work. We factor in how much these people will get paid, how many hours per day and per week they will work, whether or not they will get benefits, etc. We add all this up. On top of that, we then add company payroll tax liabilities and disability and workers' compensation, where applicable. The gross number usually surprises the client.

Sometimes this staff forecasting exercise will make people reconsider the size or layout of the kitchen, the menu, or the hours of operation. This is an example of how the planning process can define the concept and why—especially for the least experienced people—it is important, and often a cost savings (in the end), to have support from the start.

Bobby Flay

THE CHEF AS ENTREPRENEUR

Bobby Flay

Before he turned thirty, Bobby Flay, winner of the James Beard Rising Star Chef of the Year award, had accumulated the accolades most chefs only dream of. In 1991, at the age of twenty-six, he and his partners opened the critically acclaimed Mesa Grill, where he created southwestern-influenced dishes full of flair, such as shrimp and roasted garlic corn tamale and grilled loin lamb chops with jalapeño preserves. In his spare time, he wrote a beautifully designed, award-winning cookbook, Bobby Flay's Bold American Food. With a few additional years under his belt, he also has television shows to his credit—Hot off the Grill with Bobby Flay and Grillin' and Chillin' and Lifetime Television's The Main Ingredient with Bobby Flay. Between his television shows, the cookbooks, and merchandising, Flay represents not only the chef as celebrity but also the chef as entrepreneur.

When Gary Goldberg, a restaurant consultant and director of The New School's Culinary Arts program, reflects on the reasons restaurants fail (see page 236), he lists disagreement among partners as one of the leading factors. When things are running smoothly, colleagues have the highest regard for each other. When equipment breaks down, sales slip, or reviews are unfavorable, the problems begin to multiply and fights seem inevitable. Fortunately, Bobby Flay has not had to contend with a partnership gone wrong. The first set of investors to approach Flay about opening a restaurant offered him the kind of deal Goldberg would endorse—a partnership where responsibilities are divided up early and unambiguously. But Flay didn't meet his dream team right away. First he had to establish his reputation as a cook worth the investment.

Unlike many established chefs working today, Flay wasn't born with a desire to cook. He didn't grow up idolizing James Beard; nor was he planning dinner parties at age sixteen. In fact, had he done better in high school, he might never have set foot into a professional kitchen. But given his high school performance—"I got kicked out, dropped out, the whole gamut"—Flay's dad more or less vetoed college and instead helped him get a job at Joe Allen's, a popular restaurant in New York City's theater district.

Within months, Flay went from being a young man who lacked focus and hated the kitchen to one who was actually self-motivated and inspired by his work. The transformation was so complete that in 1984, after a year and a half at Joe Allen's, Flay decided to go to a cooking school, the French Culinary Institute (FCI). The FCI has a top-rated, star-studded faculty and administration (which now includes Jacques Pépin, Alain Sailhac, André Soltner, and Jacques Torres, and visiting dean Alice Waters), and its alumni typically have many job options. Flay, one of the FCI's first alumni, was no exception. Shortly after graduating in 1984, he went to work at Bud's with Jonathan Waxman, a chef who has mentored and inspired many of Flay's contemporaries. Flay admired Waxman because he was one of "the first people to bring California cuisine to New York." But it was Waxman's way with southwestern ingredients—chile peppers and blue corn tortillas—that impressed Flay the most. "I fell in love with the textures, the colors, and the flavors."

As Flay's reputation started to grow, another restaurant group invited him to be the chef at a Mexican restaurant they planned to open. Already thinking like an entrepreneur, he suggested that a southwestern restaurant would have more potential than a Mexican one, as more and more people were traveling to New Mexico and falling under the spell of things southwestern. Besides, Flay reasoned, "with the exception of Brendan Walsh, who was heading up the kitchen at Arizona 206, nobody was really doing southwestern food in New York City." The owners took Flay's advice, and he stayed at the very progressive Miracle Grill—a restaurant that still has a devoted following—from 1988 until 1990, when he met Jerry Kretchmer, owner of the Gotham Bar and Grill. "Kretchmer had taken a trip to the Southwest, and he wanted to open a southwestern restaurant." When Kretchmer started searching for a chef with whom he could form a partnership and launch a new place, everybody pointed to Bobby Flay. The ultimate success of Kretchmer and Flay's partnership, as described below, is a textbook case of how to do nearly everything right when it comes to opening a restaurant.

When Flay met Kretchmer and his two partners, including his son Laurence—a general contractor with a degree in real estate—to talk about how they might structure a deal, Kretchmer told Flay that they didn't want to be silent financial partners. Instead, they wanted a genuine partnership, where everyone would have something specific to contribute. "'We're partners,' they told me. 'Together, we'll raise the money, we'll find the space, and we'll help design the restaurant. We'll do this *together* from start to finish, so that we're all in it to win it.'" With this structure everybody got to bring his expertise to the table. While Flay started to conceptualize a menu, the other three put their real estate and banking backgrounds to work. For Flay the partnership got off to a good start because each individual complemented the others' skills:

> When my partners go to a bank to borrow money, they know who to talk to and how to make the deal. And when we're building the restaurants, Laurence, the contractor, is right there overseeing things. It saves so much time and money. As an example, we built Mesa Grill in six weeks. When you're paying $30,000 a month rent, it helps to get those restaurants open right away because you have to pay rent while you're building, which means you have no incoming revenue.

Beyond cooking, financial, and building responsibilities, they also divvied up management. Flay would manage the food, beverages, and kitchen employees; and Laurence would work as the general manager, which means among other things that front-of-the-house managers reported to him. Laurence was also to be in charge of reconciling each day's business.

* * *

With the partners' roles clearly and unambiguously defined, Flay fined-tuned the food concept. The four had already decided on a southwestern menu, but Flay refined that concept even more: bold, simple, colorful food that would combine basic ingredients in novel ways. A perfect example is Flay's Sweet Potato–Chipotle Soup, a recipe published in *Bold American Food.* The ingredients are simple—honey, onions, and sweet potato, for example—and with the exception of the bold, smoky flavor of the chipotle, not very exotic. Yet the finished dish is uniquely delicious.

With a firm idea of a menu in mind, the partners began looking for the right location. After considering several neighborhoods in Manhattan, they ultimately put down roots in an area south of the landmark Flatiron building. In 1991, though the area wasn't totally deserted, it wasn't the mecca for restaurants that it is today. Still, the rents were relatively affordable and they could see that the Flatiron District was on the rise. But they weren't the first ones there. "I didn't want to be Gorbachev, because you get no credit for trailblazing."

Once the building and the design of the space were under way, the team searched for front-of-the-house staff who could provide good service. (For more on scouting a location, see page 144; for more on offering excellent service, see page 238.) With everything in place—management team, menu, a colorful and vibrantly designed space, and a staff—Mesa Grill opened its doors. Despite an ominous beginning—the opening night coincided with the onset of the Gulf War—the business got off to a fantastic start. There was good word-of-mouth buzz almost instantly, and the reviews were enthusiastic.

Three years after opening Mesa Grill, Flay and his partners decided to capitalize on their success and open a second restaurant. The end result would have two effects. First, if things went well, it would contribute to the group's bottom line. Beyond that, it would give the press another opportunity to write about Flay and his partners. Fully committed to the idea of another restaurant, Flay and his team began brainstorming concepts:

I didn't want to do an Italian trattoria, and I was definitely not going to do a French bistro, because they were on every block. Spanish food, on the other hand, wasn't represented at all in New York City, except for all the seventy-dollar-per-person high-end restaurants that sprang up after the Olympics in Barcelona.

The only other kind of Spanish restaurant to be found, according to Flay, was the old-fashioned, red-and-white-tablecloth place that served overcooked paella and red sangria. There was nothing in the middle. So the group decided to serve "Spanish" food at their next restaurant. After a reconnaissance mission to Spain, Flay designed a menu that borrowed from, and called itself, Spanish cuisine but was in fact his own take on it. A typical dish might be something traditionally Spanish, like his oven-roasted baby shrimp with toasted garlic chips or paprika-spiced fillet of striped bass. Alternatively, some dishes were Flay's imaginative variations on traditional Spanish dishes. "Authenticity is out the window. I'm feeding New Yorkers; I'm not feeding people from Madrid. So I make adjustments and come up with dishes such as Sea Scallop Ceviche with Grilled Red Onion and Mango-Tortilla Salad." In the interim, while Flay was designing the menu, the team's real estate experts set about finding and building a space for Bolo, as they christened their new restaurant. Its opening, in November 1993, did indeed give the critics something new and positive to write about, and it taught Flay an important lesson: "Being in the media is really important, though you don't want to get oversaturated because then they stop writing about you forever. I try to find a way to keep myself in six-month cycles with the media."

From the example of Flay and his group, a philosophy of restaurateuring can be pieced together: Chefs looking to make the transition to chef-owner should first find the right partnership. But be warned that not every partnership is structured like that of the Kretchmers and Flay. There are two scenarios, in particular, that Flay advises chefs to question seriously before committing themselves to a deal. "There is the 'let's get four hundred partners together with everybody getting one percent' scenario. That's a bad situation because everybody thinks he owns the restaurant. They all bring their friends in and they want to eat free." According to Flay, this kind of structure isn't financially viable, especially in an industry where investors see only eight cents out of every dollar earned. (The other ninety to ninety-two cents goes toward rent, food, flowers, payroll, insurance, etc.) Then there's another common boilerplate deal, where the money is half and the talent is half. The money comes from an investor, someone with all the money and no face. In this kind of arrangement, if the restaurant costs $1 million, the investor puts up *all* the money and gets *half* of the ownership. The chef gets the other half, the sweat equity. Flay is very suspicious of these types of deals:

Money is easy. Talent—that's the difficult part. So whenever a young chef calls me and asks for a few moments of my time to talk about going into business with someone, I always say, "Don't sell yourself short. You've got what they want. You can go somewhere else and get what they have."

The most important point here is that chefs shouldn't sign a deal just to jump-start their career without considering all the variables closely. Once they've found the deal that fits what they're looking for, they should then design a menu, find a location, hire a manager who can train the front-of-the-house staff in the art of good service, and pay attention to the media.

Another cornerstone of Flay's philosophy is that a chef has to think and act both as an entrepreneur and as a cook. This tenet should inform everything a cook does, from designing a menu to branching out wherever possible, as Flay has done. In addition to his restaurants, he has revenue coming in from the sales of his cookbooks (*Bold American Food* was followed by *Bobby Flay's From My Kitchen to Your Table* and *Boy Meets Grill*), his television shows, and his line of barbecue and hot sauces. Through each segment of the business, he is able to cross-promote another. As a result of his cross-promoting, his status as a television celebrity, his cookbooks, and his products, Flay has been able to make a pretty comfortable living; his entrepreneurial urges have paid off. But just because he and a few of his peers—such as Emeril Lagasse, Paul Prudhomme, Wolfgang Puck, and Jean-Georges Vongerichten—have turned their love of cooking into notable financial successes doesn't mean every entrepreneurially inclined chef will see equal returns on his or her efforts. According to one survey, for chefs ten years out of cooking school, the average salary is between $41,000 and $65,000 per year. According to another survey, done in 1995, executive chefs average $38,000 per year.[21] This explains why, when Flay advises people to choose their partners wisely and to think entrepreneurially, he offers one other key piece of advice. To be happy in this business, "you need more than the desire to make money. You need passion, because even if you do everything right—if you combine good business sense with passion—you still may not make it."

Bobby Flay and Mesa Grill's

Sweet Potato Soup with Smoked Chiles and Blue and Gold Corn Tortillas

Chef's note: *People are always surprised by this thick, rich, orange-gold soup—the food writer Gael Greene has called it "pure beta-carotene." If you like, you can cut the amount of cream in half, but the consistency will change. The result will be a good but different dish.*

(Serves 8)
2 tablespoons unsalted butter
1 medium onion, coarsely cut
2 garlic cloves
3 medium sweet potatoes, peeled and quartered
4 cups chicken stock or water
½ cup plus 2 tablespoons honey
½ cup crème fraîche or heavy cream
2 tablespoons pureed canned chipotles
Salt and freshly ground pepper to taste

Garnish

2 cups peanut oil
Two 6-inch blue-corn tortillas, cut into squares
Two 6-inch yellow-corn tortillas, cut into squares

1. In a large saucepan over medium heat, melt the butter and sweat the onion and garlic for 5 minutes or until translucent. Raise the heat to high, add the sweet potatoes and stock, and bring to a boil. Lower the heat to medium and simmer for about 30 minutes.

2. Remove from the heat and add the honey, crème fraîche, pureed chipotles, and salt and pepper to taste. Puree in a food processor and set aside. *May be made up to 2 days ahead to this point. Refrigerate. Reheat before serving.*

3. In a saucepan over medium heat, heat the peanut oil to 360°F. or until a tortilla square sizzles when immersed. Fry the tortilla for about 30 seconds, drain on paper towels, and set aside. *May be made up to 1 day ahead.*

4. Divide the soup among 8 bowls. Sprinkle each with a handful of crumbled tortilla squares. Serve warm.

Bobby Flay's

Sea Scallop Ceviche with Grilled Red Onion and Mango-Tortilla Salad

Chef's note: *Contrary to what people think, ceviche does not mean raw seafood—citrus juices "cook" the scallops enzymatically. The sweet scallops, juicy mangoes, grilled onion rings, and crisp fried tortillas give this beautiful dish lots of color and texture.*

Everything in this salad can be done ahead: grill the onions, fry the tortillas, dice the mangoes, and marinate the scallops up to 1 day before serving, and combine all the ingredients at the last minute.

(Serves 8)
24 large sea scallops, about 1½ pounds, halved
2 cups fresh orange juice
2 cups fresh lime juice
2 cups fresh lemon juice
2 medium red onions, peeled and cut into thick slices
2 cups peanut or canola oil
6 blue corn tortillas, cut into fine julienne strips
2 small mangoes, peeled and diced
4 tablespoons finely chopped chives
2 tablespoons honey

Citrus Vinaigrette (recipe follows)
Salt and pepper
2 medium limes, peeled, sectioned, and membrane removed
2 medium oranges, peeled, sectioned, and membrane removed

Ceviche

1. In a bowl, combine the scallops with the orange, lime, and lemon juices. Refrigerate, covered, for 2 hours or up to 1 day.
2. Prepare a grill or preheat a broiler. Grill or broil the onion slices until just marked, about 2 minutes for each side. Reserve at room temperature.
3. Heat the oil in a large sauté pan over medium-high heat until it begins to smoke, and fry the tortilla strips until crisp, about 30 seconds. Drain on paper towels.
4. Just before serving the scallops, drain off as much citrus juice as possible and add the mangoes, chives, honey, citrus vinaigrette, and salt and pepper to taste. Gently mix in the lime and orange sections, being careful not to break them.
5. To serve, place the onion rings in the center of a larger platter, and using them as support, stand the tortillas in the middle. Surround with the scallop and fruit mixture. Sprinkle with pepper and serve immediately.

Citrus Vinaigrette

Chef's note: May be used over any kind of grilled fish; it will bring out all the natural juices.

¼ cup fresh orange juice
¼ cup fresh lemon juice
¼ cup fresh lime juice
2 fresh basil leaves, cut into chiffonade
1 tablespoon finely chopped red onions

2 cups pure olive oil
salt and pepper

Combine the juices, basil leaves, and onion in a blender and blend until smooth. With the motor running, slowly add the oil until emulsified. Season to taste with salt and pepper. May be refrigerated up to 1 day. Bring to room temperature before using.

* DESIGNING PROFITABLE MENUS— *
ADVICE FROM AN EXPERT

According to **Linda Lipsky,** a restaurant and hospitality consultant who has advised hundreds of clients, from mom-and-pop cafés to white-tablecloth dining rooms to restaurant chains, "A flashy menu that doesn't generate sales is like a race car without an engine. . . . Nice to look at, but it won't pay the bills." Here, Lipsky offers suggestions on how restaurateurs can design eye-catching menus that highlight and promote the most profitable items.

Seasonal Offerings
Change your menu at least twice a year to ensure that you are offering the most cost-effective ingredients during each season. Don't get caught offering asparagus in the middle of winter.

Sell Extras
Use every area of the menu (without cluttering it) to market your extensive product line, including specialty cocktails, wines by the glass, nonalcoholic and after-dinner beverages, salads, sides, and desserts. A wine list, if it is extensive, should be included on a separate menu.

Costing and Recipes
Do your homework when selecting menu items and finalizing the recipes. *Write* every recipe, and cost out every ingredient in it. Until this is done, you'll never be able to max-

imize your profits. There are now many software products available to help cost out your recipes, which can expedite the process.

Pricing Survey

Check the competition before you set your menu prices, and make sure you are comparing apples with apples. You and a competitor may both be offering grilled lamb chops, but this doesn't mean that the portion is the same or the overall quality is comparable. Use both cost data and competitive data before you lock in your menu prices.

Design

There are three ways to draw attention to the high-profit items—through the use of colors, icons, and typefaces. Consider designing a menu with three distinct colors of ink: one to highlight the headers ("starters"), a second to list standard menu items, and a third to distinguish special, high-profit menu items within each section. Icons can also be used to highlight the more profitable menu items and signature dishes. Typeface is another option. In much the same way as you could use three colors of ink, choose three different typefaces.

In-House Printing

Whenever possible, keep your menu flexible by printing it in house. Your ability to edit and revise your menu and keep things fresh at your restaurant will be perceived positively. Menu covers usually have to be ordered from an outside source. As with every ingredient on your menu, be sure to get several competitive bids for the menu covers as well. Also, be aware that there are many paper companies, which can provide you predesigned menu insert pages in a variety of colors, styles, and sizes. By choosing one of these predesigned products, you'll save on design fees.

Legibility

Legibility is crucial. If the customers can't read your menu, the targeted menu items won't sell. So be careful when choosing the typeface, leading (space between the lines), ink, and paper color, and make sure there is enough color contrast between the paper and the ink. Factor in the impact of your dining room lighting.

User-Friendliness

Don't intimidate your customers by excessive use of foreign phrases (without explanations) on your menu. This will keep some guests from ordering these items, since the ingredients and preparations are unknown to them. No one wants to feel ignorant, especially when he or she is paying for the privilege.

For more information on how to reach Linda Lipsky, see Appendix D.

＊

✳ CLEVER MENUS—MORE ADVICE ✳
FROM THE EXPERTS

According to another expert, **Gary Goldberg**—restaurant consultant and director of **The New School's Culinary Arts** program, poorly conceived menus are one of the prime reasons restaurants close: "The menu sets the tone for nearly everything else in the dining room." You can't design a kitchen or a dining room, let alone hire a chef (if you're an investor), until you've figured out the menu. And yet many people start restaurants without having a fully fleshed idea of what they're going to serve and at what level.

After you come up with the concept, you have to design a menu that is both cost-effective and capable of catching the customer's eye. Like Linda Lipsky, Goldberg has several tips on how to position the menu aesthetically so that it's a menu that *sells* dishes rather than a menu that merely lists them.

Design a Well-Thought-Out Menu

- Limit your ingredients. Ingredients used in one dish should be used in others. Serving a shrimp bisque? Add grilled shrimp to the menu as well.
- Limit the price spread on your menu to no more than 40 percent. For instance, if the least expensive item is $8, the most expensive should be no more than $14.
- Pick a specific theme. It's not enough these days to say Italian or Mexican. You have to be specific. Is it Tuscan or pizza? Is it gourmet Mexican or Tex-Mex?

Direct the Customer's Eye

There are several ways you can direct the customer's eye toward specific items.

- Provide a prix-fixe menu.
- Highlight signature dishes with icons or boxes.
- Use a separate dessert menu.
- Never use light lettering on a dark background.
- Avoid exotic typefaces.
- Use a *color* stock that complements the decor of your restaurant.
- Consider the lighting conditions in which your menu will be read.
- Leave approximately 50 percent margin space.

Frank Brigtsen

FROM PRUDHOMME'S ASSISTANT
TO SAVVY RESTAURATEUR

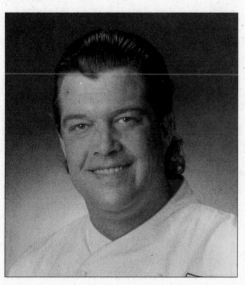

Only two things might appeal to Frank Brigtsen, owner and executive chef of the four-star restaurant Brigtsen's in New Orleans, more than creating Creole-Acadian dishes: watching the sun rise over the Louisiana bayou before he goes fishing on his day off or hosting a backyard crawfish boil for friends and family. Brigtsen won the 1998 James Beard Foundation Award for best chef in the Southeast, and his story is a regional one. But it's more than that. It's also a story of how one chef went from cook to entrepreneur and—in one lean year—from restaurateur to savvy businessman.

When the restaurant Brigtsen's got its first review, Frank Brigtsen was floored. "Absolutely floored." To this day, he can remember one line in particular: "Brigtsen's is now the place against which all other restaurants serving south Louisiana cuisine will have to be measured."[22] "I said to myself, 'Wow, I'm really a cook.' To me that was a hard climb."

It all began in 1973 at Louisiana State University, Baton Rouge, where Brigtsen was pursuing an MFA in printmaking and painting. As has been the case with so many cooks in *If You Can Stand the Heat*, Brigtsen worked at a local restaurant while he was in college simply to make money. Before long, however, he was spending more time at work than he was at school, and by 1978 he realized that he had to choose one or the other. He chose work.

Rather than stay in Baton Rouge, he decided to return to New Orleans, where he had been born and raised. As he scanned the want ads one day, he came across a job opening at Commander's Palace, one of the preeminent New Orleans restaurants. Within hours of responding to the ad, he was sitting across from the executive chef, Paul Prudhomme. In several one-hour interviews, in which Prudhomme tried to learn not only what Brigtsen could do on a grill but also what he wanted out of life, Prudhomme gave Brigtsen a choice. He could work as a line cook, and a lot would be expected of him. Or he could apprentice and, in return, expect a lot out of Prudhomme. Because Commander's was very busy and Brigtsen had no real experience in a serious restaurant, he knew he wasn't ready to be a line cook. So, at the age of twenty-four, he became an apprentice, earning the minimum wage.

The move would prove to be smart for two reasons. First, it exposed Brigtsen to high-volume gourmet food. "They served top-quality food to six to seven hundred people a day for dinner." While big volume wasn't something he wanted to do for the rest of his life, he figured it would be a solid skill to have: "When you have that experience under your belt, you realize just how manageable any place can be." He also found a mentor, a development Brigtsen thinks is integral to the growth of any chef:

> *If you are interested in the culinary profession and you have the opportunity to go to school, do it. But in combination with that, the best thing you can do is find a mentor, not only a chef whose work you admire, but also a person whom you like and can get along with. And whoever that person might be, get a commitment both ways.*

Theirs was a two-way commitment: Paul Prudhomme taught Brigtsen about the fundamentals of cooking and Cajun food, and in return, Brigtsen gave Prudhomme all of his attention, hard work, and allegiance.

Prudhomme's lessons were both metaphysical and pragmatic. First and foremost, he gave Brigtsen a love of and respect for food. "Paul taught me things like when you're in a busy restaurant kitchen and you drop an oyster on the floor, you've wasted a life, that oyster lived its whole life for nothing, because now it's in the trash." To this day, Brigtsen honors this notion of the inviolability of food by being active in local and state environmental issues and working with culinary and environmental groups like **Oldways** and **Chefs Collaborative 2000** (see page 157).

Beyond this reverence for food, Prudhomme schooled him in the practical aspects of being a cook. Brigtsen started out as a prep cook, and as he was prepping strawberries one day, two sauté cooks failed to show up for Commander's jazz brunch. With up to eight hundred people per brunch, it was the single busiest shift. Frantic, "the line cooks turned to me and asked, 'Frank, do you know how to make an omelet?' I had never made one in my life. They'd ask again every twenty minutes. Well, come ten-thirty A.M., I was over on the omelet station. A few of the omelets hit the grill, but the ones that went out were pretty good, I thought." Prudhomme must have thought so too, because not long after that, he asked Brigtsen how he felt about sauces. It was a rhetorical question—Prudhomme's way of letting Brigtsen know that he had just been promoted again, this time to saucier.

Brigtsen continued to work with Prudhomme at Commander's until 1980, when Prudhomme asked him to move to K-Paul's Louisiana Kitchen, "a businessperson's place for lunch." For the first eight months of K-Paul's life, Prudhomme ran between Commander's Palace and K-Paul's. But the new restaurant's reception was so phenomenal that he decided to add a dinner menu and a new chef—Brigtsen. From this point on, Brigtsen's relationship with Prudhomme and his understanding of Cajun food grew geometrically. "Prudhomme would go to K-Paul's at five in the morning and set up lunch there. I would come in about ten-thirty A.M., and we would talk over the menu. Then he would leave to go to his job at Commander's." It was a heady time for Prudhomme and, by extension, for Brigtsen:

> When he got hired at Commander's, Paul made the front page of the Times-Picayune *because there was no such thing as an American chef. It was an oxy-*

moron. And to have a local boy, a Cajun boy at that, have an executive chef position, it was newsworthy. And during those first years at K-Paul's, we saw the whole phenomenon of American regional food and Cajun food take the nation by storm. The early eighties were an amazing time—not only for me personally, but I think for food and chefs in America.

It would have been a phenomenal experience for any neophyte chef to work so closely with one of America's great chefs, but it was all the more formative for Brigtsen because he never went to culinary school. Essentially, his mind was a clean slate, ready to absorb all Prudhomme had to offer. "It was to my advantage that I didn't have a strong culinary background or education, because the only things I really knew were the things he taught me." Apart from reverence for food and the technical aspects of the different positions in the kitchen, Prudhomme's lessons were quintessentially Cajun, starting off with the origins of Cajun food:

> *Historically, it's really French country cooking—the food of people of this earth—farmers, sharecroppers, and fishermen. It's home cooking or pot cooking, and it often used the least desirable ingredients. Since the nice chickens were sold to the market, they might cook that old rooster who is not doing his job anymore.*

Beyond the origins of Cajun food, Prudhomme taught Brigtsen how to reinvent it into restaurant fare. Part of Prudhomme's genius lay in knowing that not everyone's taste runs to old roosters. While some ingredients were adapted for the restaurant patron—the old rooster was exchanged for a spring chicken, for instance—there were ingredients that Prudhomme struggled to keep as authentic as possible. Initially that meant introducing new foods into the New Orleans metropolitan area. Though andouille and boudin sausages may have been available before Prudhomme began his illustrious career, he was among the first to introduce tasso—a spicy aged smoked pork seasoning meat. And rather than settle for readily available substitutes, he also brought in many vegetables and spices, such as baby squash, squash blossoms, and freshly ground gumbo filé (sassafras leaves). Prudhomme "would just go knock on people's doors and ask, 'Would you grow this for me?'" As a result of his pioneering diligence, people all over the world, not just natives of new Orleans, know about Prudhomme.

* * *

After seven years of absorbing Prudhomme's respect for food, his deep-seated knowledge about Cajun food, and his passionate insistence on authentic, high-quality ingredients, Brigtsen decided to open a restaurant of his own. In 1986, he and his wife, Marna, converted a shotgun cottage built in the 1890s into a three-room, sixty-seat restaurant called Brigtsen's. The idea, or concept, was to serve *Acadian* food—"Acadian" being the word from which Cajun was bastardized. By using the original word, Brigtsen hoped to convey that his menu would be more authentic and more mindful of the traditions of the French people who came from Nova Scotia to Louisiana than the food served by the many imitation Cajun restaurants that had followed in the wake of Prudhomme's success.

At his own place, Brigtsen hoped to redress the popular misconception that all Cajun food is hot. Rather, Cajun food should be well seasoned, Brigtsen argues. For example, when Brigtsen uses pepper, he uses a *combination* of cayenne, black, and white pepper, because each one affects the palate differently:

> *Black pepper affects you toward the forward part of your palate—your lips and the tip of your tongue—and it hits you right away. White pepper sort of goes a little past that, toward the back of your throat, even in your sinuses a little bit. And cayenne gives a nice warm glow all the way down, to the deeper part of your throat. So what really happens when you're eating food that has three peppers in it, even if it's not a really hot dish, is that those peppers are working on your palate, making you salivate and jump and say, "Oh, man, that's so good."*

And for Brigtsen, building complexity of taste and depth of flavor is one of the main characteristics of southern Louisiana cuisine.

This complexity and depth get translated into Gratin of Louisiana Oysters with B&B, Spinach, Italian Sausage, and Romano Cheese; blackened yellowfin tuna with smoked corn sauce and red bean salsa; and the delicious roast pork loin with sweet potato dirty rice and pork debris sauce. These are not only dishes that Brigtsen creates as chef de cuisine, but dishes that he still executes as a line cook, twelve years after opening Brigtsen's.

Though Brigtsen could walk away from the line and pursue other avenues, such as merchandising, television, or cookbooks, his respect for the work is so great that he can't imagine being anywhere else. "I line-cook because I love it and because my name is on the door. People consider this my place, and they expect my food. If I'm not doing that, what am I doing? Cooking grounds me. It gives me the happiness I seek in this business."

As owner, however, Brigtsen has one other responsibility that is no less pressing than cooking: maintaining the restaurant's financial stability. He can't even imagine doing this without the accountant with whom he works very closely, Beauregard Parent, a professor of accounting at Tulane University. "When I opened the restaurant, I knew I was a pretty good chef, but I didn't know anything about the business." So Parent developed a financial statement, which the two review every month. Beyond profit and loss, the statement also includes key statistical histories: among others, how many business days Brigtsen's is open per year, how many meals are served per open day, the check average, and the check average per person. Brigtsen has found that the number of people who set foot into his restaurant to eat (the restaurant's bar isn't accessible to the public) is the figure that drives his bottom line. Unfortunately, he found that out the hard way.

During the recession of 1993, Brigtsen's lost money. After reviewing the books with Parent, Brigtsen realized that if they had served only ten more people per night, he would have broken even. Consequently, Brigtsen and Parent began monitoring the number of people served each evening. In the process, Brigtsen has learned that the reservationist has one of the most crucial jobs in his restaurant. "If we're booked at seven-thirty, eight P.M., which we are pretty much all the time, then we have to sell the nine or six-thirty time slot." Getting people to be flexible about when they dine can turn a financially disastrous year into a profitable one. For example, the average check at Brigtsen's totals $40 per person. If the reservationist persuades ten more people to come in at a time different from what they initially requested, the restaurant grosses an additional $400 per night. With approximately 250 open nights a year, that amounts to $100,000 more revenue annually. But getting those extra people is not as easy as it looks. Part of the problem is no-shows, or what Brigtsen calls attrition:

> Attrition is when a party of six becomes a party of four. It's people calling half an hour before their reservation saying they can't make it because their plans changed. It's human nature. And you have to build it into your plans. If you

don't, you're not being realistic. Tonight, we have 147 reservations. If we do 125, I'll be very happy. You can counteract by overbooking. We don't because we just don't have the physical room to play. But if you have 200 seats, you might be able to juggle with it more.

To overcome this natural attrition, Brigtsen came up with another way to boost income and the customer count—the originally controversial $14.95 "early evening special."

Four years after Brigtsen's opened, and having earned as many years of glowing reviews—four stars from *Menu* magazine, Five Beans (highest) from the *Times-Picayune*, Chef of the Year from *New Orleans* magazine, and others—Brigtsen did what was then unthinkable. He put an ad in the paper announcing an early-evening special. This was so *déclassé* that one critic called to warn him that gourmet white-tablecloth restaurants didn't offer early-bird specials, and that it would tarnish his image, perhaps even turn away regular customers. But Brigtsen was philosophically committed to it. "Some people can't afford to spend thirty-five to forty dollars per meal. But they can afford to spend twenty dollars. It's something I want to do for the locals, for the people who would like to eat here more often without spending as much money. It also brings new people in," people who may later return for the more expensive menu. Another business advantage is that the steady stream of locals evens out the seasonality of doing business in a place like New Orleans.

Financially, as Brigtsen and Parent concluded, it made perfect sense. "Tuesdays through Thursdays, we're standing around until seven P.M. before we get a table." Yet from 5:30 P.M. until then, the restaurant is already fully staffed, and carrying insurance and other fixed costs such as gas, electricity, and flowers. Why not get what Parent calls "revenue contribution" by offering a meal that's not only less expensive to make, but is also a way to prep and energize the staff early on in the evening. People who dine after 7 P.M. walk in and say, "'Damn, this place has got it.'" It's a win-win situation. The latecomers feel good about the place because it's hopping, the local early customers enjoy the bargain and express their goodwill by coming back, and Brigtsen gets to flex his muscles by preparing a different menu—home-style cooking—for the early diners. Whereas his regular menu might offer rabbit tenderloin on a tasso-Parmesan grits cake with spinach and Creole mustard sauce as an appetizer, the early-bird special menu offers fare like oyster stew. And where he might serve a pan-roasted red snapper with crawfish and pistachio lime butter as an entrée, he can offer broiled Gulf fish with crawfish, corn, and crawfish broth for his early customers.

For Brigtsen the increased profitability is, more than anything, a means to an end. As long as he is profitable, he can share this uniquely American food—food that dates back over 200 years and is constantly being improvised on by Brigtsen and his peers—with the public, which is what has kept him motivated for twenty-five years:

I love this business because with food you can make people happy. And the smiling faces that you see at the end of the night, the sense of accomplishment that you bring to this job, is why you work so hard. It's not for the money, although it is a good living. It's because it makes people happy. And if you can take that home with you, you've got something.

Butternut Shrimp Bisque

Chef's note: *This is our most popular soup and our most requested recipe, and it is easy to prepare. The shrimp and squash can be found nearly year-round, but fall is probably the best time to make this soup. White shrimp from the Gulf of Mexico are plentiful, and the butternut squash is at its peak.*

(Serves 6)

2 cups fresh shrimp, peeled, heads and shells reserved

2 cups water

3 tablespoons unsalted butter

2 cups diced yellow onion

1 bay leaf

4 cups butternut squash (peeled, deseeded, and diced into ½-inch cubes)

2¼ teaspoons salt

⅜ teaspoon ground cayenne pepper

⅛ teaspoon ground white pepper

6 cups heavy whipping cream

1. *To make the shrimp stock:* Place shrimp heads and shells in a medium-sized saucepan and cover with 2 cups cold water. Bring to a boil, simmer for 5 minutes, and strain. You should have about ½ cup of stock.

2. Heat the butter in a heavy-duty saucepan over medium-high heat. Add the onions and

bay leaf and cook, stirring constantly, until the onions become soft and clear, 3 to 4 minutes. Reduce heat to medium and add the butternut squash. Cook this mixture, stirring occasionally, until the squash begins to soften, 6 to 8 minutes.

3. Reduce heat to low and add the shrimp, salt, cayenne, and white pepper. Cook, stirring occasionally, until the shrimp turn pink, 2 to 3 minutes.

4. Add the shrimp stock and cook, stirring occasionally, for 6 to 8 minutes. If the mixture begins to stick to the pan, scrape it with a spoon and continue cooking. This will intensify the taste of the bisque.

5. Transfer the squash mixture to a food processor and puree. Return the pureed squash to a saucepan, add the cream, and bring to a boil. Reduce heat to low and simmer for 2 to 3 minutes. Serve immediately.

Frank Brigtsen's

Gratin of Louisiana Oysters with B&B, Spinach, Italian Sausage, and Romano Cheese

Chef's note: *Louisiana oysters are my favorite food. There aren't many dishes in which meat and seafood work in harmony, but this is one of them. The combination of anise and oysters has a history in Creole cuisine—like oysters Rockefeller. The herbaceous B&B and the anise in the Italian sausage complement the sweet and briny flavor of the Gulf oysters.*

(Serves 4)

2 tablespoons finely grated Romano cheese

2 tablespoons fine bread crumbs made from French bread

2 teaspoons unsalted butter, melted

¼ teaspoon hot Hungarian paprika

1 teaspoon olive oil

½ cup ground pork or beef

¼ cup finely diced yellow onion

¼ teaspoon minced fresh garlic

¼ teaspoon salt

¼ teaspoon crushed red pepper flakes

1 teaspoon whole anise seeds

⅛ teaspoon dried whole-leaf oregano

1 pinch ground black pepper

4 teaspoons unsalted butter, softened

4 teaspoons finely diced shallots

4 cups fresh spinach leaves

2 tablespoons Brandy and Benedictine (B&B) liqueur

24 freshly shucked oysters, preferably from Louisiana

2 tablespoons oyster liquor (the juice from freshly shucked oysters)

6 tablespoons coarsely grated Romano cheese (use the large holes of
your hand grater)

1. *To make the gratin topping:* In a small mixing bowl, blend the finely grated Romano cheese, bread crumbs, melted butter, and paprika. Set aside.

2. *To make the Italian sausage:* Heat the olive oil in a heavy-duty skillet over medium-high heat. Add the ground pork or beef and cook, stirring constantly, until the meat is browned, 3 to 4 minutes.

3. Reduce the heat to low. Add the onion, garlic, salt, crushed red pepper, anise, oregano, and black pepper. Cook, stirring constantly, for 7 to 8 minutes. Remove from heat and set aside.

4. *To cook the oysters:* Preheat broiler. Heat 1 teaspoon of the softened butter in a large heavy-duty skillet over medium heat. Add the shallots and cook, stirring constantly, for 1 minute. Add the Italian sausage mixture and spinach. Cook, stirring occasionally, just until the spinach begins to wilt, about 30 seconds.

5. Remove the skillet from the stove and add the B&B liqueur. Return the skillet to the stove and tilt it so that the B&B ignites. When the flames subside, add the oysters and cook, stirring occasionally, for 1 minute.

6. Add the oyster liquor and bring to a boil. Add the remaining 3 teaspoons of softened butter and shake the skillet back and forth just until the butter is melted.

7. Remove the skillet from the stove and stir in the coarsely grated Romano cheese. Divide the mixture evenly among four shallow baking dishes.

8. Top each dish with 1 tablespoon of the bread crumb and cheese mixture. Place the dishes under the broiler and cook just until the bread crumbs begin to brown, 1 to 2 minutes. Serve immediately.

Note: If you shuck your own oysters, reserve the oyster shells for service. Otherwise, serve the oysters in shallow baking dishes.

Frank Brigtsen's

Fresh Berries in Champagne Vanilla Sabayon with Pecan Pound Cake

Chef's note: *Sabayon is like a custard without the milk or cream. In this recipe, I use vanilla bean and Champagne, which has undertones of vanilla. I love the silky feel of the sabayon in contrast with the different berry textures—simple yet luxurious.*

(Serves 4 to 6)
Pound Cake

3 tablespoons milk
3 eggs
1½ teaspoons pure vanilla extract
1½ cups sifted cake flour
¾ cup granulated white sugar
¾ teaspoon baking powder
¼ teaspoon salt
1 tablespoon finely chopped lemon zest
13 tablespoons unsalted butter (6½ ounces by weight), softened
½ cup coarsely chopped roasted pecans.

1. Preheat oven to 350°F. In a mixing bowl, lightly combine the milk, eggs, and vanilla. Set aside.

2. In an electric mixer with a wire whisk attachment, combine the flour, sugar, baking powder, salt, and lemon zest. Mix on low speed for 30 seconds to blend.

3. Add the butter and *half* of the egg mixture. Mix on low speed until the dry ingredients are moistened. Increase to medium speed and beat for 1 minute.

4. Turn the mixer off and scrape down the sides. On medium speed, slowly add the remaining egg mixture in 2 batches, beating for 20 seconds after each batch. Scrape down sides of bowl as needed.

5. Butter and flour a 4- by 8-inch loaf pan. Fold the roasted pecans into the cake batter and pour it into the loaf pan. Bake for 55 to 60 minutes or until a toothpick inserted into the center comes out clean. Cover the cake loosely with a piece of aluminum foil after 30 minutes of baking so the top doesn't get too brown. Remove from oven and set aside to cool.

Sabayon

6 egg yolks
1 cup granulated white sugar
¾ cup Champagne
1 vanilla bean, split lengthwise

1. In a mixing bowl, beat the egg yolks and sugar with a wire whisk until light and creamy (ribbon stage). Add the Champagne and vanilla bean. Cook this mixture over a double boiler on low heat, whisking constantly, until thick and frothy, 15 to 20 minutes.

2. Using the back of a knife, scrape and fold the inside of the vanilla bean into the sabayon. Discard the bean.

To Serve

1½ cups raspberries, blueberries, and/or blackberries
2 cups sliced strawberries

½ cup crème fraîche, in a squeeze bottle, for garnish
4 sprigs fresh mint, for garnish

Place ½ cup of sabayon in the center of each serving plate. Place 1 wedge of pound cake in the center of each serving plate. Place equal amounts of berries around the edges of each plate. Drizzle the berries with crème fraîche. Garnish with mint. Serve immediately.

✳ FOUR KEY REASONS RESTAURANTS FAIL ✳

Because *If You Can Stand the Heat* is designed to provide *inspiration* as well as to give a realistic idea of what the lives of chefs and restaurant owners are like, all the chefs and restaurateurs profiled have been successful at their business and craft. Of course, some of them have stumbled here and there. A few have lived through really bad years, financially; while others have watched their businesses close, despite their years of experience and expertise. But given the number of restaurants that go bankrupt or change ownership within the first five years of opening, they are not alone.

According to Gary Goldberg, director of **The New School's Culinary Arts** program, there are four common reasons—apart from bad food and rotten service—why restaurants and food specialty companies fail. Below, he outlines the pitfalls he sees most often as a restaurant consultant whose clients include the department store Takashimaya, the Great American Health Bar, and the '21' Club.

Lack of Capital

"It always cost two times as much as one plans and takes two times as long to build a restaurant, even if you have experience." The reasons are limitless. Your contractor goes to Fiji; your local utility doesn't show up on the scheduled day; unbeknownst to everybody, the building is a historical site. "Imagine doing construction in your own home, and magnify the possibilities for what can go wrong several hundred times over."

Beyond start-up capital, anticipate that you'll need enough reserves for up to six months of operation. (For more on start-up capital, see page 201.) "The first three to six months are a critical period, when most restaurants fail." If you don't plan in advance, you may have to sell part of your equity stake to an investment group.

Insufficient Experience

Because there are no barriers to entry, everyone thinks he or she can open a restaurant. After all, we all know about food. When people are successful at one business, there may be a tendency to think that their success will transfer to the restaurant industry. Rather than assume that their skills are transferable, Goldberg advises, people should "go to school and work in the industry before trying their hand at their own place. There is an enormous range of schools out there in terms of time, money, and commitment. After school, apprentice or work your way up through the industry."

Poor Menu Planning

"You can't be all things to all people." And that applies not only to decor and ambience, but also to the menu. Too many restaurants don't have a well-defined concept. Consequently, it's difficult for them to design a coherent menu. For more on menu planning from both Goldberg and the restaurant consultant Linda Lipsky, see pages 219 and 216.

Disagreement Among Partners

As Bobby Flay (see page 205) discusses, when things are going well, there is plenty of goodwill between partners. More often than not, however, problems develop that need to be solved swiftly and competently. Goldberg's solution: Have the partners divide responsibilities up front. Who is the chef? Who is the manager? Who is responsible for design? "You need a team, which could include restaurant real estate experts, liquor lawyers, restaurant consultants, menu consultants, tabletop consultants, and—very important—designer and architects. And once the group is assembled, you need someone to manage the team. Take, for example, Danny Meyer, the entrepreneur behind Union Square, Gramercy Tavern, Tabla, and 11 Madison. He always brings in a number of experts. At Union Square, he has an excellent general manager, Paul Bolles Beaven, as well as an outstanding chef, Michael Romano."

As for finding your own dream team, the best source is word of mouth. And Goldberg offers one more word of advice: Don't just find a lawyer or a real estate expert. Find a *restaurant* lawyer, a *restaurant* real estate expert, and so on.

✳

✳ THE ART OF GOOD SERVICE AND ✳
DINING ROOM MANAGEMENT

"You can have a better experience eating a pretzel from a stainless-steel cart, if it's served with a smile, than you can have at a three-star restaurant, if your meal is served with no soul," according to Giuseppe Pezzotti, senior lecturer at **Cornell University's School of Hotel Administration.** "The most expensive meal in the world will be deflated if the service surrounding it isn't graceful and generous. A good meal with bad service is like a painting with no frame, like trying to make a good sauce with margarine. You need butter."

So what's the secret of good service?

Dominique Simon, a sommelier and maître d' who has worked in some of the best restaurants in the world—including the Ritz Hotel, Guy Savoy, and Michel Rostang in Paris; Fennel in Los Angeles; and La Grenouille, Lespinasse, and Bouley in New York—says it's as simple as treating diners as if they were guests in your own home.

This is a rule Simon has been following since he walked out of the austerely run kitchen of his grandfather's restaurant (which was said to have been the best in the Loire Valley after World War II) into its dining room. The kitchens were so hot that he "literally couldn't stand the heat."

Of course, things have changed since Simon first started twenty-five years ago. Back then, kitchens didn't have effective air-conditioning systems, and the chefs were cloistered away from the dining public. "This was before the arrival of open kitchens, which allow the chefs to interact more with the public, and I was suffering in the kitchen because I couldn't see the reason for my work—smiles on people's faces as they ate their food. I wanted to greet people, to see them happy, to watch their emotions change throughout the meal."

He got to see such smiles when he moved to the front of the house at his grandfather's restaurant. Since then, it's always been his preference, and he has the credentials to prove it. He has worked variously as a waiter, captain, maître d', and sommelier. Having worked his way across two continents in pubs, clubs, creperies, and four-star restaurants, he's seen almost every kind of dining room and has handled almost every type of crisis. This experience benefits diners at Bouley Bakery (David Bouley's successor to Bouley), where Simon is currently the maître d'. And he, in turn, benefits from working with Bouley. "I've worked with Bouley for over seven years, and I have found that there is something different, something spiritual, about his restaurants." Of course, Simon himself contributes to the ambience at Bouley's restaurants by, again, adhering to his one simple adage: Always treat diners as if they were guests in your own home.

But beyond that, he swears by very few hard-and-fast rules. According to Simon, the business is too unpredictable to accommodate a rigid way of doing things. "When you're running a dining room, the number-one rule is that there are no rules, because they'd never, never work. There are too many factors that just make it impossible." To illustrate his point, he gives an example—a 5:30 P.M. table in a twelve-seat restaurant. These customers said they wanted to leave by 7:30 for an 8:00 show, so the reservationist makes a 7:30 booking for their table. What happens when the people at the 5:30 table change their plans?

> The rule is that the five-thirty table should be out when they said they would be so that you can accommodate your seven-thirty table. But guess what? They don't show up until six because they got caught in traffic, and all of a sudden they decide they're not going to the show. They want to stay and relax instead. What do you do? What kind of book do you open to Chapter 12 that says, "Kick them out"? Or Chapter 13, "Move them to a smaller table." You won't find it. And don't look for the rule that says you can explain it to the seven-thirty table, because no one wants to hear your problems. So where are the rules? There are none. When it comes to great service, you have to improvise, particularly in a small restaurant, where you don't have the luxury of extra tables.

Managers with less experience than Simon—whose work has been widely praised in *Wine Spectator, Los Angeles Magazine,* and a number of other publications—may seek out some technical assistance in assorted reference books. According to Giuseppe Pezzotti, there is Cornell's own *The Essentials of Good Table Service* as well as *The Professional Host,* edited by the Foodservice Editors of CBI. *Serve 'Em Right: The Complete Guide to Hospitality Service,* by the hospitality consultant Edward Solomon and Shelley Prueter (Oakhill Press), is another comprehensive guide. People seeking a hands-on guide may want to consider a consulting service such as **Service Arts.** Its founder, Eric Weiss, travels around the country working with restaurant owners and, if requested, their entire staff—from chef-owners and managers to servers and busboys—teaching how to give good service.

If you pair technical information from such publications and consulting groups with the advice from Simon, which follows, then you should see more customer satisfaction. Simon's advice isn't just for managers and maître d's; it's for chefs as well. As Michael McCarty says (page 84), it's not enough just to know what's best for the back of the house. It's useful to know a few things about the front of the house too. And of course, as Weiss reminds us, good service has implications for investors as well: "Owners who realize that service is the key have the competitive edge. Good food, service, and design are all parts of one whole. Unfortunately, most restaurant owners don't get that."

If You Want to Be a Better Manager

Work in a Variety of Venues

Just as Simon worked in a variety of venues, from Fennel's—a start-up in Los Angeles—to ski resorts in Courchevelle, France, he advises aspiring managers to work in as many places as possible. The broader your experience, the more adept you'll be at handling crises. According to Simon:

> You have to learn all the aspects of the business because there is something you take with you no matter where you work. It may be the pace in one organization, the timing in another. The number of stars a restaurant has, or the price per person, should never determine good service. From your different experiences, you can concoct a little cocktail that will help you find your own style of management.

Learn to Read a Customer's Body Language

Diners' body language will tell you what they want and why they are at your restaurant. Simon suggests that you train your staff to intuit your customers' needs:

If you want to make diners happy, teach your front-of-the-house staff to put themselves in the customers' shoes; the customers will show you what they need. When you see them eating the bread and putting their fingertips in the sauce, what does it mean? It means they need another slice of bread. Their body language also tells you about their mood. Are they worried? Are they relaxed? Do they have to get back to the office in half an hour? Is it a special occasion? If you see a blue Tiffany box on the table, it's a safe guess that it is a special occasion. Every table will be different. Dining room management is about reading the body language and aura of each table. Is it hard to carry a plate from one side of the room to another? Not particularly. But figuring out what people want before they express it, that's the challenge and the beauty of this end of the business.

Select and Train Your Staff Wisely

According to *Restaurants USA,* the monthly magazine put out by the **National Restaurant Association,** there's an old adage that most dining room managers follow, "Hire for personality; train for skill." The assumption is that you can always teach your staff which side of the plate the napkin goes on, the proper way to change a tablecloth in the midst of a full dining room, or that they need to refill the diner's water glass the minute it gets below a certain point. But you can't train them how to be intuitive, as Simon knows:

The technical aspects can be taught or picked up in books. So I choose waiters and front-of-the-house people because I think they are good people inside, even if they have no clue about what they're doing, because I can teach them. When you interview them, ask them what their interests are, what movies they go to, and—most important—what made their last great restaurant experience so great. And once you've hired the right people, rotate them through different positions so they can fill in when the unexpected happens. One of the best people I've hired recently is a young man who came from Little Rock, Arkansas. With no money in his pocket and only a big dream of making it in the city, he applied for a job at Bouley Bakery. He didn't know who David Bouley was, or the first thing about what makes a restaurant great. But from one conversation with him, I knew I could train him. I hired him on the spot, loaned him the fifty dollars he needed to buy the black pants and shoes, and gave him a start. He's now one of the best on the staff because he didn't try to copy others. Rather, he drew on what he already had deep down inside.

Encourage Your Staff to Be Honest with the Customers, Even When There's a Problem

Since he arrived in America thirteen ago, Simon has been struck by the generosity of the American spirit. Simon suggests that waiters and managers take advantage of this generosity without abusing it:

I tell my waiters, if you make a little boo-boo on the table, talk to me; we can fix it. Go tell the customer, "Look, I forgot your order in my pocket, and that's why you've been waiting for twenty minutes. I really made a major mistake." The guests are good-hearted, especially Americans. If you're honest, nobody is going to blame you. If you're not, you're going to get caught. The guests don't want a hassle; they want a spiritual experience. Dining is about people coming together, breaking bread and drinking wine, which is one of the oldest symbols of sharing we have.

Devise a Comfortable Way to Communicate with the Chef

There are various ways that the dining room manager or maître d' communicates with the chef about what worked in terms of specials, menu changes, service, and customer flow. Rather than suggest a precise right way and wrong way, Simon suggests that you work out a system that best complements your chef's style:

Before the beginning of service, a dining room manager should give the chef a flow of the day or night's anticipated business. Who is coming, who was here last week and is back again, who doesn't eat shellfish, and to the extent that you can find out in advance, who has prearranged to drink a specific wine so that the chef can design a menu accordingly. During service, you should communicate with the kitchen about the pace of the room. For example, David Bouley, who is a master at reading plates, and I will examine the guests' plates to see if anything is remaining, what wasn't quite right. We'll also talk about which tables are anxious and in a hurry and which ones are taking their time with their appetizers.

The end result of all this hard work should be a dining room that looks as if it's running effortlessly. "If you can do it," according to Simon, "you have something that works."

✳

Seth Price

WHEN EGGS MAKE SENSE

Many of the restaurants and chefs profiled in this book make their bread and butter serving dinner. But according to estimates by the National Restaurant Association, 11 percent of overall restaurant traffic in 1997 involved breakfast eaters, and 37 percent of customers went for lunch. Combined, that's nearly 50 percent of the nation's restaurant traffic, to say nothing of the number of people who went for that signature American meal, brunch. In some parts of the country, brunch is more than a meal; it's an activity, a reason to get out of bed on weekends. Here, Seth Price, a co-owner of Bubby's, one of New York's most beloved places to brunch, shares a few insights about the economics of brunch.

Every town, big or small, has a few restaurants where friends and family don't really mind waiting in line to "brunch." In Philadelphia the Blue in Green is quite popular; in Seattle, there's always a wait at the Kingfish Cafe or the Hi-Spot Cafe. For many in New York, especially south of Fourteenth Street, it's Bubby's, a restaurant that the *Zagat Survey* describes as "a homey neighborhood joint where the neighbors and regulars happen to include Harvey Keitel and John F. Kennedy Jr." Here celebrities and local artists compete with families and Wall Street executives for tables. Caffeine-deprived adults choose between buckwheat pancakes with apple maple compote and smoked salmon Florentine, while kids go straight for the peanut butter and homemade strawberry jam sandwiches, flipping, in between bites, through the restaurant's dog-eared copies of Dr. Seuss.

Though some people prefer Bubby's dinners, especially the macaroni and cheese, it's the egg-and-pancake combos that have made the Bubby's name almost synonymous with brunch. Though Seth Price and his partner Ron Crimson both love brunch, initially they just wanted to sell pies—pies that in a blind tasting would be indistinguishable from those their grandmothers served. After all, for Seth Price, his grandmother is where it all began.

As with many other successful restaurateurs and cooks, Price's first mentor was a relative. Ruth Price is not unlike Edna Lewis (see page 61). Both are black women who moved from their native South to the East Coast, and both came naturally to the school of thought that almost everything can, and therefore should, be made from scratch. Apart from the cakes and pies she regularly baked when Price was growing up in her household in Brooklyn, his grandmother canned her own fruit, grew her own vegetables, and made her own vinegar, ketchup, and other condiments. Weather permitting, she'd also go fishing, if she wanted to serve fish for dinner. "Within twenty minutes, she'd gut, cut, and scale the trout, and have it ready for the skillet, because she believed that if you killed something—say, a chicken or a fish—you cooked it as soon as humanly possible."

Of all the regular meals, however, none was more sacred than breakfast. "My grandmother is from the Old World, which means that she took care of the entire family from morning till night. Every day, she'd wake up at five in the morning and cook breakfast for my grandfather, who left the house by six. By the time I woke up, the table would be set and the house fragrant with the smell of bacon and biscuits."

Growing up under the influence of a home cook so grounded in respect for food, Price inevitably fell under her culinary sway. But it wasn't clear just how attached he had become to her cooking until he was nine years old, and an aunt took him from Brooklyn to California to visit his father. Before that visit, Seth had seen his father only occasionally, a concession to the family elders who thought Price would be better served by the firm and guiding hand of his grandmother than by that of his father, who at the time was an up-and-coming artist. But this particular visit turned out to be different. The family decided, unbeknownst to Price, that the time had come for his father to get more involved with child rearing. Price's aunt returned to Brooklyn alone, leaving a shocked but adaptable preadolescent behind.

In his new home in Berkeley, Price assessed his situation. Gone were the freshly baked loaves of bread and homemade pumpkin-spice and apple pies. What remained were his finely honed taste buds, which were never quite satisfied by his hippie father's almost comic holy trinity of stir-fry, granola, and brown rice. After a year of complaining, Price and his dad struck a deal. The father agreed to purchase *The Joy of Cooking* and *Mastering the Art of French Cooking*, do all the shopping, and let Price select the menu. Price, for his part, promised to do all the cooking and make no more complaints. A handshake sealed the deal, and a trip to the grocery store inaugurated the first meal. "I wanted to make something I liked to eat. So I looked up the recipe for doughnuts. My dad bought the ingredients, including yeast, which I had never seen before, and we finally sat down to my first dinner—a plate of doughnuts."

From doughnuts to soufflés, from roast chicken to baked ham, Price cooked his way through two of the bibles of American cookery. "I made every soufflé there was in *Mastering the Art*, until finally it got to the point where friends stopped coming over." He wasn't discouraged. If anything, he was inspired, figuring that it was about time for him to get paid for his cooking skills.

Lying about his age, he found a job at a sandwich shop in Arcata, the town in northern California where he and his father had relocated from Berkeley. Within two months, at only fourteen years of age, he was managing the place. While other kids may have saved their money to buy a new bike or even a car, Price redirected his paycheck into food. Not yet old enough to drive, he used public transportation to get to the best restaurants he could find. "Here I was, this little kid in tennis shoes and jeans, and I would go in and ask for a table. In the beginning, the staff would panic, call my dad, and ask, 'Do you know your son is here alone?'" But by then his father knew that Price was an epicure in the making and simply encouraged the restaurants to offer the boy the best seat in the house.

After several of these trips, Price started sneaking into the kitchens, where he bombarded the kitchen staff with questions, checked out the equipment, and boasted to the chefs that when he got older, he was "going to have a restaurant that would be better than this one." Price's childish taunts turned out to be at least partially true. While there's no objective way to know if his food is "better," he did in fact open his own restaurant, though not before working at dozens of other restaurants.

Within a year and a half, Price moved from the sandwich shop in Arcata to a steakhouse, and then to a French restaurant, where he was rotated through various positions in the kitchen—from salads to the grill. But this was northern California before the boom in the wine industry and the many restaurants that emerged in its wake. Price felt that his options were limited. After he graduated from high school and tried his hand at working in an office—which he hated because he had to wear a suit and tie—Price moved to New York City. Once again, he worked in a variety of kitchens, getting as much experience as possible in both the front and the back of the house. "Because my family was always self-sufficient and I knew I wanted to be able to run my own place one day, I was eager to learn as much as I could about every job there was in a restaurant." In addition to cafés, restaurants, and bars, Price also worked in catering kitchens, and it was in one of them that he met Ron Crimson.

Crimson and Price catered throughout Manhattan, "garnishing their way through various ritzy parties," until they had an ethical clash with the catering company's owner, who, when cash flow was tight, refused to pay the dishwashing crew. Though they could take comfort in being morally on the right side, their solidarity with the dishwashing staff left them unemployed. Uninspired with the food that was being served at a number of trendy restaurants in New York in the 1980s, which Crimson calls a time of "high garnish," and tired of working for other people, the two started brainstorming ideas of their own. "We didn't want to prepare and cater fancy food, and Mrs. Fields had already cornered the cookie market." But when it came to pie—the dessert they loved most, the dessert that most reminded them of their grandmothers' touch—they felt they faced little competition. In their view, no one was making the kind of old-fashioned pies their grandmothers—or, in Crimson's word, their "bubbies"—made. "So we decided to open Bubby's Pie Company."

Borrowing the kitchens of various friends in the business whom they had met along the way, they would go in at eleven o'clock at night and compose their creations, such as mile-high apple pie and Michigan cherry pie; box everything up; clean the kitchen; and leave before the owners got there in the morning. Price thought he was about to realize his dream of being an entrepreneur. But instead he discovered that a wholesale food company was a difficult business to sustain. "All the fancy gourmet and retail stores didn't pay us on time. They took sixty days to pay, even though they said they'd pay us in thirty."

To avoid these cash flow problems, they decided to go into retail. After scouting for a location, they chose Tribeca, a neighborhood that was in transition from industrial to residential and was, at the time, still affordable. With less than $10,000 saved up, Price and Crimson opened Bubby's on Thanksgiving Day in 1990, offering a menu of pie and coffee, an affordable snack for the locals. Within a month, in an unplanned stroke of business sagacity, the menu was expanded to include eggs. This was an odd addition to a menu that had already grown to encompass other desserts, such as coconut layer and chocolate cakes and ginger and chocolate-chip cookies. But given how often Crimson and Price worked through the night during the start-up phase of getting Bubby's off the ground, a craving for eggs made sense: "We added eggs because that's what we wanted to eat in the mornings." They kept the eggs because eggs made financial sense. Tribeca was attracting world-class chefs and pricey restaurants: Drew Nieporent had opened Montrachet, Tribeca Grill (with Robert De Niro), and Nobu (with Nobu Matsuhisa); Brian McNally opened Odeon; and David Bouley opened the eponymous Bouley. Though the neighborhood had a surfeit of places serving premium foie gras and fish, there wasn't much competition for plain old-fashioned bacon and eggs.

From breakfast flowed brunch, now a particularly successful component of their menu. Brunch combines Crimson's and Price's favorite breakfast foods and has made Bubby's one of the most popular places to congregate on weekend mornings and after-noons. On any given Saturday or Sunday, no matter the weather, people start queuing up early. Those craving eggs can choose eggs Benedict, steak and eggs, or any of a number of other egg combos, including Bubby's "big breakfast special," consisting of two eggs any style, two pancakes, a slice of melon, smoked-chicken-and-apple sausage, toast, and cof-fee. Those more inclined toward something sweet also have a number of things to choose from, including pancakes, French toast, and pumpkin-pecan waffles with cinnamon-pear compote. Some people go for the southern-style grits and eggs after they've had one bite of the complimentary biscuits, which come warm and unexpected, yet welcome all the same, as soon as the guest is seated. Each addition to Bubby's menu—from the buttery grits to the smoked-chicken-and-apple sausage—gets to the heart of Crimson and Price's menu philosophy: Never make anything that you yourself wouldn't want to eat. Never make anything you can't imagine your Bubby making.

Price would consider it bad business, however, if his menu consisted only of things he likes. He also wants to be sure that his menu makes economic sense. Elsewhere, two restaurant consultants elaborate on what constitutes an effective menu (see pages 216 and 219), but in Price's experience, it's critical for a menu to be efficient. For instance, when he wanted some smoked fish other than salmon on the menu, he searched around until he found a man in upstate New York who smokes his own freshly caught trout. Price now serves trout and eggs with horseradish cream for brunch and trout cakes for dinner. Because the prep work for both dishes is similar, and he can allocate the overnight shipping expenses over two dishes. The alternative is a diner-style approach to planning a menu:

> Some Greek diners have everything in the world on their menu, but it comes out of the can. When they're out of tomato sauce, they open another can. That's not possible in a place like ours, when we slow-roast our tomatoes in the oven for two hours to make our sauce and we braise our ribs in the oven for five hours before throwing them onto the grill. To give our food this level of attention, we have to prep a limited number of items. Otherwise, it's inefficient in terms of space, labor costs, and time.

Beyond being efficient and tailored to their own preferences, brunch also makes financial sense for Price and his partner. The basic foods for brunch and breakfast (eggs, bread, bacon, bagels, etc.) are less expensive to buy than the foods for dinner, so "food margins"—that is, food costs as a percentage of overall food sales—are much better at "brunch than they are for other services such as dinner." (For more on the overall margins restaurants should aim at, see page 201.) There is also more volume at brunch than at other meals, in part because people are willing to wait in line, whereas they tend not to want to wait for dinner, and in part because brunch patrons are more loyal. "You tend to have more 'regulars' at brunch because people incorporate it into their Sunday-morning ritual—whether that involves watching sports, reading the paper, or having an early-morning jog." Regular customers make it easier to forecast budgets as well. That brunch and breakfast are more affordable than lunch and dinner also makes this a somewhat more reliable service. In tight financial times, people may forgo the oysters on the half shell or the sea urchins, but they can still afford eggs and coffee.

However, as Price cautions, brunch is not necessarily trouble-free financially. In fact, many industry experts regard it as a break-even meal at best. In part, this is because, as noted above, in all but the most exclusive restaurants the overall check tends to be lower because breakfast and brunch items are less expensive than dinner items and because—the occasional Bellini and Bloody Mary notwithstanding—people usually drink less alcohol at brunch. Given that most restaurants mark up their alcohol at three times cost, this is a substantial loss of revenue. Some restaurants compensate for the lower tabs by offering a service with special entertainment such as a jazz band or a gospel choir. Because people tend to frequent such restaurants when they're entertaining a parent or hosting a birthday or anniversary party, they're willing to spend more money. And there is also the added benefit that these new customers will be so impressed that they'll become regulars.

Ultimately, Price notes, a restaurateur needs to assess what works for a given clientele, competition, size, and location. What works for Bubby's may not work for other restaurateurs, particularly those who can't support a brisk business.

> There are many aspects that determine the feasibility of offering brunch. For example, if you're in a location where there is a lot of lunch traffic but not a lot of weekend traffic, it might not make sense to offer a brunch menu. For a business owner, it's important to look at each profit center (i.e., time period) and determine your potential for profitability in each specific area.

Finally, this entrepreneur who knew as a kid that he was going to be a restaurateur has one other piece of advice. Because the extra time involved in preparing and serving brunch are hours that most chefs usually reserve for catching up on sleep and spending time with their families—to say nothing of prepping for the lunch and dinner service—chef-owners who want to open mornings and weekend afternoons had better love the very ritual of brunch, this meal that was once considered the food of heathens. As far as Price is concerned, the pleasure he takes in brunch is the reason for Bubby's success. "From the time I was a kid, breakfast was always one of my favorite things. And I think that is one of the reasons we're so popular. You have to love what you do."

Seth Price's

Banana or Plantain Walnut Pancakes

Chef's note: This dish was inspired by the pancakes with sautéed plantains that my grand-mother used to make when I was a kid, but it works equally well with bananas. I've added sour cream to the batter, which perfectly balances the sweetness of the bananas. The batter holds up well overnight in the refrigerator.

(Serves 6 to 8)
Pancake Batter

2 cups all-purpose flour
1 teaspoon baking soda
2 tablespoons sugar
¼ teaspoon salt
¼ teaspoon cinnamon
2 eggs
2 cups sour cream
1 teaspoon vanilla extract
¾ cup milk
3 tablespoons unsalted butter, melted
¼ cup chopped walnuts

1. In a large mixing bowl, sift together the dry ingredients. Set aside.
2. In a medium bowl, combine eggs, sour cream, vanilla, milk, and melted butter.
3. Make a well in the dry ingredients and add the sour cream mixture and the walnuts, stirring until the dry ingredients are incorporated thoroughly. Be careful not to overmix. Set aside.

Sautéed Bananas or Plantains

2 tablespoons unsalted butter
2 bananas or plantains, sliced diagonally, ½ inch thick
½ teaspoon sugar
Pinch cinnamon
Powdered sugar (optional garnish)

In a medium nonstick sauté pan, heat the butter until melted and bubbling. Add the sliced bananas or plantains, sugar, and cinnamon. Sauté until crisp and golden brown on each side. Set aside.

Pancake Technique and Assembly

1. Grease a seasoned pancake griddle or nonstick pan and place over moderate heat. The griddle is hot enough when a few drops of water dance on the surface. Using a scant ¼ cup of batter for each pancake, pour batter onto the hot griddle.
2. Cook the pancakes on the first side until they are puffed and full of bubbles, looking dry at the edges; then turn and cook for 1 minute or until cooked through.
3. Garnish the pancakes with sautéed bananas or plantains and powdered sugar (optional).

✳ KEY FINANCIAL RATIOS ✳

In addition to some of the financial data and statistics that Frank Brigsten (see page 221) and his accountant examine regularly (number of business days Brigsten's is open per year, number of meals served per open day, average table check, average check per person, etc.), chefs, restaurant managers, and accountants should also keep track of various costs as a percentage of sales. Below are recommended spending limits for the key expenses incurred by most restaurants.

Expense	Percent	Sales of
Food	25–33	Food
Liquor	18–20	Liquor
Wine	25–40	Wine
Staff (pretax)	30–35	Gross sales
Rent	8–12	Gross sales
Linen	1–2	Gross sales
Kitchen equipment, supplies, plates and glasses (replacement)	1–2	Gross sales
Flowers	½–1	Gross Sales

Source: Karen Karp of Karp Resources.

For example, if you sell $10,000 worth of food in a week, your food costs should run no more than $2,500 to $3,300 for that same period. If your restaurant sells only food and beverages (for instance, there's no bakery attached), and your total gross sales are $25,000 for one week, replacement for kitchen equipment, supplies, plates, and glasses should cost approximately $500, or 2 percent of $25,000, for that same week.

Steve Poses

RUNNING A RESTAURANT
VERSUS A CATERING COMPANY

A whole chapter could be devoted to how Steve Poses turned a quaint one-room restaurant in Philadelphia with secondhand furniture into Shooting Stars, an 11.5-million-dollar-a-year eating empire. At its height, Shooting Stars included six restaurants, a bakery, a gourmet market, food service to a local science museum, and a catering company. At its nadir, the empire was draining money faster than a falling star. Poses's accomplishments earned him respect and a hefty moniker: "father of the Philadelphia restaurant renaissance." But this vignette isn't just about Poses's rise and subsequent fall as a restaurateur, it's about his transition into catering, and his preference for it. Thoughtful, visually oriented, and compulsively creative, Poses, author of the best-selling Frog Commissary Cookbook *and one of Philadelphia's most highly sought-after caterers, offers insights into how restaurateuring and catering differ.*

Writing in *The New York Times* in October 1961, Craig Claiborne called Simone Beck, Louise Bertholle, and Julia Child's *Mastering the Art of French Cooking* "the most comprehensive, laudable and monumental work" on French cuisine to be published in the United States. He went on to write that "it will probably remain the definitive work for nonprofessionals." History may prove otherwise. It seems many *professional* chefs also count it as one of their seminal texts (see Rick Bayless, page 147; Seth Price, page 244; and Scott Peacock, page 62). Not only did Child introduce many cooks to French techniques, her books and television programs also paved the way to a whole new appreciation of the role of food in our culture.

Steve Poses is one professional chef who was influenced by Child, though when he first read *Mastering the Art* he was an amateur, not yet a professional. In fact, he was an idealistic student at the University of Pennsylvania—newly arrived from Yonkers, New York—and he had no desire to cook. Instead, deeply affected by Jane Jacobs's groundbreaking book on urban planning, *The Death and Life of Great American Cities,* he wanted to study architecture and sociology and become an urban planner. He was particularly mesmerized by Jacobs's discussion of the role of the neighborhood candy store as a place that "brought people together" in cities where they were otherwise anonymous. Later he would adapt Jacobs's idea to his own interest, cooking. Like a candy store, a restaurant could function as a place where people gathered to talk about the relevant issues of the day, and at the time of the Vietnam War and the protests against it, there was certainly a need for communal reflections. The only difference between a restaurant and a candy store, Poses reasoned, was that customers would eat great food instead of candy. And so an urban planner–in–the–making decided to become a restaurateur instead. In addition to providing him with direction, Poses's new goal suited his 1960s idealism. "Back then, I didn't want a traditional kind of career. I pooh-poohed business as sort of dirty."

After graduating from college in 1968 and working with disabled children and the antiwar movement, Poses took his first restaurant job—working his way up from a glass polisher to a line cook at La Panetière, a French restaurant in Philadelphia. In 1973, when he had what he thought was enough experience, he turned to his parents for a $35,000 loan—enough not only to build and stock the restaurant, but to also procure a liquor license. A plant lover, he decorated an old antiques store with tons of plants and supplemented this "design" with secondhand furniture and artwork given to him by his uncles. That wasn't the only help he got. Apart from a brand-new South Bend six-burner commercial stove, grill, and broiler, almost everything else in the covered kitchen was used or borrowed, including the kitchen appliances and equipment. As he explains in *The Frog Commissary Cookbook*, Frog's inventory consisted of

> *a used one-thousand-dollar Jackson dishwasher (our single most expensive piece of equipment); a used refrigerated worktable; a borrowed junked refrigerator from a friend's basement; and a bridge table (borrowed from the same friend) that served as our salad station. We had to tie a leg of the bridge table to something so it would stand up.*

With the hardware in place, he began casting about for a name for the sixty-five-seat restaurant. His mother suggested *La Grenouille,* to which he responded, "What's a Jewish kid from Yonkers doing opening a restaurant called *La Grenouille?*" Preferring, instead, something simple and unpretentious, he considered Frog, the English translation of *La Grenouille.* It suited the down-home, plant-filled, funky, storefront feel of the place, as did the handwritten menus, which Poses laboriously wrote out daily on a small black chalkboard. The name stuck.

In no time, Poses had a standing-room-only hit on his hands. Whether it was the casual atmosphere or the delicious food—omelets, quiches, and brochettes—the city took to it with more ardor than even Poses had projected. "It was pretty successful from its inception. And not because we were wonderful. Certainly by today's standards we were extraordinarily amateurish. But by the standards of the alternatives that people had back then, we were quite an adventure." In 1977, four years after Frog opened, Poses launched the Commissary, a multiplex food service enterprise modeled, in part, after Jacques Pépin's Potagerie, a forward-thinking "fast-food soup cafeteria" in Manhattan. With a hundred-seat café, a table-service dining room overlooking the café, a piano bar, a bakery, and eventually a gourmet takeout service, the Commissary revolutionized the way Philadelphians ate. To the standard bill of fare for lunch, Poses added dishes like bouillabaisse salad with saffron mayonnaise and caviar.

The Commissary's success changed the way Philadelphians regarded this self-proclaimed amateur from Yonkers. Some called him a culinary genius, others the father of the city's restaurant renaissance. He credits his good fortune to being in the right place at the right time, and to good marketing strategies. As an example of a sound marketing strategy, he offers his use of caviar: "Hardly anyone ate caviar, but people sure felt good about *going* to a cafeteria that served it." Location was another strategic consideration. Situated right in the middle of Center City, the complex was a draw for both the lunch crowd and the dinner crowd, serving up to 1,500 people a day in its heyday. (For more on choosing the right location to suit your concept, see page 144).

As Frog and Commissary continued to prosper, Poses was approached by investors, who wanted him to launch two other restaurants—Eden and Eden II—using Commissary as a model. Meanwhile, with the help of Don Falconio—a graduate student who happened to see the "Help Wanted" sign in the window of Frog before it opened, and who has been with Poses ever since—he opened up a catering company that operated out of the Commissary's basement. Even as Poses continued to open restaurants, the catering company, which now does business as the Frog-Commissary, continued to attract important corporate customers.

Despite having four restaurants and a catering business, Poses was still not completely content. He has an innate need for continual changes of scenery. "I never had it in me to do only one thing. Despite your ability to do nightly specials and evolve your cuisine, if you're in only one restaurant, it's still the same four walls and the same kind of setting night after night." A former student of architecture, Poses had an almost insatiable need for new stimuli, both visual (the design of a restaurant) and food-related (the menu). Fortunately, for a while at least, his need for something new paralleled the eating public's need to dine at the trendiest spots. "When you're in the high end of the restaurant business, people want what's new, and by definition you can't sustain what's new at any *one* place." Poses's solution was to open up more and more new restaurants. In 1980, for example, he opened the 16th Street Bar and Grill, which joined Eden I and II and Commissary, and formed Shooting Stars, Inc. At its height, the company employed 300 to 400 people[23] and served up to 5,000 meals a day.

Poses thought it would never end. In 1984 he opened up City Bites, a restaurant that was, arguably, ahead of its time. "It was our neatest-looking restaurant, but it was beyond what Philadelphians were used to." Customers sat in crumbling *faux* Greek temples, the menus were posted on television screens, and much of the art came from the East Village, then a fringe area on Manhattan's Lower East Side, where artists like Jean Michel Basquiat had their studios. "We had an early Keith Haring and a Kenny Scharf.

It was wonderful art and a fabulous-looking place." But it was a far cry from the second-hand look that charmed the patrons at Frog, and Philadelphians didn't take to it. "City Bites was my first failure and it took a while to recognize what failure looked like, then to admit to it, and to just let go."[24] Even though he could admit that City Bites was draining money from the Shooting Stars enterprise, he could not let go emotionally.

Shoring up City Bites drained him of the resources—physical, mental, and financial—necessary to keep the others afloat. (For more on why restaurants fail, see page 236). The stars in Poses's empire came crashing down as one restaurant after another began to fail, and Poses went into more and more debt. "We exhausted both our resources and the life cycles of these restaurants."

The only aspect of the business that wasn't losing money, as it happened, was the catering company, Frog-Commissary. For Poses, the catering company turned out to be an unexpected blessing:

> Ultimately, catering is a better business. If you're going out to dinner with a friend or with another couple, you go to a new restaurant. What's the worst thing that can happen? You have a bad meal, not the end of the world. But if you're entertaining a hundred clients, you want to go where you know someone has done it before and you can depend on it. So catering is a much more relationship- and performance-based business. And while you certainly have to stay fresh, you get rewarded for longevity—whereas ultimately, I think, you get penalized for longevity with restaurants.

In addition to relying on a customer base that tends to be more stable, catering also allows Poses to work in ever-changing environments. For Poses, catering is to cooking in just one restaurant what street theater is to Broadway. With catering the props and a scenery change every night. Is it going to be an engagement party or a corporate bash? With a restaurant, by contrast, he found it too expensive to change much beyond the flower arrangements. "Some people are more cut out for street theater. With caterers, the audience, the setting changes and you're on the road. With a restaurant, you design it, and that's wonderful, but then it's done. And, yes, you repaint it periodically and occasionally change the artwork, but it's much more static than catering."

Another reason Poses prefers catering is that it allows the head chef to be much more anonymous than a chef de cuisine at an intimate restaurant. Always a back-of-the-house person, Poses was never comfortable greeting diners at his restaurant. As a caterer he's not expected to meet and greet. Instead, he's able to focus on the management essentials: making sure he meets the payroll from week to week, feeding new ideas into the menu book, and introducing new design concepts into the "prop shop." The food and prop ideas come from his imagination or are inspired by any of the hundreds of cookbooks in the library at the Frog-Commissary warehouse, where the bulk of the prep work is done. The rest of the work—soliciting and meeting clients, hiring and managing up to 300 seasonal workers (wait staff, cooks, and art school students in need of money who act as designers)—he leaves up to his operations and accounts managers.

While he's more temperamentally suited to catering, he acknowledges that there are undeniable operational drawbacks, not the least of which is the seasonality of the business. Most of Frog-Commissary's events occur in the spring and fall. "We could go from two to three events a week in our slow season to as many as thirty to forty in our busier season." With such a cyclical business, Poses finds it hard to keep more than a small, dedicated core on staff. Consequently, he uses a lot of freelancers. "It's a huge challenge to manage the amount of people you'll need. You may need three hundred people one week and thirty people the next. So there is this huge process of recruiting that you go through because people move on with their lives." With the workforce constantly evolving, Poses must continually train new people.

The sheer physicality of the work is another major drawback. "There is a tremendous amount of schleppage involved. Schlepping there is not bad," but ten hours later, when the crews are absolutely exhausted after having prepared the food and then having stood on their feet all day, "it's hard to schlep home." Not only do Poses and his staff cart huge quantities of food around; they also move cooking equipment and tables. Caterers rarely go into places that have kitchens:

> We often go into a place that is not designed for food service and create the infrastructure we need to make it work. Usually, that's a combination of heat and tables. That's very different from having your carefully planned restaurant kitchen with your 500- and 350-degree ovens, your finishing broiler, and your salamander.

The challenges continue unabated once all the food and equipment arrive on the scene. Caterers tend to serve in one of two styles—buffets and food stations or sit-down dinners. Buffets and food stations are the easiest. If the theme of a buffet is Chinese food, Frog-Commissary will do a stir-fry station. For another buffet, a food station might have a raw bar or a Mediterranean grill. Sit-downs are a much more complicated matter. Timing can be extremely difficult, particularly for entrées—enough to try the nerves of the most experienced food professional:

> The moment of high drama in a catering kitchen is when you try to assess, "Is the speech a little longer than planned or a little shorter?" Remember, we need to know when speakers are going to stop twenty to twenty-five minutes ahead of time, so that we can begin preparing the food so that it will arrive on the table just in time—not overdone and not cold. There is a tremendous amount of stress building up to that point and then a tremendous sense of relief when the last plate is out.

Despite the complications involved, Poses doesn't believe in preplating food. His goal is to cook as much as he possibly can as close to the time of service as he can. If he has an order for fifty filets mignons, for example, he will, at most, sear them beforehand and then roast them at the event. He does not believe in simply rewarming plates. He sticks to this philosophy whether he's serving fifty or five hundred. Of course, it's more difficult with five hundred, but he firmly believes it can be done, even if it requires hiring more people per event. "We don't preplate; we always turn out on line because my standard is always that little table for two in the corner of Frog, our original restaurant. And we recognize that there are certain things that don't work. We are not going to do sautéed calf liver for three hundred people, for instance. The challenge is to know and understand what works and what doesn't work for different-sized audiences."

Fortunately, desserts are easier to serve, if only because they can be served cold and the caterer doesn't have to worry about timing. The same holds true for first courses. Poses and his crew can offer a starter as complicated as fried wonton stuffed with Asian greens and grilled salmon fillet marinated in star anise, glazed with black sesame seeds, and topped with frizzled green onions. Though the dish is fairly fancy, that it can be served cold gives the caterer an opportunity to be creative.

Despite these differences, Poses is the first to point out that there are some similarities between a restaurant and a catering company. Catering is still a *business,* where a payroll has to be met; insurance premiums have to be paid; and food, appliances, and vans have to be purchased and maintained—to name but a few of the issues he and his staff have to manage daily. In both businesses, there's also the challenge of keeping himself motivated throughout a long, however varied, career. For an analogy, Poses turns to a competitive sport—basketball. "Basketball players have a very long season. They went into it because it was fun, but by the eightieth game of the season the novelty wears off. The ones who are great find some internal way to drive themselves, to find something novel and fresh. Michael Jordan is not just a basketball player but a role model for how someone at that level keeps reinventing himself or herself and finding new reasons to be great." Cooks, he advises, have to do the same.

So, thirty years after Poses first synthesized the ideas of Child and Jacobs, the question must be asked: Did his restaurants function as the candy stores of his era, places where he and others could touch base with their community, discuss the issues of the day? "Not exactly," he admits. But as an older, wiser person, he doesn't have exactly the same values he had as a kid. He doesn't necessarily view the candy store as the proper paradigm. This former idealist who shunned business now thinks that "going into business is one of the most creative things" he's done and new generations can aspire to. "I've had vastly more impact on the life of this city as a restaurateur and caterer than I ever would have had as a city planner because I've created jobs and careers for people, and I've come to think that's one of the most important things a person can do."

Bluefish Provençale

Chef's note: *Summer brings out the bluefish in full force along our neck of the eastern seaboard. . . . This was one of the most popular seafood plates at the Commissary. The Provençale sauce—consisting of a thick, aromatic tomato puree combined with a chunky tomato sauté spiked with olives—truly complements the full-flavored fish. The resulting combination is delicious even to those who have sworn that they won't look at another blue.*

(Serves 6)

Tomato Puree

2 tablespoons olive oil
2 cups chopped onions
2 teaspoons minced garlic
1 pound tomatoes, chopped (about 3 cups)
½ cup dry white wine
1 tablespoon fresh lime juice
½ teaspoon salt
¾ teaspoon chopped fresh rosemary or ¼ teaspoon dried
¾ teaspoon chopped fresh basil or ¼ teaspoon dried
¼ teaspoon ground fennel
¼ teaspoon grated lime zest
¼ teaspoon pepper
⅜ teaspoon fresh thyme leaves or ⅛ teaspoon dried

1/8 teaspoon cayenne pepper
1 bay leaf

Bluefish

Six 6-ounce skinless bluefish fillets
1 tablespoon fresh lime juice
1/2 teaspoon salt

Tomato Sauté and Assembly

2 tablespoons olive oil
1 cup finely chopped onion
1 1/2 teaspoons minced garlic
1/2 teaspoon salt
1/2 teaspoon pepper
1 pound tomatoes, chopped (about 3 cups)
2 tablespoons Greek black olives, chopped
Minced parsley (optional)

1. *To make the tomato puree:* In a large saucepan, heat the olive oil. Add the onions and then the garlic. Sauté until soft and translucent. Add the tomatoes, cover the pan, and let the mixture simmer 15 minutes. Add the remaining ingredients and simmer uncovered until very thick. Remove the bay leaf and puree the mixture in a food processor or through a food mill. Strain and set aside.

2. *To make the bluefish:* Preheat the oven to 400°F. Arrange the fish in a single layer in a baking pan. Sprinkle with the lime juice and salt. Bake for 12 to 15 minutes.

3. *To do the tomato sauté and assembly:* While the fish is baking, heat the olive oil in a large skillet. Add the onion, garlic, salt, and pepper. Sauté until the onion is wilted and translucent. Add the tomatoes, olives, and reserved puree. Keep hot. As soon as the fish is done, serve it topped with the hot sauce. Dust with minced parsley (optional).

4. *Serving suggestions:* This is especially good accompanied by oven-roasted potatoes. Use the sauce for other dishes, too, such as on eggs, chicken, eggplant, and other fish.

✳ STARTING YOUR OWN CATERING BUSINESS? ✳ HOW TO GET STARTED, PLAN AN EFFECTIVE MENU, AND SIGN THE DEAL

"Catering has to be one of the most over-romanticized businesses there is. Nobody, for instance, dreams of opening a dry cleaner the way people think about starting their own catering business. People may open a dry cleaner because a corner becomes available and, after running the numbers, they see they can make a good living. But when it comes to catering, people go into it simply because they know how to cook and love parties." As a result of this naiveté, cautions Nicole Aloni—the founder of Nicole Cotrell Productions in Orange County, California, and author of *Catering Confidential,* a book about entertaining at home—most new caterers try to make every bite of food themselves. Unless they are graduates of **Johnson & Wales** or the **CIA,** with years of professional cooking experience, they shouldn't bother, says Aloni. "The fact is that you can do a much better job if you specialize in one area and find good subcontractors to do the rest." It's frequently the niche caterers who stay in business. Below, Aloni elaborates on the efficacy of specializing and offers additional considerations for aspiring caterers who want to open their own business.

Getting Started

1. Specialize

Develop a specialty, an area of expertise that you are familiar with and, where necessary, have all the special equipment for. If, for example, you have a nice commercial grill in your kitchen or backyard and you know how to maintain a hot fire and also know at what temperature to grill vegetables and a variety of produce, meats, and breads, then grilling could be your specialty. When you go out and meet clients, you can offer them a diverse menu: grilled pizzas, grilled mozzarella, grilled lamb, grilled vegetables, and so forth. Other areas caterers might specialize in include vegetarian, southern food, Mediterranean, hors d'oeuvres, omelets, kosher, and so forth. When you are coming up with a specialty, make sure it dovetails with the preferences of your geographical region. If you're a caterer in the Midwest, your menu selection will have to be different from what it would be if you were in southern California, New York City, or Florida.

Develop Relationships with Other Food Producers

After you've picked an area of expertise, you'll save both your money and your sanity by supplementing the things you do well with wonderful purchased products made by businesses that specialize in other areas. For example, if your specialty is grilled foods and the client wants a pasta to accompany the grilled pizzas and vegetables you're making, find a pasta company in your neighborhood with which you can work to develop dishes complementary to your own. There is a man near my kitchen, for example, who specializes in handmade fresh ravioli. I worked with him to customize a special filling of chicken, sun-dried tomato, and arugula that I use fairly often. I also work with a person who makes only sorbets and ice cream to order, a breadmaker who makes all my breads, and a pastry chef who has taken a look at what I do to come up with a few special desserts. So at any given event, I may concentrate on the main course, finish the sauce for the customized pasta, and garnish the dessert. Relying on other tested sources is a way to maximize your energy.

Rental Subcontractors

In addition to people who make specialty menu items for you, you'll also want to develop a Rolodex full of reliable business from which you can rent equipment, from chairs and linens to vans and stoves.

Planning a Menu

Once you have worked out an area of expertise as well as the regional preferences and the produce of your area, you'll want to start bidding on projects. Below you'll find some of the key considerations you should include in your first meetings with the prospective clients. The better structured the initial meetings are, the more likely you are to win the deal.

1. Ask Clients About Their Food Preferences

Five percent of the clients with whom you'll meet will know exactly what they want to serve. These are the easy meetings. The other 95 percent have no idea. Part of your job as a professional caterer, however, is to know how to help potential clients articulate their preferences. While drawing their preferences out of them may feel like a group psychotherapy session, it will distinguish you as a real professional. Start by asking them for their favorite restaurants and types of cuisine. And don't forget to inquire about special dietary, religious, and ethnic considerations. Do they eat red meat? Can they eat nonkosher food? Is anyone allergic to nuts? And so on.

2. Factor In the Client's Budget

Once you've picked a menu that takes the client's needs and preferences into consideration, your next step is to quantify what clients mean when they say, "We don't want to spend very much" or "Cost is no object." In my experience, the latter comment always turns out to be inaccurate. The first time clients said to me that they didn't care how much it cost, I proceeded to plan my dream menu, only to find out that when they said cost is no object, they meant they were prepared to spend up to but no more than $10 per person. To them, that was the top of the market. Of course, I had to redo my menu. Now when I'm chatting with somebody and we're just starting to rough out menu ideas, I throw out numbers for what something we're discussing might cost. This saves everybody a lot of time. Let's say, for example, that on the basis of clients' answers to my questions about their favorite restaurant experiences, we've determined that they'd like to serve salmon on a buffet for fifty people. On the basis of a few more details—the equipment I'll need to rent, the number of servers required, and so forth—I estimate that this is going to cost $30 to $35 per person. If clients freak out when you give them this ballpark number, you know you have to change the menu before you invest a lot more time preparing their bid.

3. Check Out the Location and the Equipment You'll Be Using

Ideally, you should inspect the party site, be it beach house, home, or clubroom, *before* you submit the contract for the party, because until you've surveyed the site you won't know what your limitations are. And until you know that, it's hard to plan a menu and therefore a budget. Say, for example, you're cooking in a kitchen where everything is open and exposed. It's wonderful on a personal level, but God help the caterer who wants to fry or assemble something. You can ruin the party because people don't want to see all the details. If you know ahead of time that the kitchen isn't out of sight, you'll know during the interview that you should avoid certain menu items, and your final estimate will accurately reflect what you discussed in those first meetings.

In real life, however, caterers frequently don't get a chance to survey the site until after they've submitted their menu. Sometimes, clients just aren't comfortable letting a contractor into their home until they at least know what the price range is. So, logistically, most inspections seem to happen *after* the caterer has submitted his or her proposed budget and menu. Whether it's before the estimate (which, again, is optimal) or after, you'll want to inspect the site.

What are you looking for during an inspection? The locations of the water source and storage spaces are important, and you'll want to make sure you have all the appliances you need. But there is more, beyond just visually assessing the setup. I learned a monumental lesson at a formal fund-raising dinner for a political candidate, where the host was charging $500 a plate. When I went to look at the house, I noted that the hostess had a beautiful, newly installed commercial kitchen. The night of the event, I put the veal in the Wolf Range Oven, with the temperature turned to high. Several minutes later, I noticed that it wasn't getting warm. I found the hostess, and she suddenly remembered that she had never had the gas or electric lines connected. After several quick trips to a neighbor's house, I learned a critical lesson: *Don't just look at things. Turn on every living thing and make sure it works properly.*

During a site inspection, you should also keep a list of what, if any, special equipment—such as stoves, grills, portable lights, tenting, power lines, and garbage cans—you'll need to rent. Then, the minute you're awarded the contract, make plans to rent the equipment. There's a 99 percent chance that you will not get the equipment you need if you try to rent it on the day of an event.

Submitting a Menu and Closing the Deal

Once you've designed a menu combining your areas of expertise with the client's preferences and budget, and inspected the site, your next step is to submit a menu, which is your bid for the contract. As your deal maker, it should reflect everything you've talked about with the client: equipment rental, number of servers, etc. It should be well written, and its quoted prices should be within the ballpark of what you've previously discussed. Also, write out the key ingredients in all the dishes, or you're going to be sorry. I can't emphasize this too much. You're going to have people saying, "I thought that flan meant custard with raspberries because that's the way the restaurant where we eat out at serves it." And then they're completely bummed out when you serve a flan with no berries. It ruins the whole party for them.

✳ THE WORLD OF PERSONAL CHEFS ✳

If you love to cook but think working in a restaurant may be too stressful or simply in-compatible with your schedule, there are several cooking-related jobs to consider—such as catering (see page 267), working as a cook at a hunting club (as Scott Peacock did), or cooking for private clients. These are but a few of the options available.

Personal chefs, like cooks in restaurants, make their living cooking for other peo-ple, but the similarities pretty much end there. Because most personal cooks are self-employed, one of the most pronounced differences is that they don't have to put up with the temperamental chefs that the industry is renowned for, nor do they have to suffer through the "military-like" environment that has come to characterize most kitchens. Among other things, this means they don't have to make their way, inch by painful inch, up the chain of command. Personal chefs can also make their own schedules. Another major difference is that most personal chefs get to know their clients' preferences and eating habits fairly well, whereas a restaurant chef has a rather tenuous relationship with most of his or her clients. That personal chefs can change the menu as often as they like is also a plus, particularly if the idea of cooking half a dozen entrées and a few salads night after night sounds unappealing.

Candy Wallace, a former corporate executive, started working as a personal chef in 1993, when her employer relocated from southern to northern California. With no de-sire to uproot her life, she decided to try her hand at working as a personal chef. One client led to another, and within ten months Wallace was making well over $50,000 a year, with a client base of twenty people. She named her company The Serving Spoon. Once every two or three weeks, depending on the client's needs, Wallace goes into his or her home, equipped with enough kitchen regalia to stock a small restaurant. She cooks two to three weeks' worth of meals at a time, then packages and freezes them and writes precise handling and reheating instructions for each meal.

Having been in the business for nearly six years, she gets a lot of referrals, but she also gets clients from the marketing work she does. A mother, for instance, was worried that her son, who had just moved to San Diego to start a business, would overdose on junk food. After spotting a newspaper article about The Serving Spoon, she arranged for Wallace to feed the son. Wallace, whose business has grown substantially, has not once regretted her resignation from corporate life.

Charles LeGalos, a former corporate consultant based in Paris, also tried his hand at cooking for private clients after working in a more traditional job. The decision to work with food may have been an odd one for a businessman whose specialty was advising clients throughout Europe on implementing strategies for mergers and acquisitions. But in fact his choice was a natural extension of his lifelong interest in food. It began when, as a kid, he would read about and prepare meals from the first cookbooks ever published—written in Old French, no less! While he was still working as a consultant, he developed a technique for cooking meats in a beautifully decorated, multicolored salt crust, and selling them for as much as $300 a pop. When he moved back to the United States, he wanted to try working with food full-time and decided to give being a personal chef a try. But he didn't find it quite as rewarding as Wallace did. Within just seven months, he learned that while being a personal chef was a nice way to earn extra income, it was not a way to build a business that could operate without his being there every single second.

The biggest obstacle he encountered was the law prohibiting a cook from bringing food made in one client's home into another client's home—even something as basic as sauces. If, for example, LeGalos wanted to make a chicken stock that he planned to use in a soup for household A on Monday and in a reduction for a sauce for household B on Tuesday, he'd have to make two separate stocks. It was neither very time-effective nor very cost-effective. For LeGalos, who was used to developing efficiencies in the workplace, this was frustrating. Another drawback is that personal chefs are dependent on the unpredictable whims of a small group of clients. "If someone calls up and says, 'My husband has the flu and he can't stand the smell of cooking right now, so I'll call you when he feels better'—or, 'We're going on vacation for two weeks, so stop by on the fifteenth of the month'—it's very difficult to earn a consistent living," says LeGalos. He found it much more efficient to lease a properly licensed kitchen from which he could cook customized meals for multiple families.

Rather than cook one meal at a time in individual households, LeGalos and his staff at Personal Chefs cook from two to three weeks' worth of meals out of a kitchen attached to an organic farm in Amherst, Massachusetts. On average they charge just over $30 for an entrée and two sides, for two people. The meals are then properly packaged and delivered, with instructions for thawing and handling, directly to the client's home. Though the meals are fully customized and incorporate the dietary requirements and food preferences of LeGalos's clients, there is still room for crossovers. If LeGalos and the staff are cooking for nine different families, for example, there may be overlaps in as many as ten to thirteen sides or entrées. By operating out of a fully licensed kitchen, Personal Chefs achieves an efficiency that chefs who cook for one client at a time simply cannot. LeGalos's business falls between the personal chef and an area of the business known as "home meal replacement," which runs the gamut from businesses like LeGalos's to high-end corner-store gourmet takeouts to chains such as Eatzi's, and is estimated to be a $100- to $125-billion business.

Although Wallace and LeGalos take different approaches, they both reflect the flexibility of this segment of the business. According to Wallace—who, in addition to running Serving Spoon, directs the **American Personal Chef Institute,** which trains personal chefs nationwide—"The beauty of this fledgling industry is that no two personal chef services need look alike." Having watched more than 300 people break into this growing field, she's upbeat about how diverse the population of personal chefs is. The "personal" in "personal chefs" can be interpreted in two ways. Cooks tailor menus to fit the needs of their clients, *and* they customize their business to fit their own schedules.

These businesses may be operated on either a full-time or a part-time basis. Part-time work is great for chefs who are parents and want to be available to their children, but who also want to be able to express their culinary creativity and earn money. I know of one cook who is also an operatic soprano. She cooks three days a week, studies voice two days, and performs on weekends. On the other hand, I know a woman who has made a very comfortable living from working only for partners of one law firm in California. Each week, she'll go to the house of a dif-ferent family and cook two to three weeks' worth of meals. Between that and catering the firm's private parties, she's set. Part-time or full-time, you can make it work for you.

Below, Wallace and LeGalos offer tips for anyone thinking of cooking for private clients.

How to Build a Successful Business as a Personal Chef

Who Uses Personal Chefs? Know Your Client Base

When LeGalos examined who uses personal chefs, he found that it's not just people who can't or don't have time to cook; it's people who have enough discretionary income to be able to afford it. LeGalos advises personal chefs to seek out clients who fit the following profile: "Two-income family, professional, between thirty and forty-one years of age. Don't target people much over forty years old. A forty-five-year-old female attorney has long ago found a way to provide food and do all the other things that she needs to do for her family as well as have a career. The twenty-six-year-old female attorney, fresh out of law school and totally overwhelmed by building a practice, never learned how to cook and, in many cases, doesn't care. She's not interested."

Wallace adds that "career-obsessed singles who spend ten hours at the office, be-fore going straight to the gym and coming home to a dinner of yogurt and cereal, are also a good target market, since they too can afford it and would love to eat delicious, healthy food prepared in their own home." Senior clients who prefer living in their own homes to living in a retirement facility, and are otherwise pretty self-sufficient, are another ex-cellent group to target. Wallace knows of one personal chef in California who will cook only for senior citizens. "A lot of them have traveled the world and know about good food; they simply don't have the energy or desire to shop for groceries or eat out nightly, let alone cook."

Go After Your Client Base

Professional organizations are a good place to meet new clients, according to LeGalos, because they "can put you into contact with clients or organizations whose members can become clients. For example, I'm a member of the New England Women's Business Owners' Association, which numbers 350 successful women who own their own business. They're all potential clients. I was on the membership committee of the Boston Business Council, an organization of about 1,300 gay- and lesbian-owned businesses and major corporations that have nondiscrimination policies. Two-thirds of the members are in long-term relationships, with very high two-person household incomes. Because they both tend to be working and they don't have kids to send to college, there is a lot of discretionary income."

As one of the pioneers in the industry, who has helped over 300 private chefs get started, Wallace stresses that it is important for a personal chef to spend as much time developing a client base as he or she does preparing food. With the following example, Wallace demonstrates how newcomers can cleverly tap into their own communities: "One chef told her OB-GYN about her new venture, and that doctor subsequently referred the chef to new mommies all over town. The service is so popular that the chef is now referred to as the 'gift certificate queen of southern California for new mommies.'"

Screen Clients to Prevent "Churning"

The key to a successful business as a personal chef is to provide your clients with exactly what they want. This entails a fair bit of legwork. At Personal Chefs, LeGalos interviews potential clients extensively to find out data such as what their dietary needs are, what they're allergic to, and what their favorite foods are. He and his staff also keep a database on which meals their clients responded favorably to and which they'd rather not have repeated. In short, too much work goes into building the relationship to let it falter only a couple of weeks later. "It usually takes about two to three months to get to know a client." Because of the work involved, LeGalos will turn down clients if he thinks the relationship will be short-lived. People who make too many references to cost, and people who call because their doctors told them they have to change the way they eat "or else," usually don't work out. As a psychologist friend told LeGalos, "People would rather die (literally) than change the way they eat." If people say they want a personal chef because they want to lose weight, but they're not members of Weight Watchers or they haven't joined a gym, he "recommends that they do those things first to get their weight under control, and then give us a call."

Training Materials

Everyone who enjoys working in the kitchen is getting into this business, from home cooks to four-star chefs. If you haven't worked at a place like Personal Chefs or a restaurant before and don't want to learn through trial and error, you may want to get the training materials produced by one of the two personal chef organizations. In addition to Wallace's organization, the **American Personal Chef Institute,** there is the **United States Personal Chef Association.** Materials run from $350 to $2,100.

For information about contacting these organizations, see Appendix D.

Thomas Keller

IT TAKES TWO:

A CHEF AND HIS DINERS COLLABORATE

When Ruth Reichl writes in the New York Times that your restaurant "is the most exciting place to eat in the United States" and the James Beard Foundation names you the "Outstanding Chef in America" one year and the "Best Chef of California" the next—the first time anyone has ever walked away with such an accomplishment—it would seem that the pressure to excel must be extremely high. But according to Thomas Keller, the chef-owner of The French Laundry, it's the same as it ever was—dicing vegetables, reducing sauces, deboning fish, all the little things that constitute the miracle of food with its myriad shapes and colors, tastes and textures. What's changed over the course of a twenty-year career is Keller's audience.

Concomitantly with the evolution of his own career, a sophisticated group of American diners have come of age. It is projected that, collectively, they will spend $117.3 billion in 1999 eating out at full-service restaurants. To know anything about the success of Keller and the other chefs profiled in this book, or their peers, is to appreciate the people for whom they labor—American gourmets.

When Thomas Keller bought The French Laundry in Napa Valley, a rustic restaurant that was originally built in 1900 as a French steam laundry, he didn't realize how well nearly everything about it would suit him. He only knew that its setting would impress potential investors and that the ambience of the place—a two-story stone building nestled in a country garden, right in the heart of Napa Valley—spoke to him instantly. What he hadn't considered, but now counts as a major benefit, is the serious appreciation of food that people who visit this northern California wine valley would bring to the table, and how that intensity would, in turn, inspire him. While all chefs are beholden to their diners, Keller's reverence is almost palpable. For him, the customers—the people who call dozens of times before getting through to the reservation line, and then travel up to thousands of miles to claim a place at one of The French Laundry's sixty-two seats—are more than his livelihood. These diners are the last arc in a circle that starts with his whimsical yet French-inspired and classically grounded cuisine, continues on to the restaurant's idyllic setting and excellent service, and is completed with its outstanding wine menu.

Of course, it all begins in the kitchen, where Keller, who opened the restaurant in 1994, has chosen to preserve a tradition instituted by The French Laundry's previous owners—a multicourse tasting menu of miniature portions, known as *dégustation*. Though there are two other dinner options—a multicourse dinner of no less than seven courses or a five-course vegetable menu—it is the *amuse-gueule* (taste teasers), or canapés, as Keller sometimes calls them, for which The French Laundry is renowned. On any given night, guests who select the tasting menu are served at least nine of these canapés.

No more than three bites each, the canapés range from humorously named dishes such as "macaroni and cheese" (a butter-poached lobster with creamy lobster broth served on a bed of orzo mixed with mascarpone cheese) and "oysters and pearls" (a sabayon of pearl tapioca with poached Malpèque oysters and a touch of caviar) to salads and soups such as the much-praised chilled English pea soup, which is infused with white truffle oil and served with a Parmesan crisp. And just in case the canapés listed on the menu are not filling enough, the kitchen sends out several complimentary dishes as well, including a salmon *tuile*—a miniature wafer shaped like an ice cream cone and filled with Atlantic salmon tartare and crème fraîche. A signature dish, it is said to have been inspired by a visit Keller made to Baskin-Robbins.

After these "appetizers," the meal builds with fish, poultry and game, and meat. All diners are offered different wines as their meal progresses, with each suggestion meant to complement the course being served. Though French cooking methods are used throughout, Keller isn't afraid to canvass the world for ideas. For example, one late fall evening he served a yuzu reduction sauce with a Pacific mo'i, a Hawaiian fish that was reserved for royalty until relatively recently. After the fish and meat dishes, the meal slowly winds down with a cheese plate and at least two desserts from the award-winning pastry chef Stephen Durfee, then ends with a plate of mignardise.

Keller's imagination is inexhaustible—though the salmon *tuile* canapé may be the only dish on the menu to have originated in an ice cream store. It is reported that Keller "invents six to eight new dishes per week, some spontaneously created mid-meal," which his staff then rushes to the dining room.[25] On a typical night, the kitchen will send out over 800 of these little *dégustations*; on particularly busy nights, it may send out as many as 1,000. To eat all these courses takes time. But the time required—dinner lasts no less than three and a half hours—is part of an unspoken pact Keller makes with his diners. "Americans go to France and they'll eat anything. They'll sit down to dinner and spend two and a half hours. And they'll enjoy it. They come home and they want a steak and they want to be out in an hour. Not here."[26]

For his customers, apart from giving freely of their time, there's another component to the pact. When it comes to the food they eat, they have to be adventuresome. Sometimes the kitchen offers the familiar done in an unusual twist, such as a salad of California green asparagus with morel-mushroom vinaigrette and curry-infused oil. But more often than not, the diner is asked to go beyond the familiar, to be a little daring, as is the case with The French Laundry's classic canapé "tongue in cheek," which marries a braised beef cheek with veal tongue, baby greens, and horseradish cream.

Why so many plates? Why such detail? For Keller the answer is twofold. First, he has to keep himself as well as his staff challenged. "Even if the customer has never seen it, I have, and we have to keep ourselves excited."[27] But it is just as important to please the diner—this is the linchpin of Keller's whole philosophy. For Keller, a number of small dishes, as opposed to a starter, a main course, and a dessert, are the ideal way to share with his audience all that has been brought together by him, his staff, and his purveyors—a select group from around the world, including a woman in Maine from whom he's been buying lobsters for over twelve years, a stockbroker–turned–lamb breeder from Pennsylvania, and a Japanese middleman who turned him on to yuzu, a kind of citrus fruit. "We want to offer the enjoyment of these different products that we've been able to assemble, and arrange them in a way that we feel complements each one before and each one after."

More than just showing off what he's been able to assemble and create, however, a tasting menu is a way to circumvent what Keller calls the law of diminishing returns. To illustrate the point, Keller recalls the time a friend unexpectedly dropped by The French Laundry just in time to taste the white truffle custards. Keller brought him a custard, and after eating it, the friend said that he "wanted to weep, it was so good." But then Keller tried to send him another custard, only to be rebuffed. A second one, the friend said, would not have had the same impact, physically or emotionally. After nearly bringing someone to tears, what more could Keller expect? Keller applies this psychology of diminishing returns to his patrons. He knows that even if he comes up with a wonderful dish, the most he can expect is that the first bite will be judged "excellent," the second bite "great," and the third "good." A chef's tasting menu that changes daily according to what Keller's purveyors can provide, and according to feedback from the wait staff and customers, is Keller's line of defense against the customer's ever getting to "okay."

For Keller, this theory of diminishing returns governs the way he staffs and trains his kitchen. Where other successful restaurateurs might have increased the number of seats in the dining room once they achieved popular success, Keller elected, instead, to increase the number of kitchen staff from four in 1994 to over twenty in 1998. Like a school principal concerned about the student-to-teacher ratio, the more culinary professionals Keller has in his kitchen worrying over each dish, the more assured he is of having customers who walk away feeling "restored." (The original meaning of *restaurant* was "restorer.") Likewise, when Keller expanded the staff, he wasn't looking just for people with cooking skills. He was looking for cooks who buy into The French Laundry's philosophy of putting the customer first. When people approach Keller about working at The French Laundry, he tries to screen out those who are there just to collect another impressive restaurant for their résumé, as if a restaurant were a trophy. In the end, he warns them,

This business isn't about media hype or becoming famous overnight: It's about the true responsibility that all chefs have toward themselves and their guests. People who are coming here have been thinking about this for two months or longer, and

every time they think about it, it builds up a certain level of expectation, of de-
sire. You have to treat that with respect, because if you don't, then you lose the in-
tegrity of what you're trying to do.

Keller holds to his philosophy of keeping the customer in mind when it comes to train-ing the team in the front of the house as well. The kitchen staff meets daily with the waiters to go over all the changes in the menu, so that the waiters are able to answer any questions concerning food that the people in the dining room may have. In addition to those meetings, everyone on the wait staff is required to spend two days a year working in the kitchen, learning firsthand what's involved in the preparation of each dish, and to attend the food seminars that Keller and others give five times each year, on topics rang-ing from fish to pastry. Because of these meetings—and the direction of Laura Cun-ningham, Keller's general manager, who combines an astute knowledge of wine with an ability to train and motivate the front-of-the-house team—Keller doesn't have to worry about the service. "When you have an expert up front, it really frees you to concentrate on the food."

The French Laundry owes its success not just to Keller's devotion to his customers but also to the customers' reciprocal enthusiasm, which might not have been so re-sounding at another juncture in America's culinary history. Steve Poses, owner of Frog-Commissary Catering, theorizes that his restaurant City Bites closed because it was "ahead of its time" (see page 259). Had it opened years later, the script might have been different. Similarly, had Keller attempted to open The French Laundry ten years earlier, or even in another part of the country, his concept may not have worked. It's precisely because Napa and Sonoma valleys attract foodies and wine enthusiasts (300,000 people visit Napa alone each year) that Keller can count on people to go through so many hoops in order to be guests at his table. "People don't come to Napa to take in the shows, the sights, or the museums, or to swim at the beaches; they come to eat and drink."

The good news for food professionals around the country is that it's not just in Napa that a gourmet audience can be found. In the last twenty-five years, a period that's nearly concomitant with the evolution of Keller's career, Americans have, in general, gone from eating iceberg lettuce salads and Cheez Whiz on a cracker to arugula salads served with shavings of Parmesan and goat cheese served on olive bread. As a result of this shift, chefs like Keller and his peers are free "to do what we do." Again, Steve Poses, a name synonymous in Philadelphia with good food, is a relevant example. His first restaurant, Frog, succeeded because in an era where omelets were considered sophisticated, he was able to stand out by serving quiche and brochettes. If he were to start a restaurant today, he'd have to factor in how much more cultivated the American palate is. That Americans are more interested in food can be attributed, in no small part, to "four noncooks—M. F. K. Fisher, Craig Claiborne, James Beard, and Julia Child," who, as Mark Ruhlman notes in *The Making of a Chef*,[28] used writing and television to foment a food revolution. In his memoir *Nobody Knows the Truffles I've Seen*, George Lang points out the other contributing factors:

> . . . *in the 1950s, Americans' favorite foods were surf and turf, luaus à la Trader Vic's, groaning pseudo-smorgasbords, fondue, beef Wellington, flaming shish kebabs, and dishes known as "continental" that were not too disturbingly different from Americans' accustomed fare. But after the 1958 recession, the early sixties became an era of prosperity and affordable travel to faraway places, which stimulated restaurant goers and restaurateurs alike.*[29]

Keller would also credit World War II, which pushed a significant number of women into the workplace, many for the first time. Most continued to work after the war. With more money and less time, more families started going out to eat. Add to the mix an American economy that despite its ups and downs has been *the* great economy of this century, and you have a situation that has, in Keller's opinion, given more people more money and more opportunity to go out to eat:

> *What's happened with American cuisine in my lifetime has been phenomenal. From the time I started to today, we've gone from buying canned, frozen, precut, prefabricated, and precooked goods to a point where we're growing our own herbs and lettuces and having people fly tiny mussels in from Maine. Our awareness has grown so much that it has enabled us as professionals to reach the level that we always aspired to—that great French chef that we all held as an idol.*

In the twenty-year arc of his career, Keller has experienced this American culinary evolution firsthand. But until he was nineteen, Keller didn't even aspire to be a cook, though he certainly knew a lot about kitchens. As he admits in a *Food & Wine* feature on

Bouchon—the new restaurant that he and his brother, Joseph, opened in Yountville, Napa Valley, in 1998—growing up with a mother who was a restaurant manager meant that "after-school activities had a lot to do with peeling vegetables." But something changed when his brother enticed him away from dishwashing toward cooking. Since then, he's done nothing but cook.

Keller first started cooking at the Palm Beach Yacht Club in Florida, which his mother managed. After other jobs in Florida, he moved to Rhode Island and then New York, before deciding to go to France to really hone his craft. After eighteen months abroad and many apprenticeships, including one at the Michelin three-star Taillevent and one at the two-star Guy Savoy, as well as others with Gérard Besson, Le Toit de Passey, Chiberta, and Le Pré-Catalan, Keller returned to New York.

Like most cooks who serve an *estagière* in France, Keller returned with a more nuanced palate and better technique, and he emerged with a renewed sense of discipline, which is best expressed in an interview with the food journalist Corby Kummer in *Departures*. Working in French kitchens isn't, Keller noted, "about making a veal stock." It's about "being consistent, organized, and clean."[30] He also returned from France with heroes and a set of standards to which he could aspire. "When I was a young cook, my mentors were the great French chefs, the ten or twelve who came out of the Ferdinand Point era of the fifties and exploded on the scene in the late sixties and seventies. They became what are known as the 'superstar' chefs—Michel Guérard, Alain Chapel, Paul Bocuse, Roger Vergé, and Pierre Troisgros."

Back in America, Keller worked at Rakel in New York and then joined the Ayala Hotel Group as executive chef of Checkers Hotel Los Angeles, earning critical acclaim, including a *New York* magazine cover story by Gael Greene. Ready to strike out on his own, Keller started looking for a place where he could offer both the food and the service that one would expect to find in the restaurants of his French mentors. (The French Laundry is a member of two French-based service associations, **Relais and Châteaux**—whose 400-plus member restaurants and hotels must all comply with the "rule of the 5 Cs: character, courtesy, calm, charm, and cuisine"—and **Relais Gourmands and Traditions and Qualité.**) At that point, Keller got a call from Jonathan Waxman, the restaurateur-chef whom both Bobby Flay (page 205) and Patricia Williams (page 3) praise for bringing California techniques and flavors to the East Coast. A restaurant housed in an old French laundry was for sale in Napa Valley, Waxman told Keller. Maybe he should go check it out. As noted earlier, the place spoke to Keller immediately, he knew that investors would love it, and the building suited his type of cuisine. But he hadn't predicted that all the different components would come together—the kitchen skills inculcated by his family and enhanced by French training, a hardworking staff, dedicated purveyors, a valley where people go specifically for food and wine, and a group of worldly diners, the beneficiaries of an American culinary revolution.

With all that and a little bit of "dumb luck or destiny," Keller is finally getting what he hoped for as a trainee in France—a group of restaurant-goers eager to collaborate with him. "As a young cook, I kind of hoped that I would be like those great French chefs, which meant that one day I'd have a customer base that would appreciate what I was trying to do. Because that is what this is all about. How can I express more to my customers? Because giving them more in turn gives me more."

Thomas Keller's

Chilled Soup of Spring Peas Infused with Garden Mint

Chef's note: *This dish heralds the arrival of spring and has long been a favorite at The French Laundry. The pairing of the mint and the peas makes the dish particularly vibrant. For the best flavor use fresh peas, preferably those from a farmer's market, as peas from most supermarkets won't have the sweetness that this soup requires.*

(Serves 6 mini- or 4 bowl-sized portions)
3 tablespoons salt
4 cups shelled fresh peas (use very sweet peas, such as sugar snap
   peas; be careful to avoid starchy peas)
2/3 cup fresh mint leaves
1 to 2 cups vegetable broth diluted with water (or 1 to 2 cups water only)
Freshly ground white pepper
6 tablespoons crème fraîche, whipped
2 teaspoons mint-infused oil (optional)

1. Fill a large pot with at least 6 quarts of water (there must be enough water to keep boiling when the peas are added, so that they retain their color). Bring the water to a rolling boil and add at least 3 tablespoons of salt; it should taste like seawater.
2. Add the peas and cook for 5 minutes or until they are cooked through. About 1 minute before they are done, add the mint leaves.

3. Drain the peas and plunge them into ice water. This stops the cooking and helps them keep their color. Drain them well.

4. Combine the peas and up to 2 cups of vegetable broth or water in a blender. (Vegetable broth can overpower the delicate pea flavors; dilute it at least half-and-half with water.) Puree the peas until the mixture is very smooth and pourable, adding more water if necessary. Season to taste with salt and freshly ground white pepper. Refrigerate for at least 3 hours.

5. Serve the soup with tablespoon-size dollops of whipped crème fraîche and, if you wish, a drizzle of mint-infused oil.

Crème de Farine with Poached Golden Delicious Apples, Candied Apple Ice Cream, and Cinnamon Stick Syrup

Chef's note: *The inspiration for this dessert came to me when I was having breakfast with my five-year-old son, Alex. We were eating one of his favorite dishes, cream of wheat with applesauce, when I thought a variation on the theme might make for an unusual dessert. For presentation ideas, I turned to the braised veal breast with polenta and roasted root vegetables, which was then being featured on Thomas Kelller's menu. I thought the similarities in texture between the polenta and the cream of wheat would leave an unexpected yet pleasant impression on the palate.*

(Serves 6)

6 to 10 ounces Candied Apple Ice Cream (recipe follows) or 1 to 1¼
    cups vanilla ice cream

6 slices, ¾ inch thick, Poached Apples

6 Cream of Wheat "biscuits" (recipe follows)

1 cup cinnamon stick syrup (see step 2 of Poached Apples, recipe follows)

6 cinnamon-twist cookies (optional)

biscuit cutter

ice cream maker (optional)

1. Brown the Cream of Wheat "Biscuits" as described in the recipe below. Drain and blot them well on paper towels. Keep them as warm as possible.

2. Spoon 2 to 3 tablespoons of cinnamon stick syrup onto each plate. Place a "biscuit" on each pool of syrup and top with a slice of poached apple and a small scoop or rounded tablespoon of ice cream. Rest a cinnamon-twist cookie on this stack, if desired.

Cream of Wheat "Biscuits"

4 cups water
1 cinnamon stick
1 vanilla bean, split and scraped, seeds reserved
1 star anise pod, lightly crushed
1 cup Cream of Wheat
¼ cup superfine sugar
1 cup mascarpone
flour
milk
finely sifted bread crumbs
canola oil

1. In a saucepan, simmer the water with the cinnamon stick, the vanilla bean halves and reserved seeds, and star anise for 5 minutes. Strain out the spices and return the water to the pan. Stir in the Cream of Wheat and cook it according to package directions. When the Cream of Wheat is ready, stir in the sugar and mascarpone and pour the resulting mixture into a lightly oiled 8- by 10-inch baking pan. It should be about ¾ inch to 1 inch deep. Be sure to avoid lumps.

2. When the Cream of Wheat is cool and has firmed up, cut out disks with a biscuit cutter. The biscuits should be the same size as the poached apples after they've been cut with the biscuit cutter. Just before serving, dust each "biscuit" with flour, dip it in milk, and then coat with very finely sifted bread crumbs. At The French Laundry, pastry chef Stephen Durfee deep-fries these to crisp the surface and warm the interior. At home, you can brown each side in a pan with a few tablespoons of canola oil. Set aside. While waiting for the Cream of Wheat to firm up, poach the apples.

Poached Apples

1½ cups dry white wine, such as sauvignon blanc
1½ cups water
1 cup sugar
2 Golden Delicious apples, peeled and cored
1 cinnamon stick

1. Combine the wine, water, and sugar in a medium-sized saucepan. Bring the mixture to a boil to dissolve the sugar. Reduce the heat. Cut the apples crosswise into round, ½-inch-thick slices and poach them in the wine syrup for 10 to 20 minutes, or until they are no longer the slightest bit crisp.
2. Remove the apples from the syrup and set them aside to cool. Add a cinnamon stick to the poaching liquid and continue boiling until it reduces to a thick syrup. You should have enough to yield 1 cup. Let this cool.
3. Use the biscuit cutter to cut the apple slices.

Candied Apple Ice Cream

2 cups fresh, unfiltered apple juice
1 pint vanilla ice cream.

1. In a wide saucepan, simmer the apple juice until it has been reduced in volume to ¼ cup. Chill the resulting dark, sweet syrup. It should be very cold.
2. Soften the ice cream and blend in the syrup. Return the ice cream to the freezer to firm up, if need be. If you prefer to make ice cream from scratch, add the syrup to a vanilla base for 1 pint and freeze it in an ice cream maker. Makes 1 pint.

In January 1998, Sullivan's closed its doors, leaving New Yorkers to speculate on why a restaurant in such a coveted spot was not successful. The *New York Times* hypothesized that Sullivan's "was serious about food in an area where theme restaurants like Hooters and Planet Hollywood are more the rule." Meanwhile, after taking six months off to write book reviews and magazine articles and to polish screenplays, Anthony Bourdain resurfaced in the kitchen of a popular French bistro, Les Halles, in New York. He wrote about both Les Halles and his life as a chef in *The New Yorker*.

Some months later, news came of another closing—Mesa City. Though Bobby Flay and his team had put their usual expertise to work at their third restaurant, it nonetheless closed within a couple of years of opening. That it didn't survive is perhaps the best example of how many unknown factors are faced by even the most experienced professionals.

Andrew Pforzheimer, who had at one point turned against the idea of owning a restaurant because he didn't want to spend time away from his family in the evenings, has gone on to open two new restaurants, neither of which is the burger joint he has long wanted. In 1999, he opened Luna, an Italian restaurant, in Westport, Connecticut; and later that year, he and his partner opened an Argentine grill in Greenwich. He makes an office out of his Volvo, which he uses to drive from one location to the other. With a good team in place, he gets to spend time with his family and has, indeed, watched more than one person advance from busboy to dishwasher, from dishwasher to cook.

In 1998, the owners of the Café Sunflower and their new partners opened a higher-priced restaurant. "As is usually the case with these things, we were a little late in opening and there was a lot of pressure to do large numbers from the get-go," Marc Jolis says. In the process of that opening, Jolis learned that he and the new partner weren't exactly simpatico. These kinds of tensions are "also part of the food industry." After an amicable split, Jolis decided to work as the executive chef of a catering company and to join the **American Culinary Federation,** in the hopes of studying to be a Certified Chef de Cuisine. This would enable him to teach—his ultimate goal.

In addition to restaurant openings and closings, some chefs underwent major personal changes. In an episode that reveals how vested in the lives of their chefs diners can become, some customers at Peristyle tried to fix Anne Kearney up, though others worried that they'd have less of her as a chef if she ever got married. Nonetheless, in October 1998, Anne Kearney did indeed get married—to someone outside the business, Tom Sand. He now manages the restaurant. Though she goes to work no later than ten in the morning and gets home no earlier than midnight, she's determined to strike a balance between home and work. She also joined Corina Mazo of Boston's Truc, Suzanne Goin of Lucques in West Hollywood, Diane Forley of Verbena in New York City, and Alison Barshak of Venus and the Cowboy in Philadelphia in a national advertising campaign for T-Fal Integral cookware. In 1999, she was nominated for the James Beard American Express Best Chef: Southeast award. And in this same vein, when Linda Rodriguez opened Nobu London, she made a number of friends who made her departure quite difficult, including the man who is now her husband—a fellow chef who followed his heart and moved to the United States in 1999.

Finally, just before *If You Can Stand the Heat* went to press, Longteine De Monteiro's cookbook, *The Elephant Walk,* was nominated for an International Association of Culinary Professionals (IACP) award and Frank Brigtsen won the *Nation's Restaurant News* 1999 Fine Dining Hall of Fame Award. His celebrity notwithstanding, he still works the line five days a week.

COOKING SCHOOLS
THAT APPEAR IN *IF YOU CAN STAND THE HEAT*

For a more complete listing of schools in the United States, see The Shaw Guide to Cooking Schools, *which provides an array of information from cost of tuition to student-teacher ratio.*

Baltimore International College
17 Commerce Street
Baltimore, MD 21202
Phone: 800-624-9926/410-752-4710
Fax: 410-752-3730
URL: http://www.bic.edu/

Beringer Vineyards' School for American Chefs
Allison Simpson
Administrator
P.O. Box 111
St. Helena, CA 94574
Phone: 707-963-7115, ext. 2162
Fax: 707-963-1735

California Culinary Academy
625 Polk Street
San Francisco, CA 94102
Phone: 800-BAY-CHEF/415-771-3536
Fax: 415-771-2194
URL: http://www.baychef.com

Cambridge School of Culinary Arts
2020 Massachusetts Avenue
Cambridge, MA 02140
Phone: 617-354-2020
Fax: 617-576-1963
E-mail: info@cambridgeculinary.com
URL: http://www.cambridgeculinary.com

Career Education Corp.
2800 West Higgins Road, #790
Hoffman Estates, IL 60195
Phone: 847-781-3600
Fax: 847-781-3610

The Cooking and Hospitality Institute of Chicago
361 West Chestnut
Chicago, IL 60610
Phone: 312-944-0882
Fax: 312-944-8557
E-mail: chic@chicnet.org
URL: http://www.chicnet.org

Culinary Arts Academy in Cincinnati
425 Ezzard Charles Drive
Cincinnati, OH 45203
Phone: 513-977-8076
Fax: 513-977-8090

Culinary Institute of America
433 Albany Post Road
Hyde Park, NY 12538-1497
Phone: 1-800-CULINARY
URL: http://www.ciachef.edu/cia.html

CIA at Greystone
2555 Main Street
St. Helena, CA 94574
Phone: 707-967-1100

Florida Culinary Institute
2400 Metro Centre Blvd.
West Palm Beach, FL 33407
Phone: 800-TOP-CHEF/561-688-2001
Fax: 561-842-9503
E-mail: info@floridaculinary.com
URL: http://www.floridaculinary.com

French Culinary Institute
462 Broadway
New York, NY 10013-2618
Phone: 212-219-8890 or
1-888-FCI-CHEF
URL: http://www.frenchculinary.com

Johnson & Wales University
College of Culinary Arts
8 Abbott Park Place
Providence, RI 02903
Phone: 800-342-5598
Fax: 401-598-2948
E-mail: admissions@jwu.edu
URL: http://www.jwu.edu

Kapiolani Community College
4303 Diamond Head Road
Honolulu, HA 96816
Phone: 808-734-9111

Le Cordon Bleu
404 Airport Executive Park
Nanuet, NY 10954
Phone: 800-457-CHEF ext. 130
E-mail: info@cordonbleu.net
URL: http://www.cordonbleu.net

New England Culinary Institute
250 Main Street
Montpelier, VT 05602-9720
Phone: 877-223-6324
Fax: 802-223-0634
URL: http://neculinary.com

New School Culinary Center
66 West 12th Street
New York, NY 10011
Phone: 212-255-4141
Fax: 212-807-0406

New York City Technical College
Hospitality Management
300 Jay Street, #N220
Brooklyn, NY 11201
Phone: 718-260-5630
Fax: 718-260-5997

New York Restaurant School
Director of Admissions
75 Varick Street, 16th Floor
New York, NY 10013
Phone: 212-226-5500
Fax: 212-226-5664

Pennsylvania Culinary
717 Liberty Avenue
Pittsburgh, PA 15222
Phone: 800-432-2433
Fax: 412-566-2434
URL: http://www.paculinary.com

School of Culinary Arts of the Arts Institute International
c/o Education Management Corporation
Phone: 800-275-2440
URL: http://www.aii.edu

School of Hotel Administration at Cornell University
172 Statler Hall
Ithaca, NY 14853-6902
Phone: 607-255-9393

CULINARY AND
HOSPITALITY SCHOLARSHIPS

In addition to the scholarships offered through the financial aid offices of most culinary academies, the following organizations also distribute scholarship funds. Information about contacting the organizations listed can be found in Appendix D.

American Culinary Federation (For information about the organization, see page 303.)

Arizona Women in Food and Wine (For information about the organization, see page 169.)

Black Culinarian Alliance (BCA): Two scholarships are administered through the BCA, a nonprofit educational and networking organization devoted to the professional development of blacks within the hospitality industry. The Leah Chase Scholarship Award is given annually to a student enrolled in Johnson & Wales, whereas the Jefferson Evans Award is given to a student enrolled at the Culinary Institute of America.

Careers Through Culinary Arts Program (C-CAP): For inner-city high school students in Arizona, California, Illinois, New York, Pennsylvania, Washington, D.C., and Virginia. High school home economics teachers are provided with basic culinary techniques, which they teach to their students. Students then intern at local food service establishments.

Educational Foundation of the National Restaurant Association: Scholarships for students specializing in food service, hospitality management, culinary arts, food technology, dietetics, or related areas.

IACP (For information about the organization, see page 114.)

International Food Executives Association: Members include chefs, food and beverage managers, procurement specialists, dietitians, consultants, and educators in the areas of catering, restaurants, clubs, schools, health care, the military, and bars. The organization has given away over $1 million in assistance to hospitality and culinary students.

James Beard Foundation (For information about the organization, see page 113.)

Les Dames d'Escoffier International (For information about the organization, see page 169.)

Network of Executive Women in Hospitality, Inc. (NEWH). Offers scholarships to students interested in pursuing a career in the hospitality industry. The scholarships are based on merit and need. There are chapters in Arizona, California, Colorado, Florida, Georgia, Illinois, Massachusetts, Nevada, New York, Texas, Virginia, Washington, and Washington, D.C. Applicants should apply to the state closest to where they live.

Roundtable for Women in Foodservice (RWF). (For information about the organization, see page 170.)

State Restaurant Associations. Many state chapters of the National Restaurant Association (NRA) offer scholarships for students intent on enrolling in a culinary or hospitality program. For example, since 1987, the Colorado Restaurant Association has administered over $120,000 in scholarships to more than eighty people. Likewise, the Texas Restaurant Association also administers a scholarship fund. (For information about your state's Restaurant Association, contact the NRA. See page 305.)

CULINARY EXPERIENCES ABROAD

Italy

La Scuola Pettirosso

c/o Parker Company
Seaport Landing
154 Lynnway
Lynn, MA 01902-1811
Phone: 800-280-2811
URL: http://www.theparkercompany.com

Master Chef Angelo Chiavroli teaches up to fourteen people the basics of Italian cooking. Classes are held at the four-star Hotel Montinope and are taught in the morning. There is also a visit to a nearby market.

Lorenzo de' Medici School

Via Faenza, 43
50123, Florence
Italy
Phone: 39 055 28 71 43 or 39 055 28 73 60
E-mail: LDM@dada.it

"Apicius: The Art of Cooking" is a cooking program offered at the Lorenzo de' Medici School in Florence, Italy. The courses run for eleven days and vary from season to season to include Wine Appreciation, Regional Food in Italy, Restaurant Management, and Renaissance Culture Through Cooking.

Mangia Firenze
2130 Comistas Drive
Walnut Creek, CA 94598
Phone/Fax: 925-939-6346
Also   Via Taddea 31
50123, Florence
Italy
Phone/Fax: 39 055 29 25 78
E-mail: judy@mangiafirenze.com
URL: http://www.mangiafirenze.com

The art of eating and preparing the food of Tuscany. Classes are held in the "typical Florentine apartment" of the host, Judy Witts Francini, the director. Participants can enroll in a one-, three-, or five-day session. The one-day programs include a walking tour of the central market, wine tasting, and lunch. It's also possible to do three days of cooking. The five-day program includes all of the above as well as a day in Chianti.

Mangia Firenze can also help arrange custom-designed food-oriented trips for groups of four to eight in Tuscan villas.

Villa Crocialoni
Tuscan Cooking School
Via delle Cerbaie 60
50054 Fucecchio
Italy
Phone: 39 571 296237
E-mail: houseview@flownet.it
URL: http://flownet.it/tuscan-cooking-school

Villa Crocialoni offers a five-day seminar on the basic Tuscan fare, some of it cooked in a wood-burning oven in a Tuscan villa on thirty acres of property. All demonstrations and accommodations are taught in English by an American who has been living in Tuscany for many years. Classes are held in the villa, which is located between Florence and Pisa. Visits are made to the central market in Florence as well as to the fish market in Viareggio.

Villa Micheaela (Tuscany) or Le Mas des Oliviers (Southern France)
Rhode School of Cuisine
216 Miller Avenue
Suite 8
Mill Valley, CA 94941
Attention: Tim Haydon-Stone
Phone: 888-254-1070
URL: http://www.to-gastronomy.com

The Rhode School of Cuisine offers a package that includes hands-on cooking classes for dinner and lunch, with special emphasis on the food of France or Tuscany. The chef instructors, Frédéric Rivière and Valter Roman, have trained and worked throughout Europe. Demonstrations, classes, and accommodations are in a villa on the Mediterranean coast of France or in a villa in the hills of Tuscany and run for one week.

Mexico

Culinary Adventures Inc.
6023 Reid Drive, NW
Gig Harbor, WA 98335
Phone: 253-851-7676

Culinary Adventures Inc. organizes annual culinary tours to various regions of Mexico, including summer tours with Diana Kennedy. These hands-on classes are held in Ms.

Kennedy's home in Michoacán, with additional activities in and around Mexico City. Classes are limited to six skilled cooks.

Rick Bayless is the guest instructor on the winter trips, which are held in different states from year to year, all known for their regional cuisine. Each area offers a different weeklong experience. Demonstrations by local cooks, market visits, and cultural activities are parts of each trip.

FOOD ORGANIZATIONS AND BUSINESSES IN *IF YOU CAN STAND THE HEAT*

American Culinary Federation
10 San Bartola Drive
St. Augustine, FL 32086
Phone: 800-624-9458
Fax: 904-825-4758
E-mail: acf@aug.com
URL: http://acfchefs.org

American Institute of Wine & Food
1550 Bryant Street, Suite 700
San Francisco, CA 94103
Phone: 800-274-AIWF
Fax: 415-255-2874
URL: http://aiwf.org

American Personal Chef Institute
Candy Wallace
American Personal Chef Institute and
   Association
4572 Delaware Street

San Diego, CA 92116
Phone: 800-644-8389
E-mail: ChefCandy@personalchef.com
URL: http://www.personalchef.com

Arizona Women in Food and Wine (AWFW)
Cindy Selby
1350 E. Northern Avenue
#236
Phoenix, AZ 85020
Phone: 602-678-0718

Black Culinarian Alliance
P.O. Box 2044
North Babylon, NY 11704
E-mail: BCA1993@aol.com
URL: http://www.blackculinarian.com

Bogdanow Partners, Architects, PC
75 Spring Street
New York, NY 10012
Phone: 212-966-0313
Fax: 212-941-8875

**Careers Through Culinary Arts
Program (C-CAP)**
155 West 68th Street
New York, NY 10023
Phone: 212-873-2434
Fax: 212-873-1514

Chefs Collaborative 2000 / Oldways
25 First Street
Cambridge, MA 02141
Phone: 617-621-3000
Fax: 617-621-1230

Frog-Commissary Catering
435 Fairmount Avenue
Philadelphia, PA 19123
Phone: 215-923-6500
Fax: 215-923-6519
URL: http://www.phillycater.com
E-mail: frogcomm@erols.com

Gary Goldberg
Director
Culinary Center
100 Greenwich Avenue
New York, NY 10011
Phone: 212-255-4141
Fax: 212-807-0406

The Greenbrier
Director of Personnel
The Greenbrier Hotel
300 West Main Street
White Sulphur Springs, WV 24986-2498
Phone: 304-536-1110
Fax: 304-536-7883

**International Association of
Culinary Professionals (IACP)**
304 West Liberty Street
Suite 201
Louisville, KY 40202
Phone: 502-581-9786
Fax: 502-589-3602
URL: http://www.iacp-online.org

**International Food Executives
Association**
3739 Mykonos Court
Boca Raton, FL 33487
Phone: 561-998-7758
Fax: 561-998-3878

James Beard Foundation
167 West 12th Street
New York, NY 10011
Phone: 212-675-4984
Fax: 212-645-1438
URL: http://www.jamesbeard.org

Karp Resources
P.O. Box 515
Southold, NY 11971
Phone: 212-352-7210 or 800-269-8089
E-mail: karp2food@aol.com

Les Dames d'Escoffier International (LDEI)
P.O. Box 2103
Reston, VA 20195-0982
Phone: 703-716-5913
E-mail: ldei@ldei.org
URL: http://www.ldei.org

Linda Lipsky Restaurant Consultants, Inc.
216 Foxcroft Road
Broomall, PA 19008
Phone: 610-325-FOOD (3663)
Fax: 610-325-3FAX (3329)
E-mail: lipsky@restaurant.consult.com
URL: http://www.restaurantconsult.com

National Restaurant Association
1200 Seventeenth Street, N.W.
Washington, DC 20036-3097
Phone: 202-331-5900
Fax: 202-331-2429
E-mail: info@dineout.org
URL: http://www.restaurant.org

National Restaurant Association Educational Foundation
250 South Wacker Drive
Chicago, IL 60606
Phone: 800-765-2122
Fax: 312-715-0807
URL: http://www.edfound.org

Network of Executive Women in Hospitality, Inc. (NEWH)
Phone: 800-593-NEWH
Fax: 800-693-NEWH
URL: http://www.newh.org

New York Women's Culinary Alliance (NYWCA)
305 West 98th Street
Apartment 5E North
New York, NY 10025
Phone: 212-316-4213

Perini Ranch Mail Order Catalog
1-800-367-1721

Relais and Châteaux Relais Gourmands
11 East 44th Street, Suite 704
New York, NY 10017
Phone: 800-735-2478 or 212-856-0115
Fax: 212-856-0193
E-mail: nyrelais@aol.com
URL: http://www.relaischateaux.fr

**Roundtable for Women in
Foodservice (RWF)**
1372 La Colina Drive
Tustin, CA 92780
Phone: 800-898-2849 / 714-838-2749
Fax: 714-838-2750
E-mail: webmaster@rwf.org
URL: http://www.rwf.org

**United States Personal Chef
Association**
David MacKay
3615 Highway 528
Suite 107
Albuquerque, NM 87114
Phone: 800-995-2138
URL: http://www.uspca.com

Service Arts
Eric Weiss
P.O. Box 6973
FDR Station
New York, NY 10150
Phone: 212-338-9054

Texas Restaurant Association
Phone: 800-395-2872
URL: http://www.txrestaurant.org
(See also National Restaurant
Association)

United States Pastry Alliance
1810 Grand Junction
Alpharetta, GA 30004
Phone: 888-APASTRY
Fax: 706-637-9728
E-mail: Maison1@CompuServe.com
URL: http://www.uspastry.org

**Wider Opportunities for Women
(WOW)**
815 Fifteenth Street NW
Suite 916
Washington, DC 20005
Phone: 202-638-3143
Fax: 202-638-4885
URL: http://www.W-O-Wonline.org

**Women Chefs and Restaurateurs
(WCR)**
304 West Liberty Street
Suite 201
Louisville, KY 40202
Phone: 502-581-0300
Fax: 502-589-3602
E-mail: wcr@hqtrs.com
URL: http://www.culinary.net/cgi-bin/
iccentry.cgi

COOKBOOKS BY CHEFS
IN *IF YOU CAN STAND THE HEAT*

Rick Bayless

Authentic Mexican: Regional Cooking from the Heart of Mexico, by Rick Bayless with Deann Groen Bayless, Morrow, 1987.

Rick Bayless's Mexican Kitchen: Capturing the Vibrant Flavors of a World-Class Cuisine, by Rick Bayless, Deann Bayless, and Jean Marie Brownson, Scribner, 1996.

Salsas That Cook: Using Classic Salsas to Enliven Our Favorite Dishes, by Rick Bayless, Jeanmarie Brownson, and Deann Bayless, Scribner, 1998.

The Elephant Walk

The Elephant Walk Cookbook, by Longteine De Monteiro and Katherine Newstadt, Houghton Mifflin, 1998.

Bobby Flay

Bold American Cooking, by Bobby Flay with Joan Schwartz, Warner, 1994.

Bobby Flay's From My Kitchen to Your Table, by Bobby Flay, Potter, 1998.

Bobby Flay's Boy Meets Grill: Get Busy in the Backyard with More Than 125 Bold New Recipes, by Bobby Flay, Joan Schwartz, and Tom Eckerle, Hyperion, 1999.

Thomas Keller

The French Laundry Cookbook, by Thomas Keller, Artisan, 1999.

Edna Lewis

The Taste of Country Cooking, Knopf, 1976.

The Edna Lewis Cookbook, by Edna Lewis and Evangeline Peterson, Bobbs-Merrill, 1972.

Michael McCarty

Michael's Cookbook: The Art of New American Food and Entertaining, Macmillan, 1989.

Steve Poses

The Frog-Commissary Cookbook, by Steve Poses and Rebecca Roller, Doubleday, 1985.

Alan Wong

Alan Wong's New Wave Luau: Recipes from Honolulu's Award-Winning Chef, by Alan Wong and John Harrisson, Ten Speed, 1999.

SELECTED INDUSTRY
AND TRADE PUBLICATIONS

Culinary

Art Culinaire
40 Mills Street
P.O. Box 9268
Morristown, NJ 07960
Phone: 201-993-5500

Art of Eating
P.O. Box 242
Peacham, VT 05862

Beard House Monthly
c/o James Beard Foundation
167 West 12th Street
New York, NY 10011

Bon Appétit
P.O. Box 7196
Red Oak, IA 51591-2196

Cook's Illustrated
Boston Common Press
17 Station Street
P.O. Box 569
Brookline, MA 02147-0569

Food & Wine
P.O. Box 3004
Harlan, IA 51537-3004
Phone: 800-333-6569

Food Arts
387 Park Avenue South
New York, NY 10016
Phone: 800-848-7113

Food Forum
c/o IACP
304 West Liberty Street
Suite 201
Louisville, KY 40202
Phone: 502-581-9786

Gourmet
P.O. Box 51422
Boulder, CO 80321-1422
Phone: 800-365-2454

Martha Stewart Living
Box 60001
Tampa, FL 33660-0001
Phone: 800-999-6518

National Culinary Review
c/o American Culinary Federation
P.O. Box 3466
San Bartoia Drive
St. Augustine, FL 32085

Saveur
P.O. Box 59652
Boulder, CO 80322-9652
Phone: 800-462-0209

Vegetarian Journal
P.O. Box 1463
Baltimore, MD 21203

Vegetarian Times
P.O. Box 446
Mt. Morris, IL 61054-8081

Wine Spectator
P.O. Box 50463
Boulder, CO 80323-0463

Pastry

American Institute of Baking ALB Research Department Technical Bulletin
1213 Baker's Way
Manhattan, KS 66502

Baking Update
Lallemand, Inc.
1620 Prefontaine
Montreal, QC
H1W 2NB
Canada

Pastry Arts and Design
P.O. Box 333
Mt. Morris, IL 61054

Business

Cater Source Journal
P.O. Box 14776
Chicago, IL 60614
Phone: 800-932-3632

Chef: The Chef's Business Magazine
20 North Wacker Drive
Suite 3230
Chicago, IL 60606-3112
Phone: 312-849-2220

Cooking for Profit
P.O. Box 267
Fond du Lac, WI 54936-0267

Nation's Restaurant News
425 Park Avenue
New York, NY 10022
Phone: 800-944-4676

Restaurant Report
URL: http://www.restaurantreport.com

Restaurant USA
c/o National Restaurant Association
Phone: 202-331-5900

Restaurants & Institutions
1350 East Touhy Avenue
P.O. Box 5080
Des Plaines, IL 60017-5080
Phone: 847-635-8800

1. Ruth Reichl, *The New York Times*, April 28, 1997.
2. Andrew Dornenburg and Karen Page, *Becoming a Chef* (New York: Van Nostrand Reinhold, 1995), p. 139.
3. Beverly Savage, "Learning to Cook," *Beard House* magazine, vol. 12, no. 2.
4. *Becoming a Chef*.
5. Mark Ruhlman, *The Making of a Chef: Mastering Heat at the Culinary Institute of America* (New York: Henry Holt, 1997), pp. 17–18.
6. Source: Shaw Guide Survey of Leading Chefs, 1995.
7. Edna Lewis, *The Taste of Country Cooking* (New York: Knopf, 1976).
8. Peter Farb and George Armelagos, *Consuming Passions* (Boston: Houghton Mifflin, 1980).
9. Others include Mondavi's wife, Margrit Biever, Kate Fireston, Alice Waters, Jeremiah Tower, and Marion Cunningham. The founding members were Child, Graff, Mondavi, McCarty, Jeremiah Tower, Fritz Maytag, Joseph Phelps, D. Crosby Ross, Richard and Thekka Sanford, Audrey and Barry Sterling. From Noël Riley Fitch, *Appetite for Life: The Biography of Julia Child* (Garden City, NY: Doubleday, 1997).
10. *Appetite for Life*.
11. Hal Smith, "No Frills Ranch Cooking in Buffalo Gap," *Texas Highways*, June 1997.
12. "No Frills Ranch Cooking."
13. Ronald Takaki, *Stranger from a Different Shore*, revised and updated (New York: Back Bay Books, 1998).

14. For more information, see Janice Wald Henderson, *The New Cuisine of Hawaii: Recipes from Twelve Celebrated Chefs of Hawaiian Regional Cuisine* (New York: Villard, 1994).

15. Steven Pratt, "Good Eating," *Chicago Tribune*, October 16, 1996.

16. Victor Valle and Mary Valle, *Recipe of Memory: Five Generations of Mexican Cuisine* (New York: New Press, 1996).

17. Moira Hodgson, *New York Observer*, September 28, 1998.

18. Ruth Reichl, *The New York Times*, September 27, 1996.

19. Amanda Hesser, "Too Many Cooks? Not Nearly Enough," *The New York Times*, October 25, 1998.

20. Carol King, *Professional Dining Room Management* (New York: Van Nostrand Reinhold, 1988), p. 163.

21. "Too Many Cooks?"

22. Gene Bourg, New Orleans *Times-Picayune*, June 1986.

23. Barbara Whitaker, "The Fall and Rise of Steve Poses," *Inquirer* magazine, February 9, 1997.

24. Ibid.

25. Scott Ostler, "This Laundry Insists on Clean Plates," San Francisco *Chronicle*, July 31, 1998.

26. Harvey Steiman, "Doing the Laundry," *Wine Spectator*, June 15, 1998.

27. Corby Kummer, "Bite Size," *Departures*, October, 1998.

28. Mark Ruhlman, *The Making of a Chef: Mastering Heat at the Culinary Institute of America* (New York: Henry Holt, 1997), p. 265.

29. George Lang, *Nobody Knows the Truffles I've Seen* (New York: Knopf, 1998) pp. 200–201.

30. "Bite Size."

Cooper, Ann. *A Woman's Place Is in the Kitchen: The Evolution of Women Chefs*. New York: Van Nostrand Reinhold, 1998.

Dornenburg, Andrew, and Karen Page. *Becoming a Chef*. New York: Van Nostrand Reinhold, 1995.

Egerton, John. *Southern Food: At Home, on the Road, in History*. Chapel Hill, NC: University of North Carolina Press, 1993 (originally published by Knopf, 1987).

Escoffier, Auguste. *The Escoffier Cook Book: A Guide to the Fine Art of French Cuisine*. New York: Crown, 1969.

Farb, Peter, and George Armelagos. *Consuming Passions: The Anthropology of Eating*. Boston: Houghton Mifflin, 1980.

Fitch, Noël Riley. *Appetite for Life: The Biography of Julia Child*. New York: Doubleday, 1997.

Food Service Editors of CBI. *The Professional Host*. Boston: CBI Publishing, 1981.

The Guide to Cooking Schools. New York: Shaw Guides, 1999.

Henderson, Janice Wald. *The New Cuisine of Hawaii*. New York: Villard, 1994.

King, Carol A. *Professional Dining Room Management*. New York: Van Nostrand Reinhold, 1988.

Lambert Ortiz, Elisabeth. *The Complete Cookbook of Caribbean Cooking*. New York: Ballantine, 1973.

Lang, George. *Nobody Knows the Truffles I've Seen*. New York: Knopf, 1998.

Lefever, Michael M. *Restaurant Reality: A Manager's Guide*. New York: Wiley, 1989.

Lewis, Edna. *The Taste of Country Cooking*. New York: Knopf, 1976.

Mondavi, Robert. *Harvests of Joy: My Passion for Excellence*. San Diego: Harcourt Brace, 1998.

Raichlen, Steven. *Caribbean Pantry Cookbook*. New York: Artisan, 1995.

Reichl, Ruth. *Tender at the Bone*. New York: Random House, 1998.

Root, Waverley. *The Food of France*. New York: Vintage, 1992 (originally published by Knopf, 1958).

Ruhlman, Michael. *The Making of a Chef: Mastering Heat at the Culinary Institute of America*. New York: Holt, 1997.

Solomon, Edward, and Shelley Prueter. *Serve 'Em Right: The Complete Guide to Hospitality Service*. Greensboro, NC: Oakhill, 1997.

Soltner, André, Seymour Britchky, and Henry Kibel. *The Lutèce Cookbook*. New York: Knopf, 1995.

Takaki, Ronald. *Strangers from a Different Shore*. Boston: Little, Brown, 1989.

Trager, James. *The Food Chronology*. New York: Holt, 1996.

True, Margo. *Gourmet*, October 1996.

Tsuji, Shizuo, and Koichiro Hata. *Practical Japanese Cooking*. New York: Kodansha, 1986.

Valle, Victor, and Mary Lau Valle. *Recipe of Memory: Five Generations of Mexican Cuisine*. New York: New Press, 1995.

Waxman, Jonathan, xi, 16, 93, 95, 206, 284–85

Weiss, Eric, 240

Western Chuckwagon Association, 106

White, Marco Pierre, 33

Wholesale food business, 248

Wider Opportunities for Women (WOW), 170

Williams, Patricia, ix, 3–12, 284, 292

Wine and food, pairing, 89–90, 93

Wine Merchant, 89–90

Wine Spectator, 197, 240

Women, 7–8, 283
   assumptions about, 36
   resources for, 169–71
   social life, 8–9
   special challenges confronting, 3, 7–8, 159, 161, 162, 192

Women Chefs and Restaurateurs (WCR), 170–71
   Web site, 185

Wong, Alan, ix, xi–xii, 85, 113, 115–26

Wong, Robert, 127

Working capital, budgeting for, 202–3, 236

Working pastry chef, 27

Wressel, Donald, 173

Xavier, Paris, 88

Yamaguchi, Roy, 31, 95

Yamamoto, Michiko, 163

Zagat Survey, 245

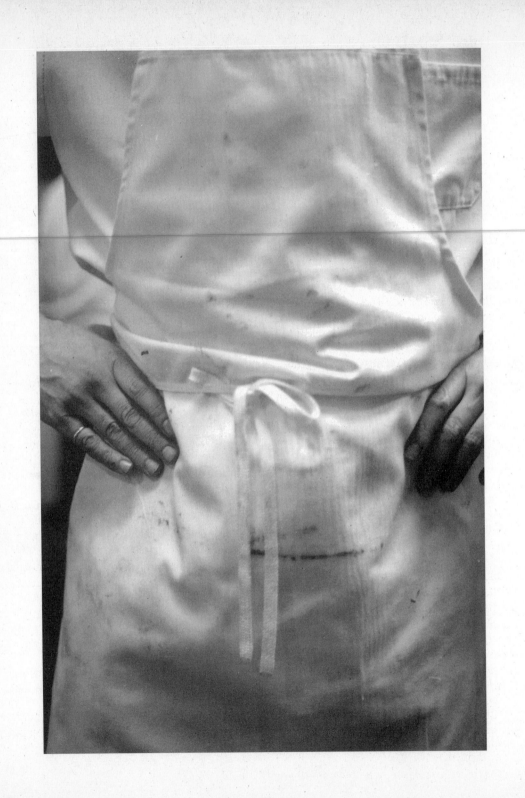